Reparenting Myself

The Mother Lode Journals, Volume 1

Anony Mom MD

Published by Anony Mom MD, 2024.

Reparenting Myself: A memoir to my daughters on growing up, getting it wrong, and giving my best

Copyright @ 2024 by Anony Mom MD

For privacy reasons, some names, locations, and dates may have been changed or omitted.

First Edition (May 1, 2024)

Written by Anony Mom, MD

Cover Photo Credit: Crisher P.H[1] from Pexels[2]

---

1. https://www.canva.com/design/DAGA5YkMzNg/WGNpxqAbNZHy6tb_oLy_pQ/edit#

2. https://www.canva.com/design/DAGA5YkMzNg/WGNpxqAbNZHy6tb_oLy_pQ/edit#

Table of Contents

Origins: Whos and Whys | 1. Who am I?..1

2. Why am I like this? 5

3. Who made me this way? 8

4. What changed me? 11

5. How did I turn out?.............................16

6. How I met your dad? 20

7. My Core Childhood Memories 23

8. Why am I writing this? 26

Growth: Evolution & Authenticity | 9. Never ending metamorphosis 31

10. March To The Beat Of Your Own Drummer 33

11. Grow At Your Own Rate 36

12. Know Your Strengths 38

13. Know your weaknesses 41

14. Find Yourself, Repeatedly.......................45

15. Seek Transformative Experiences 49

16. You Are Your Words...........................53

17. You Are Your Actions 56

18. Don't Outsource Validation 58

19. Embrace The Struggle-fest 61

Friendship: Kindness & Community | 20. Find Your Tribe 64

21. Treasure your siblings.........................69

22. Take My Word For It, This Stuff's Hard!..............72

23. Jealousy Isn't Cute On Anyone 77

24. Tone and Intent..............................80

25. Beware the Friendship Cliff......................84

26. Quality Over Quantity.........................87

27. Sparkly Peeps 90

Love: Lust & Vulnerability | 28. Kiss Some Frogs.................92

29. They Might Be Into You If.......................96

30. Teenage Lust, The Ultimate High 100

31. Have (Some) Sex! 103

32. What We Give Is What You'll Seek 106

33. Love Languages Exist.........................108

34. Relationship Red Flags 111

Loss: Despair & Redemption | 35. Embrace Your Shadow Self 115

36. Hard Times/ Defining Moments 117

37. Don't Fight The Feelings! 120

38. Grace and Grit For The Win! 126

39. Crisis Mode Rituals 128

40. Music Therapy Options 131

41. Screentime Therapy Options.. 145

42. Other Therapy Options 149

Partnership: Teamwork & Harmony | 43. Say No To The Dress 152

44. Teamwork Makes The Dream Work... 154

45. Hope For The Best, Plan For The Worst.................................. 158

46. Partner As Catalyst To A Better Self 161

47. Fingers Crossed We Don't Mess You Up!................................. 163

48. If You Choose Not To Partner 165

Parenting: Leadership & Caretaking | 49. Pregnancy and Birth Stories 167

50. Expectations, Inversely Proportional To Joy 174

51. Testing Your Sanity And Partnership 180

52. Battling Birth Order Dynamics 185

53. Kids As Catalyst To A Better Self... 188

54. Where's The Line?!? 192

55. If You Choose Not To Have Kids.. 197

Wellbeing: Health and Respect | 56. Age Gracefully 199

57. People Pleasing And Patriarchy 202

58. Respect Nouns! 205

59. Know Your Addictions 208

60. Find Your Purpose 211

61. Recognize Your Privilege 215

62. Spirit, Worship, And Communion 218

63. Role Models And Mentors 222

Grief: Sickness & Death | 64. The Ocean Of Grief...................... 226

65. If I Die, Know This.. 228

66. The Body Dies, But The Spirit Lives On.................................. 231

67. Honoring The Dead 233

68. Funeral Requests 236

Enlightenment: Insights & Intentions | 69. Perpetual Growth Goals 239

70. Karma 242

71. What Money CAN Buy 245

72. Financial Advice 247

73. Regrets 252

74. Parting Wisdom, Words, and Wishes 255

Afterword 261

Acknowledgements 262

About the Author 264

Dedication

To my children who inspire me to keep trying and growing. Being your mom is the best choice I ever made and I sincerely hope I don't mess it up too much. All my blood, sweat, tears, quirks, apologies, and love.

If you would like to join the virtual book group/discussions about this book, please check out Instragram @ReparentingMyselfBook
If you feel moved to do so, please consider leaving a review
https://www.amazon.com/dp/B0CY5Y29C9

Preface

Welcome to the stream of conscious chronicles of my motherhood in all their neurotic glory!

My toxic trait is hearing about a lovely little idea, like mother-to-daughter journals, and then taking it ten thousand steps too far and way too seriously. I suppose I can beat the fun out of a casual hobby better than The Rock can beat down his WWF besties. You are now reading the product of those efforts.

What is now this book started as journal entries to my two young daughters. I have been writing to them for years and finally organized those letters into book format. Once the book was finished, I realized that it would sit collecting dust for a decade before my girls (currently 6 and 8 years old) would be ready to read it.

There it sat, burning a hole in my proverbial pocket. So, I decided to share it with the world, in case another daughter or mother somewhere would find it useful or amusing. Maybe no one will ever read this, but I'm putting it "out there" in case anyone wants some motherly love and reflection.

To any daughters reading this: Some of my advice might not apply to you, but I think the love and nurturing from a mom *should* be universal. I think everyone deserves to hear the voice of their mom telling them that they are working to break generational cycles, that they apologize for the inevitable parenting mistakes they made, and that they cherish their children. I believe this book contains messages all daughters deserve to be told; may they be familiar, healing, or helpful in some way. I hope you feel warmly enveloped in maternal loving energy as you read this.

To other moms reading this: I'm in the trenches with you, embracing the messiness of motherhood and continually falling short despite striving to do my best. Bravo to our openness, our effort, and our beautiful imperfections. May the universe pair our children with the right therapists when they are ready. May the traumas we unintentionally inflict be all micro and never macro. May our apologies be sincere and may the love be painfully genuine and earth-shatteringly strong.

A note on my anonymity: names have been omitted to protect the innocent, aka my daughters. I am dedicated to maintaining my children's online privacy and thus wanted to do so here, as well. Even though the book is my stories to them, I didn't want to embarrass them via the world wide web. I'm certain I will embarrass them enough in person, just by being myself. Professionally, I didn't want these stories to pop up when a patient googles my name (I am a primary care doctor). I also figured my ex-boyfriends and terrible roommates would not appreciate my candid reviews of my time with them, even though I expect they will never know that this exists. Naming them would put yucky energy out into the universe and I do my best to avoid that; karma is a biatch, afterall. I did have some fun dreaming up a bunch of dorky pen names, but ultimately they felt like a sham. Authenticity is my premier goal, so I didn't want to start off sharing these honest, vulnerable journals with a big fat lie. No thanks.

If you don't like this book, I totally understand. I'm not for everyone and as a recovering people pleaser, I am trying to be OK with that. None of us are everyone's taste, except the incomparable Drew Barrymore. If I'm not for you, please feel free to move on. Or feel free to roast me online, though I'm probably not worth your time and the zen thing to do would be to move on without putting negative energy into the universe. Just sayin'.

If you do like the book, I would really appreciate feedback about what I should add or delete, what approaches I might reconsider, or what experiences you have in common. I love commiserating with other moms and tend to look to moms of older girls as light posts and spirit guides.

I made an Instagram to host possible discussions since I imagine most fellow moms don't have time for formal book clubs, but usually get some bedtime procrastination Instagram scrolling. Feel free to engage with me there and maybe even other readers, if those exist.

Instagram (@ReparentingMyselfBook)
By email (MotherLodeJournals@gmail.com)
Watch in awe as I overthink every single step of this process!
Love, Anony

Introduction

Hello, girls! How old are you as you read this? As I am writing it, you are six and eight years old. It has been sitting in your keepsake bin since that age and is either being handed to you by me, alive, because you have reached your late teens or by your dad or grandma because I have tragically died. If that's the case, what a bummer.

But, lucky for you, I live in constant fear of being ripped from your life with no notice, so I have compiled all of my motherhood messages into a book for you. Being a primary care doctor has caused a level of paranoia surrounding death that I am not proud of but has provided motivation to live in the present and prepare for the worst, so I suppose it's OK.

In the following pages, I have written down all of the things I want to tell you but you are currently too young to hear. It is a detailed evaluation of my mistakes and regrets; a biased retelling of my upbringing and generational micro traumas; an honest and impassioned explanation of my parenting approach and motherhood struggles; and finally, most importantly, a declaration of my undying, unconditional love and hopes for you girls.

Reparenting is a current trend among "geriatric" millennials like me. I'm firmly on the bandwagon of psycho-analyzing myself, my childhood, my parents, and my parenting. Perhaps that's not a GOOD thing, but here I am, haunted by the fear that my best parenting still might not be good enough. I worry that all of my mistakes will echo and reverberate into your adult lives, and that the seemingly small parts of motherhood that I get wrong will outweigh all of the parts I do right. Will my worst parenting moments live immortal, rent free in your head? Will they become your inner voice? What will be my little missteps that completely change the course of your journey?

And which ones will fade into nothingness? I suppose this book is my inner people-pleasers attempt to rectify my blunders through over-explaining, and in no less than 300 pages. Classic. Part of me wonders which messages are for you, my daughters, and which ones I wrote for my own wounded inner child.

Janet Lansbury, author and leader in "respectful parenting", says that the pervasive attitudes and behaviors of parents will always trump their intentional words and lessons. Terrifying, right? I have to not only control what I say, a seemingly impossible task, but also the way I act at all times? Where do I learn the self control for that? Which parenting book am I missing? I already have hers, but she seems to be a well of patience and compassion, never losing her proverbial $h!t. Me, not so much.

I'm not hiding anything in these journals, though I try to maintain the illusion that I have it all together in person. Lurking just under my calm and collected surface lies an ocean of self doubt and questioning. Maybe it's better that you see my messy parts now, instead of waiting until you're older. You girls are both so intuitive and discerning that I doubt anything will get past you. You have a deep knowing that transcends my words and actions, and you probably already know that I'm kooky on my best days and neurotic on my worst.

I will try not to dramatize, whine about, nor trivialize events from my past. I want to allow myself to process the little failures in my upbringing genuinely, without making them bigger than they were or need to be. Hopefully, writing this can help me to reconcile the fact that my childhood was great but also had some issues, and that recognizing those weak spots does not ruin my past. Luckily, I suffer from toxic positivity (thanks, mom!), so I won't be critical of your grandparents. I know that they did their best and loved me. I tend to see everything through rosy-colored glasses, but I am beginning to appreciate that a more truthful recollection of my past may help me in moving forward as a mom.

I don't claim to have a mother wound or that my parents were emotionally immature nor narcissistic. My parents were perfectly imperfect humans, just like I am now. I don't hold anything against them, though I wish they were open to discussing the past without becoming defensive or denying my reality. Gotta love those Boomers, or at least that's what they've told me. Parts of this book could be termed micro trauma or intergenerational trauma by a therapist. However, my wounds are tiny paper cuts compared to others. After years of denying any pain existed, I have come full circle to accept that I can acknowledge my own paper cuts while having compassion and empathy for those with gaping knife wounds. I was lucky and I am grateful.

Currently, I am in a particularly reflective and introspective phase of adulthood. Doing the "deep inner work", where I once again am questioning who I am and who I want to be. Honestly, it's probably early phases of a mid-life crisis and I might go full new-age spirituality soon. Next stop, menopause! Oh, the joy!

In my darker moments, I ask myself the following questions: Am I a victim of my generation's near-obsessive need to pathologize then heal every thought we have ever had? Does that make me a whiny little biznatch? Is personal growth a complete fallacy, perpetuated by participation trophy recipients looking to validate themselves and their perceived failures? Is my claim to be growing actually just a convenient excuse to deny accountability for past bad behavior and help me feel less $hitty about yesterday's mistakes? Today, my answer is a resounding "Nope! Personal growth is real and I embrace it!". Tomorrow's answer is pending, so stay tuned.

You're about to learn how much I love metaphors, so I wanted to start with a note about the cover photo I chose: a dandelion.

What do you see? A roadside "weed", a whimsical wildflower, or a resilient, pretty blossom? Wayne Dyer says that "the difference between a flower and a weed is a judgment". According to the Merriam-Webster dictionary, a weed is defined as "a plant that is not valued where it is growing" and a wildflower is defined as "an uncultivated plant". The only difference is our perspective. Weeds can be equally beautiful but are tough, stubborn, and resilient. Weeds sprout in places where they are not wanted; they are wildflowers that become victims of circumstance.

Here are ten reasons why I find weeds and dandelions cool. I will let you read between the lines:

1) They are sturdy and can survive or thrive where other plants perish. They will stay dormant until there is an opportunity to sprout, then grow rapidly, adapting to drought or attempts to destroy them. They are fast-growing, long-living and with deep roots up to 15 feet in the ground.

2) They remind me of childhood nostalgia and wonder.

3) They are transformative from yellow flower to whimsical seed poof.

4) They can take root anywhere, even in rock or rubble. I often find them growing through cracks in the concrete. When I see these along the sidewalk, it's a little glimmer of inspiration and makes me wonder how they pushed through. Were their roots left behind before the concrete was laid? Did a dormant seed sprout through or get dropped there by a bird? Is the flower resilient and tough? Or delicate and limited due to its location and circumstances?

5) They need wind to propagate. Without wind, they will be stagnant.

6) They have a very long flowering season from early spring to late fall, much longer than traditional "pretty" flowers.

7) Dandelions are edible and actually nutritious. They have more vitamin A than spinach, more vitamin C than tomatoes, as well as lots of iron, calcium and potassium. Weeds can nourish you.

8) Despite rumors, they are good for lawns. Their wide-spreading roots loosen hard-packed soil, aerate the earth and help reduce erosion. The deep taproot pulls calcium from the soil, making it available to other plants. While many pick them as "weeds", they actually make the grass and plants around them better.

9) Dandelions are a symbol of hope, strength, and transformation.

10) Traditionally, when you blow the seed puff, you make a wish. Many people believe the seeds can carry thoughts and dreams to loved ones through the wind. This book is filled with my wishes for you, so I thought it was an appropriate cover.

Dandelions are visible reminders that you never know what little seeds have been planted and will bloom years down the road. I won't insult your intelligence by interpreting the potential metaphors for you, instead I will bite my tongue. As your mom, that is something that I am striving to do: to let you figure things out on your own, while supporting you and shining a light in the direction that I would like you to go without pushing you that way.

Weeds are a great example of the power of perception and that few issues are black and white. In these pages, I will attempt to illustrate that life is full of gray zones and near misses, that often mistakes are our greatest teachers, and that you learn the most about yourself through struggles. Hopefully, the overall tone of this book is one of love, support, hope, and humor.

I hope that my "reparenting" journey will help you to avoid becoming a people pleasing perfectionist and an emotionally stunted doormat, like I once was. I'd like you to learn emotional intelligence through my example, but have been unable to fast forward my growth as much as I would like. I have come to accept that emotional intelligence takes time and desperately rushing to progress through it will be in vain. So, I have to grow alongside you and reconcile my shortcomings while trying not to pass them on.

You and I will learn and grow together, reparenting myself as I parent you girls, and your little brother. Fingers crossed that the pervasive memories of your childhood are happy ones, and that you have plenty of room for personal growth and cultivating a genuine self love that took me far too long to find.

Above all, I wish for you joy, friendship, confidence, resilience, humor, and clarity of purpose. My parenting success does not hinge on what college you get into or how much money you make; it will be determined by your kindness as an adult, your success in relationships, your willingness to work hard, your passion for living, and whether you choose to have a close relationship with me.

I love you, I am rooting for you, and I'm sorry for any pain I may have caused.

Origins: Whos and Whys

1. Who am I?

Where do I start? How did I become this way? I ask myself that question a lot. Honestly, who is self indulgent enough to write an entire book of childhood stories and self-described wisdom for her daughters? What weirdo makes their kids a playlist of preferred songs for their own funeral? Who has the time? (NOT me!) Who has the desire? (Me!) Who is narcissistic enough to think that anyone would want to read their innermost thoughts, failures, struggles, and advice? (Maybe me?)

I fully accept that you may never read this. Maybe I'll live long enough to gradually tell all these stories in person, though honestly that would be more annoying than this book, because all my sentimental and preachy energy would be in your actual face. But maybe one day you'll want to hear me and I won't be around, so I'm hedging that bet by writing everything I want to tell you down on paper. You're welcome!

I'll start by briefly reviewing my childhood, so you can see what molded me. I know there are a lot of nature versus nurture theories out there, and the pendulum swings between the two, but I tend to favor nurture as the origin of my own maladies.

By all accounts, including my own, I had a great childhood. I had two loving parents, who gave me everything they possibly could. Before I can even remember, my parents divorced when I was five and began 50/50 joint custody. I became accustomed to moving every 3.5 days, having two homes approximately 15 minutes away from each other. In retrospect, any kid is incredibly lucky to have one loving parent and one home, so I was twice blessed, though it didn't feel that way at the time. I got used to it, but life felt like a tug-of-war and I was the rope.

I have one older sister. SPOILER ALERT: we are currently estranged. More on that later.

After the divorce, I was the protected baby of the family. I was not my mothers' emotional friend, as I believe my sister was. Therefore, we grew up in the same household, having completely different experiences. I was sporty and my dad was a coach; my sister was musical and my mom loved theater. So, the logical arrangement seemed to be my dad pairing off with me for activities and my mom pairing off with my sister. My mom and sister shared long drives to attend special theater coaching. My dad was my soccer coach and has been my cheerleader my entire life. In the last decade, he has tried to reverse his favoritism and give my sister more attention. That has led to our relationship being a bit strained, but his relationship with my sister growing stronger. I actually fully support that, since I had all the fathering that I needed as a child and she feels she did not. I think I got what I needed, when I needed it.

Despite the divorce, my parents were able to semi-peacefully co-parent and I grew up in a pretty blissful, suburban, middle-class existence. My parents were both teachers, and worked 2 or 3 jobs each to support us. They definitely demonstrated a solid work ethic, and though we were not rich, my sister and I had all of our basic needs met and more. I lived in a safe neighborhood with tons of kids, at a time when computers and cell phones did not exist. We could run over to the park or a friend's house without much thought, as long as we were back for dinner. We would ride our dirt bikes down the street and go fishing in the neighborhood creek. I wish growing up was more like that today.

I did well in school and sports and prided myself on being a hard worker. I probably wasn't the smartest nor the fastest, but I worked my little booty off to have straight As and be MVP. My mantra was that I could out work someone else's talent. While I have found that to be true through most of my life, having some talent sure would have been nice at times.

After high school, I went away to an awesome university, which was the first of many life-changing experiences. I majored in pre-med Biology and competed for two years as a walk-on to the Cross Country team. After college, I took a year to work, apply to medical school, and save money. I got accepted to a few schools and chose one an hour from home.

After medical school, I completed residency and now I'm a primary care doctor. I met your dad online during intern year and he proposed during my final year of residency. We married one year later and got pregnant with you, my oldest daughter, around our first wedding anniversary. That's the basic outline, but skims over all the struggles and growth that happened along the way, so I'll get to that in a bit.

And that brings me to the present day as a part-time primary care doctor and married mom of three. It's great AND it's a lot. I like to think of myself as a passionate social justice advocate and outdoorsy granola person, but in reality am way more complacent, suburban, boring soccer mom than I care to acknowledge. I'm working on it, though!

As I write this, you girls are ages 8 and 6, and your brother is 3. I'm not sure at what age it will be appropriate for you to read this book; maybe as teens, though I can't imagine you will want to hear anything I have to say at that stage. Maybe in adulthood, when I'm dead and gone. Maybe never and all these thoughts will go unread into the void. At least they'll be out of my head.

My subconscious child-mind coping mechanism for my parents' divorce was to become a desperate people-pleaser. At home, I would go with the flow and be the "easy kid" with no feelings or problems. While this served me well in my youth and led to adoration as the high-achieving, "well adjusted" baby of the family, my people pleasing tendency still haunts me to this day. I'm trying so hard to break out of it, but it is ingrained in every fiber of my being. Your poor dad married a bend-over-backwards people pleaser who he is now emotionally supporting through "becoming her own person" and asserting her needs, aka I'm becoming more and more difficult with age. Poor guy. But, yay for me!

Currently, I identify as Dr. so-and-so and "(your name)'s mom"; I'm certain some people in the neighborhood don't know my actual name. But before I was a doctor and your mom, I was a complete person on my own which is hard to imagine at this point. Like every human, I had a unique set of circumstances and challenges that made me who I am today. Some made me funny and quirky, others made me neurotic and unbearable. I want to share my coming of age, in an effort to break cycles of generational microtrauma and move you along on your own path to self discovery. My hope is that by sharing my trials and tribulations, illuminating what I am trying to do differently than my own parents, and laying out all the little signs on the road that I may have missed, I can spare you some of the heartache, self-doubt, and grief I experienced. This might turn out to be a rambling mess but I'll give it a try anyways.

2. Why am I like this?

Define "this", you ask. Competitive, perfectionistic, and emotionally stunted. I have positive qualities, too, but this isn't the place for highlighting those.

I tend toward being competitive and while this may have served me well in sports and school, it no longer serves me as an adult. In my family, everything was a competition. The person with the best grades, or the fastest time, or the most trophies, or the prom date, or the cutest outfit was better. We were always made to feel competitive with the people around us including friends and siblings. I never, ever want that for you, especially as siblings. And I never want that for myself, as a mother. Now that I'm an adult, I have re-programed how I see differences. Differences shouldn't be organized into a hierarchy of best to worst, they can be appreciated like different colors of the rainbow. What another person is doing has nothing to do with me. There is no need to compare yourself to anyone else, every human is on their own journey, in their own time.

Competition and comparison culture are directly correlated to feelings of inadequacy, judgment, and failure. Trust me, I lived it for at least 25 years. Previously, I was a very jealous person, but now I am channeling that into admiration for awesome women. Instead of comparison culture, I hope that I raise you in a culture of gratitude. One where you can appreciate another woman's beauty, brains, and bad-ass-ness without feeling threatened or less-than. One where you can understand others' inadequacies from a place of wanting to do their best but sometimes falling short, and not holding their human-ness against them. One where you gladly celebrate other's victories without longing for them yourself.

When you meet someone new, I want you to assume that they are a potential ally rather than a potential enemy. I want you to see everyone as a possible contributor to your happiness rather than a threat to your resources. I don't want you to feel that if someone scores a goal or gets a better grade on a test, that they are more worthy of other peoples' love and attention. You are worthy of love and attention because you are breathing in this world, and because you are my child who I will always love no matter what.

Perfection does not exist. I want you to know your worth regardless of accomplishments, grades, or other outward measures. In the past, I have suffered from impossibly high, self-imposed standards. High standards are well and good, but unrealistic standards set me up for perceived failure and disappointment. I competed against myself in a losing battle. I was a straight A student, never missed a game or practice, and (almost) always strove to do the right thing. It led to frequent praise which reinforced my desire to perform. Perfectionism still haunts me because I believed for too long that my worth came from outside of myself. It's a slippery slope to live on and I do not recommend it.

Some people focus on perfecting their appearance, others their career, and worst of all I see some moms channeling their perfectionism into parenting (tutoring and coaching their kids to oblivion). Hopefully I am raising you to feel good enough at LIFE that you are free to relax, explore, struggle and find your passions. You have my unwavering support to be brave enough to fail and to joyfully relax into your imperfections, which make you your unique and wonderful self.

As a (former?) people-pleasing perfectionist, I still question my likes and dislikes at times. When I was dating your dad and he asked where I wanted to go for dinner, my most common answer was "wherever you want". Sad, right? Even now, I ask myself if I really genuinely like something or if I convinced myself I liked it because it was convenient to others and led to approval. At this point, I will never know.

Lastly, expressing and embracing the full spectrum of emotions is challenging for me. I always wondered why until I heard grandma tell you girls, "don't cry!". It's funny, as a parent, how the inner mysteries of who we are can become unlocked through our "re-parenting" journey. Witnessing my parents' interactions with you can be a bit triggering, but is immensely helpful in understanding why I'm like this. Emotions are tricky and I catch myself messing up this part of parenting all the time: trying to soothe your feelings and dry your tears, instead of encouraging them.

As a kid, I was praised for "always being so happy" and it irks me when my mom praises you girls for being similar. Don't get me wrong, I love grandma, but I can love her while acknowledging flaws and wanting to do things differently in certain aspects of child-rearing. I was once nick-named "cupcake sunshine" because I was always so positive and happy. I took pride in it at the time, but now recognize it was a label to my toxic positivity and inability to show any negative emotions.

In medical residency, I had a wonderful friend encourage me to keep a "feelings journal" after they pointed out my limited range of emotions (basically, happiness and anger). That exercise helped me realize there were (gasp!) OTHER feelings like sadness, jealousy, fear, frustration, guilt, excitement, embarrassment, and pride. I literally had to look up a feelings chart (which I highly recommend) to name my feelings. I realized that when I felt any negative emotion, I would transform it into anger, which was super lame and unhealthy.

Post-feelings-journal epiphany, I hope to support and encourage you to feel all the feels. It is incredibly difficult, because as your parent I want you to BE happy. At times, I have the power to MAKE you happy. So, when you are UN-happy, my intuitive knee-jerk reaction is to fix it. Hopefully, I succeed at convincing myself not to fix your feelings, but to instead hold space for them, help you name them, and support you through them. I am often overcome by worry that I will repeat my mother's mistakes and royally screw this up, but I promise I am trying my best. *fingers crossed*

3. Who made me this way?

In short, my mom and dad molded me into the person I am: the beautiful parts and the broken parts. By reflecting on all they did right and wrong, I hope that I can parent you without passing down too much generational trauma. Both of my parents loved me unconditionally and did their absolute best, which is all anyone can really ask for. However, after becoming a mom, I spent a year only being able to see their parental mistakes; only recognizing their inadequacies; only feeling frustration and resentment at the things I would have done differently. I think that that's a natural progression, if you ever choose to have children yourself. You'll criticize my choices, rage against the parenting that messed you up, and eventually come full circle to accept that it's just plain hard and everyone is doing their best with the tools they have available.

Right now, they call that process re-parenting. It can only be done by those with enough emotional maturity and resilience to ask the tough questions of themselves; only those who are not so fragile as to fall apart at self reflection can do it. So, by the fact that I'm on that journey at all, I know my parents did many things right. Remind me of that when you're older and criticizing me: that it's a part of the personal growth process and it means you're evolving.

I have a running list of the things I intend to do differently than my parents. The biggies are letting you feel all of your feelings, encouraging closeness among siblings, emphasizing the importance of friendship, and modeling a happy and healthy adulthood.

I often wish my parents had managed my sibling relationship differently. Perhaps there are those who will say that that relationship was always mine to manage and not theirs. But they wedged themselves in there, so I'm going to blame them (partly, at least). I hope that you all stay close as you age. Your sibling is your first friend and the most likely to stick around for life. As you know, my sister and I barely speak. I'll explain all of that later, in hopes you can avoid my siblinghood mistakes. I fear projecting my own hopes of what siblinghood can be onto your sisterhood bond. Perhaps it is too much pressure and will throw a wrench in your natural sibling progression. I don't have the answers and it's a tricky tightrope to walk, but I will aim to help you avoid my mistakes without obsessing about them.

Because my parents were divorced, I also did not get to witness adult friendship or self care. I saw two adults, at separate times, who loved me and were 100% present and never had any personal needs. It literally occurred to me after my second child that they were able to sustain that level of enthusiasm, patience, and availability because they had 50/50 custody. They gave me EVERYTHING when they were with me because they had 3.5 days per week to put in extra time at work, go grocery shopping, exercise, have a romantic life, and see friends. When I became a parent, I tried to emulate their level of love and COULD NOT. It finally occurred to me why and I felt like an absolute idiot. Of course, one cannot sustain 100% effort, 100% of the time in modern day parenting, but they could sustain 100% effort, 50% of the time.

I should add the things my parents did right, because I don't want to rag on them or trash talk them. They were great parents. I always knew that they loved me, trusted me, and wanted the absolute best for me. My dad was so FUN and supportive. My mom always praised me for "marching to the beat of my own drummer" which built my self esteem, helped me navigate peer pressures, and allowed me to feel comfortable off the beaten path. Both of them seemed to genuinely like me, which as a people pleaser helped me to like myself. They say what you hear during childhood becomes your inner voice, and thankfully mine is kind, loving, confident, and secure. Though not flush with cash, I was well cared for with food, clothing, and shelter. I was born into a great deal of privilege, as were you, and it was something I was aware of from an early age and encouraged to transform into social justice action.

There are probably a million other little things that my parents did right and wrong. I'm still learning and processing many of them. But, the bottom line is that I'm a big girl now and it is my responsibility to move through those experiences so that they don't reflexively become YOUR experiences.

I always thought I would parent so consciously and pre-think all of my words and actions to carefully cultivate your childhood experience. But this $h!t is HARD. In the hurried desperation of a moment, I hear my mother's voice and words from my childhood leave my mouth as my own. All my impulses are carbon copies of the parenting I experienced for 18 years, which I suppose makes sense. But those reflexive impulses are in direct contrast to my conscious intentions. I want to be more gentle and speak more slowly and calmly, but instead my words and actions sometimes trigger my inner child. I don't like it and I'm trying to fight it. So wish me luck, your life literally depends on it! :)

4. What changed me?

What helped me grow into the person that I am today was getting out of my comfort zone and having opportunities to struggle. Don't you wish I could stop with such a short answer? If "brevity is the soul of wit", I must be witless, so obviously I will elaborate.

Leaving my comfort zone included going off to college, where I was exposed to new points of view, people, and places. It was a chance to build a new friend group and be the person that I wanted to be. Going away to college was an important first step in my reinvention and exposure to new ideas. Finding a new town was invigorating and pivotal for me, but it could be done by simply moving out of the house and starting life on your own.

My next chance for growth was a struggle and one that I now appreciate. In college, I "walked on" to the cross country team, which brought me a new friend group of teammates and a sense of pride in being able to compete at a college level. However, after working hard and training all summer, I was cut from the team my junior year. This came as a shock because I ran a personal best at tryouts and had done well my previous two years, running faster than some recruits.

I believe the coach saw that I didn't take running very seriously. As a walk-on pre-med, I never put all my eggs in the athlete basket. Instead of focusing on training, I took school seriously and knew that it was my ultimate purpose. The team was full of recruits who were admitted to the school specifically to run. The recruits treated being on the team very seriously, while I was there for pure joy and pride. I would laugh at practice, make jokes, flirt with the boys, and probably didn't push myself physically as much as I should have. I won't mention how the coach was a bitter little man, who treated walk-ins like second class citizens compared to his recruits. Or how he proved his character by cutting me in an email listing the new team (my name was missing) and not giving me the courtesy of an explanation or farewell. Or that cutting me was likely based on nepotism and not my playfulness. Nope, I will be the bigger person by omitting those details.

The fact that I was cut devastated me and was a huge blow to my ego, but was ultimately a blessing, as so many disappointments are. After I was no longer spending hours per week at practice, my grades went up which ultimately set the stage for getting into medical school. The most difficult part of being cut was that my previous teammates, who I had considered my "best friends", were nowhere to be found. There was not one call or text or contact from those teammates ever again. I thought that I had a solid group of friends who would grow with me into adulthood, but instead I was ghosted.

I was left scrambling for a new social group. I had moved in with new roommates that I met in the dorms, but they were not my tribe. I did have friends at church who I enjoyed and a few former runners who had left the team, too, of their own volition. Finding my way through that experience was gut wrenching. However, it led to a defining moment: On the day that I was cut from the team, I was crying and devastated, not knowing where to turn. I was too afraid to tell my dad, because I felt like I had disappointed him, so I didn't call home right away. So, what did I do? I sat down and thought deeply about my disappointment. I thought about all that competitive running had given me and also what it may have taken away. I realized that while running in college, I put pressure on a passion which had stolen the fun. I was so focused on keeping up with the recruits and competing, that running had lost some of its joy. I couldn't remember the last time I went casually jogging. So I strapped on my running shoes, went to my favorite trail, and started run-frolicking around without a watch. I hadn't run watchless in years. It was the perfect medicine for that moment.

After that, I was forced to find new friends, buckle down in school, and reinvent myself. The devastation offered a unique opportunity to rebuild from scratch, just like a fire burning through a forest leaves fertile soil for new growth. I am glad to have had that opportunity at that age. In hindsight, I was lucky to learn that those teammates were not my true friends early on.

I imagine that having trusted people disappear when postpartum or later in life would have been even more difficult. Not making a team is pretty trivial, looking back. Those girls gave me the gift of telling me who they really were: teammates not soulmates.

My next big time of growth and disappointment was not getting chosen for the medical residency that I had hoped for. I desired to attend a very well respected hippie-filled residency near my former college town. Instead, I "matched" in the same city as my medical school, an hour from my hometown. I felt stuck and stagnant, when I was determined to enter a time of growth. I was looking forward to another opportunity to reinvent myself and felt that was being denied. The residency match process is applying for all jobs simultaneously and then getting chosen for only one. There is no negotiation and your "match", i.e. the job site that selects you, is legally binding. But some don't get chosen at all, so I should have been glad to have a spot and a great one at that. All things considered, it was for the best because this town is where I met your dad, I received excellent training, and I stayed close to my parents. The universe really knows what it's doing. Of course, I didn't see it that way at the time. It felt like I wasn't good enough, like I wasn't chosen for the team, and that I was doomed to stay the same.

Ironically, when I interviewed at the residency of my dreams, I heard about an elective that peaked my interest. It was a month-long integrative medicine focused co-op living retreat in the redwoods at the end of medical school, to de-program all the inhumanity of medical education. Obviously I signed up immediately and it became my next big life changing experience. It plucked me out of my hometown and deep into the redwoods with a group of like-minded individuals. It was the first time I was surrounded by people who felt like my tribe. No TV, limited cell service, and nothing but time and space to learn and grow. That elective became instrumental in me becoming the person that I am today. I made lifelong friends, had time to process my disappointment over my residency match, and reflected on what I wanted out of life. In many ways, because I learned about the elective while interviewing at the residency that rejected me, it felt full circle. That residency DID give me an amazing experience, just not the one I sought or expected.

Another time of growth and challenge was residency itself. I met your dad during intern year, so everything was colored by the excitement that new love provides. Unfortunately, some of the sting of not getting my intended match never left. Part of this had to do with the death of my dream: returning to my college town where I had my first big personal growth, where I could be the idealized hippie version of myself. I struggled to connect with other residents, likely due to subconsciously distancing myself from the group and pre-determining that the residency culture was not my vibe.

In an irony that can only be understood by reading the last few paragraphs, while in residency I attended a redwoods group reunion. There, one of my elective mentors hosted an open healing circle for everyone to discuss their current stressors. There were people who discussed infertility, divorce, struggling to find a job that they love, and some questioning whether they belonged in medicine at all. My struggle was the disappointment of my residency match. Trivial in comparison, I know. Without missing a beat, my mentor verbalized what I had not been able to articulate until that moment: "well, they're just not your tribe". And that summed it up perfectly.

I liked and respected the colleagues in my residency program, but I did not feel the kinship that I had hoped for. I was the only vegetarian in the program, carried my own camping spork (to avoid single-use plastics), and preferred to escape into nature than hit up the downtown dance clubs. In my mind, people thought I was kooky and weird, though no one ever said that. It was a convenient assumption to confirm my belief that this wasn't the spot for me. I wanted to sing and dance and be goofy, but didn't feel comfortable enough to do so. In retrospect, if I had been more authentic, perhaps people would have appreciated my quirks. It's hard for anyone to get to know you or fully accept you, when you don't let them in. I made one friend in residency and she's super cool. I did receive an excellent education, I met your dad, and I made connections that have lasted into my current career.

So, that is basically how I came to be. My childhood, in all of its stumbling glory, and my challenges, which took me out of my comfort zone and chiseled me into the person that I am today. I hope that you have the same opportunities for growth, reflection, and struggle without danger. Those are the things that make life worth living. If it were happy and easy all the time, we would not be as compassionate, as hard-working, or as resilient when trouble does arrive.

5. How did I turn out?

By most accounts, people would say that I turned out well. From my parents' perspective, I turned out awesome! Yay boomers! I have been married for ten years. I have three healthy children. I am a doctor. I am a financially stable home-owner. I guess I would agree, though my opinion has nothing to do with the above checkboxes, but rather that I feel content and healthy, like I am currently on the right path.

Still, though, there are parts of me that I think could've turned out better. I have struggled socially and with people pleasing. Asserting my needs and setting boundaries does not come naturally. My need for approval and to be liked has often clouded my judgment and led me to play it safe. I wonder what would differ had I not played by society's rules and listened to my heart more often, or at all.

Friendship is so difficult and important to me, that I have written countless journals to you girls outlining my mistakes and recommendations. Though I now have a few treasured friends who fully know and love me, I've lost friendships along the way because I didn't know how to be a good friend, was immature, or just plain lacked social skills.

I stumbled through meeting people and clinging onto whoever would tolerate me. I did not choose my company very intentionally, and then even if I lucked into a lovely group, didn't make an effort to maintain those friends. I expected to always be on the receiving end of invitations, but was not confident enough to pass them out. Various friend groups came and went, some who I wish I would have integrated into more fully. Now, as a mom, I see you struggling with so many of the same situations. I try to coach you through it, but social settings are genuinely not something that comes naturally and I hope I am not leading you astray. Hopefully the social skills books I bought are helping me to figure it out.

As I said, I am a doctor. I used to think that's what I wanted to do from a young age, and specifically a doctor for the homeless. However, in my older age, my mom revealed that her childhood dream was to be a doctor. So, I began to wonder, was it ever really my dream? Was I led down this path by someone else? I am, after all, an immeasurable people pleaser. Did I choose my career to please my mom? Did I choose my career because it is well respected by society? Did I choose my career because I was naturally gifted at science and it would prove my smartness, which always really mattered to me? Or did I choose my career out of my own interest and passion? These questions are unanswerable. And maybe it doesn't matter. I am happy, able to support a family on a part-time schedule, and have the general approval and respect of both my parents and society. I just wish that approval didn't still matter to me.

I also think there is something to be said for taking the road less traveled, perhaps by having a less typical career and schooling path. I was never confident enough to do that. I was raised to do well in school, be competitive, and go to a well respected university. I thought that by going to a top school it would prove something and help my confidence. This is true to some extent, but if I had been more secure in my own intelligence I could have gone to a small liberal arts college and had the same wonderful college experience. I was too afraid to think outside the box. I never once questioned the expectation that I would attend college. I never once stopped to think if an MD-adjacent field would have been a good fit, such as becoming a nurse, an acupuncturist, or a physical therapist. Too late now. I love my job and am good at what I do, but spending an additional seven years in school and residency is a huge chunk of life. I postponed living during some of my best years in order to study and I'm not sure that's a track I would recommend to you.

Given that I have played by all of societies' rules, an outsider might consider me to have turned out well. I have never majorly failed at something I attempted, I have never been arrested or in big trouble, and in general I have not lied, cheated, or betrayed anyone. Some of my notable failures are: my relationship with my sister, my move from underserved nonprofit medicine to for-profit medicine, my switch from vegetarian to meat-eater, and my lapse in social justice activities since becoming a parent. I'm still working on being the parent that I want to be.

About a year ago, I switched from full-time nonprofit medicine to part-time for-profit medicine. I needed more time for our family but it felt like selling out. After all, I pursued medicine to give back to those in need and switching patient populations felt like a betrayal to my soul. Now I can see clearly that it was the right move. Of course I miss that part of my life, my old patients and coworkers, but I know I gave them 10 years of my best effort and can always volunteer during retirement. My new job has allowed me the time and space to work on myself physically, mentally, and emotionally, and to be more present as a parent. I get to volunteer in your classes, attend school functions, and stay home with you when you are sick. Part-time work has also afforded me the space to breathe, but it came at the cost of my original dream of being a doctor to those in need. But now I tell myself: everyone is in need, just in different ways, and I am still helping people. This is exactly what a sellout might say.

After cutting back my work hours, I finally feel balanced and like I am swimming, instead of treading water and barely staying afloat. I know so many moms who are close to drowning and I wish everyone were so lucky to have this time and space. I'm still finding the right balance. I have trouble allowing myself to rest. When I am not with you kids or at work, I aim to busy myself but I am learning to be OK with naps or quietly journaling. There's a productivity bias deeply ingrained in me and I find myself feeling a need to justify "non-productive" endeavors.

Having time to work on myself is helping me to deep dive into my self improvement goals. I am building up tolerance for my imperfections and decreasing tolerance for other people's BS. I identify as a "recovering people pleaser", though I relapse often. As a parent, I want to please you kids; as a wife, I want to please your dad; as a doctor, I want to please my patients. However, I have come to acknowledge that I cannot please everyone and should not do so at my own expense. In parenthood, I am trying to reconcile keeping you happy all the time with needing to help you build up your frustration tolerance. You NEED to experience disappointment, sadness, and anger; it actually HURTS you when I try to prevent situations which will cause those emotions. My reflex is to protect you from bad things, but I'm trying to allow in the emotional diversity I deprived myself as a child.

I still have a constant need to feel approval from people who will never give it to me, such as my mother-in-law and my sister. I have to accept that and take ownership of my own sense of self-worth. It is harder said than done but something I am working toward. Your dad has actually been helpful with that. One of the most attractive things about him is that he has zero impulse to please people. As his wife that can be frustrating, but overall it is a very healthy and a rare trait to witness. I appreciate that he encourages me to dissolve my desires for outside approval.

My hope for you is that you will feel successful no matter what you do in life and always feel loved and worthy. Bumps happen along the road and historically these make us better over time. Your sense of approval should come from the inside and not from me, but I will always love you and be cheering for you to be your best self.

In reality, as to how I have turned out, the jury is still out. I say that because my most important judgment in life will be from you, likely after I'm dead and gone. I want you to define your own success. Make your own timelines, admit mistakes and learn from them, fail wholeheartedly then try again, and go off path and blaze your own trail. Be brave enough to stumble around while finding your way and secure enough in yourself to fully explore your passions (hobbies, career, people) before committing. These are my hopes for your version of success. You will be glorious, because you already are!

6. How I met your dad?

I floundered a bit in the dating department, due to my general awkwardness, inability to open up, and lack of time and focus on romance. At 27, I entered medical residency single and eager to mingle. So, I did what any smart girl whose biological clock is ticking does: I dove head first into online dating. Initially, I messaged back and forth into oblivion without meeting many people in person. When I would finally meet someone, I was disappointed when we didn't click, his picture was very different from his profile, or he was 6-8 inches shorter than advertised.. Thankfully, a bit of wine and some goofy friends helped change that.

I had a girls night with two friends from medical school and the wine flowed freely. For fun, we projected my dating profile onto the big screen and my friend went on a flirtation rampage (while signed in to my profile). With her driving the mouse, someone drunkenly, we sent winks and flirty messages to a variety of people who I otherwise would not have messaged. I was absolutely mortified. I had been approaching online dating way too seriously and not really putting myself "out there". My typical approach was painstakingly reading through profiles, looking for red and green flags, and barely messaging anyone at all or waiting for the right guy to make the first "move".

That all changed with that drunken night of debauchery, thank goodness! After tolerating someone else putting me out there and surviving, I was less scared to send messages. I started emailing more freely and avoided in person let downs by meeting people right off the bat.

With this new method, I ended up going on not quite 50 first dates, but probably 20. There were many first dates and very few second dates. I had a few dates with a wanna-be stand up comic, who was bald and ALWAYS wore a newsboy cap. Baldness doesn't bother me at all, but I just couldn't be the potential wife of the "newsboy cap guy". Then, I went on a few dates with a funny and nice graduate student but the sparks just weren't there. Then, one day, I came across your dad's profile and I was really excited for the first time in a long time. I eagerly emailed him and he replied to set up a date.

On our first date, your dad and I hiked up a nearby mountain. Initially, we were both sort of shy and quiet. On the way up the mountain, I remember thinking: "we aren't hitting it off but at least I'm getting some exercise". But by the time we hiked down the mountain, conversation was flowing and I didn't want it to end. He agreed and suggested we get post-hike pizza. When we were done eating, we were still caught up in conversation, so we found a little café where we sat and talked. I remember when we were talking at that cafe, I sat criss-cross applesauce style on a bench and marveled a little bit on the inside at how comfortable I felt and how easy the conversation was flowing. I don't think I had ever experienced that before. I felt utterly open and eager to talk more. On our first date, your dad told me that he had been previously engaged. Many would think this was a huge faux pas and red flag, but I took it as a sign that he trusted me and was an honest person. We immediately talked about scheduling another date, but I wasn't sure if he would ever call. Spoiler alert: he did.

On our second date, he took me out to dinner at a very cool vegetarian restaurant. Once again we could not stop talking, so we went to an Irish pub for drinks afterwards. Our first date was something like eight hours long and our second date I think was six hours.

On our third day, we hiked a different local mountain and had our first kiss at the top. Afterwards, he cooked me dinner at his house with cinnamon rolls for dessert. He suggested dating exclusively. We always joke that he won me over with his Pillsbury Cinnamon Rolls. From then on we were pretty serious, pretty fast.

Our early days involved quite a bit of drama, with me feeling insecure and worrying that I liked him more than he liked me. I suppose I worried about putting myself out there too far, being too vulnerable and getting hurt. But, love is a leap of faith and once I surrendered to the risk and stopped getting in my own way, things went more smoothly. We always had great communication and were able to work through the issues. As the relationship grew, I was more confident in us as a team.

He proposed on the top of his favorite home mountain, with a gorgeous ring he designed all by himself and obviously I said yes. We got married at the beach in November, which is risky weather-wise. It rained the morning of our wedding, which is supposedly good luck. There were rainbows and in the evening, a gorgeous pink sunset. It was a lovely little reminder that you can't have a rainbow without a little rain.

In an interesting twist, when I met your dad online I met another gentleman, who was one of the two best internet dudes I had ever found, but definitely second to you dad. I went on one date with him, and he pursued a second, but I turned him down because I had met your dad. Had I not met your dad, I probably would have been very excited about pursuing something with dude #2. This just goes to show that when it rains, it freaking pours! It also lends to a very "Sliding doors" version of our lives. If one thing had been different, I could have lived a totally different life.

I fully believe someone can live one hundred different lives and be happy and fulfilled in each of them. I don't believe in one soulmate or one path or destiny for each person. I believe each person makes their own path, perhaps guided by a higher power or the universe or whatever you want to call it, and there are seemingly small forks in the road that take you to vastly different destinations. Imagining all of the different possibilities is mind boggling. I could have gone to medical school in Ohio. I could have NOT been cut from my college cross country team. I could have met someone other than your dad. I'm happy all roads converged here, to you being my children.

So, it all worked out. It involved me being vulnerable and putting myself out there to a bunch of random dudes online, and waiting until the moment and the person were right. It also involved being choosy, knowing what I wanted out of life (and therefore from a partner), and not ever feeling an inclination to settle or force something that was a little off. Hold out for your best match, girls! You will know when it "feels right".

7. My Core Childhood Memories

Childhood memories are funny, because you live so many years, but have maybe a dozen or so moments that stick out in your mind. We don't get to choose which memories they are. Perhaps they are the ones where our emotions are at their highest. Perhaps they are the stories that our parents tell us about ourselves. Perhaps they are the ones captured in pictures to help us recall the details. Perhaps they are randomly selected by the universe. My core memories have become embedded into my consciousness, and some of them have begun to define who I am. I'll share a few of mine that I recall clear as day, in chronological order.

My first core memory is searching for our family cat underneath the bed in my sister's room. Weird, huh? I'm not sure if the cat had died, if he was about to die, or if he was lost, but I remember a sense of dread and worry. I've had recurrent dreams about this memory where I am frantically searching and cannot find this cat. I must have been less than five because I remember knowing that my parents were both in the house, so it was pre-divorce. In the dreams, I never find the cat. In reality, I don't recall if I found him or not, but I do know that he died around that age. I'm sure a lot of psychoanalysis can go into more detail about what this dream might mean and why it's my first core memory, but I will spare you. You're welcome.

I also remember my dad bringing home donuts on Saturday mornings, before the divorce. After the divorce, my mom would make French toast or pancakes on Saturday mornings at her house. Now, I make French toast or pancakes for you on the weekends. I'm not the best cook, I'll admit, but it feels nice making something that people look forward to eating.

During my parents divorce, I watched the movie "Annie" every afternoon. My parents say it "got me through" the divorce; screentime for the win, I guess? I know every word and every song in that movie, and oddly enough I still get uncomfortable every time they are climbing up that ladder.

The sense of worry and danger never escapes me, even though I know the happy ending as clear as day. It is interesting that even knowing how things turn out, it can be stressful in the process. If you grow up to be a therapist, you can tell me how watching a movie about a distraught orphan struggling to find a home was perhaps NOT the best subject for a kid whose family was disintegrating. But, as they say, I "turned out fine" so I won't overthink it.

I remember my dad's mom making pot roast and Christmas cookies when she would visit. The smell of onions in a crockpot brings me right back to my childhood kitchen. I remember my mom's mom asking me to help her garden during Easter, and I threw a fit because I didn't want to get out of my Easter dress and get all dirty. In retrospect, my mom's mom was so incredibly cool. She lived in a little shack by the ocean, listened to NPR, watched PBS, was a patron of the arts, and recycled before anyone else did. She was so stylish, too; her house was full of mid-century modern gems and eclectic beach art. I saw pictures of her from the 1940s with her hair done up, looking incredibly elegant. In her older age, she was equally beautiful but never wore a speck of make-up, which I think is so cool. The little wooden whale on your shelf was hers. She would clip newspaper articles for my mom, which my mom found incredibly annoying but now I see them as her love language. I regret not gardening with her that Easter, since I know now that she was trying to pass down her love of plants to me. I wish I had just dove into the mud and soaked up all the time with her that I could. I am happy to say that I realized how cool she was and appreciated her before she died (when I was in medical school).

On a road trip with my mom and sister, my mom once asked for a piece of candy. We handed her a starburst and she ate it immediately, still wrapped. We STILL laugh sometimes about her eating that Starburst wrapper. We went on annual summer road trips with many treats along the way and funny occurrences, but this seemingly small memory is the one that sticks. All the others coalesce into vague general remembrances of my childhood.

During the summers, my dad worked at a summer camp and my sister and I would get to tag along for a week. It was awesome getting to run around by ourselves in nature, eat in a mess hall, and have the quintessential summer camp experience without being away from a parent. I remember wild boar rummaging around our cabin in the middle of the night, scrounging for scraps of food. The cabins did not have doors, so the employee dads slept on the bottom bunks while all the tag-along kids slept on the top bunks to stay safe. I remember not being scared at all, but rather thinking those boars were super fun and exciting.

A funny story you may appreciate about me: laundry eluded me as a freshman in college. I have been doing my own laundry since middle school because grandma always encouraged chores. However, she purchased the detergent and dryer sheets. Once in college, that became my responsibility. I lived in the dorms without much space, so I was looking for the smallest possible container and saw one with that little bear logo. Having seen commercials about how nicely the clothes smelled and felt after washing with it, I bought the Snuggles brand, believing it was detergent. I washed my clothes with only fabric softener (no soap!) for my entire first year of college, until a friend asked to borrow my detergent and clued me in. Clean or not, all of freshman year my clothes were very soft and smelled great!

There are a million other little memories like building couch forts, tying my favorite uncle up with masking tape, my dad dancing like a dork to supermarket music (and me feeling embarrassed), playing putt-putt into a glass in the living room with my dad, camping with my mom and hiking across log bridges, and screaming the song "Build Me Up Buttercup" while on the team bus in high school. I am so fortunate that so many of my core childhood memories are happy ones. I know many are not so lucky.

Your dad and I are aiming to create a childhood for you filled with mostly positive memories. I know that it can't all be positive and that fighting the hard feelings is not in your best interest. I hope that you remember our family dance parties and blasting music in the living room, your first time seeing dolphins swim in the ocean, and rascalling around with your siblings. I hope you remember our home being fun and loud and comfortable, even if it was not always clean and tidy. I hope you remember me being loving and supportive, and not uptight and controlling. These are my wishes for your childhood.

8. Why am I writing this?

Why would I write a book to you?

1) To take my monologue tendency to new heights!

2) To be insufferable, but silently on a shelf.

3) Because I heard that other moms write letters to their children (to read in case mom dies) and I decided to take it ten steps too far, as I do everything.

4) Because I'm probably a narcissist but if I channel it into parental advice, it's not as obviously pathologic.

5) To haunt you for eternity.

6) Because I'm hilarious?

Real talk, though: I live with a fear of being plucked from this earth and ripped from your lives without notice. Unfortunately, I see it happen at work more often than I would like: someone is grieving a loved one who died very suddenly, tragically, and they are not sure where to turn. I want to be there for all of your greatest and worst moments, to cheer you on and support you. Currently, I have things to say that you're too young to hear. I have annoying advice up the wazoo that nobody really wants but I think you might one day NEED. So, putting it on paper and out into the universe helps me sleep at night.

I like knowing that if you are ever without me, you will know how much I loved you because I have written it to you (ad nauseam). If I die young, you might think "wow, what foresight!", and if I live forever we can all laugh "paranoid, much?". Plus, I fully know and expect there will be a time in your teens when you naturally pull away and won't want to listen to me, but perhaps I'll be tolerable in written form. If you can't bear to read any farther, I understand. Please skip ahead and check out my playlists in "Music

Therapy", organized by emotion. My hope is that you can find joy, solace, inspiration, and reflection through listening to some of the songs that have helped me through big feelings. If you take anything from this collection of my thoughts, let it be the playlists.

I started writing journal entries to you when you were babies. I saw an Instagram post with the idea to create an email address for your kids, send messages and pictures to it, and then give your kids the password when they turn 18. When we would do a memorable family activity, I would write to you about it. When I saw a teen at work struggling through something who needed motherly counsel, my thoughts would wander to you and wanting to give you that counsel NOW, before it was too late. So there have been scattered mother-to-daughter journals since your birth. Fast forward a few years and here we are.

About a year ago, I started dictating these journals during my work commute and going back to edit them later. Your dad says I should focus on driving (insert me shrugging), but I like feeling in communion with you on my way to and from work. I like being able to consolidate and clarify my thoughts when I am all alone in the quiet. As a working mom of three, I don't get much quiet. So, I talk to you while I drive and my handy-dandy phone transcribes it. As the journals began gathering, I realized the rambling was disorganized and sometimes repetitive, so I curated them into categories and then filled in the topics that I felt were missing. Is it super weird of me? Yes! But, I always say weird is good!

I have a fear while writing this: that my intended tone (gentle love, humor, and support) will come through, but that that tone will be SO remarkably disparate to my actual real-life personality that you won't even recognize me. Hopefully my actual voice matches the voice in this book, though as I have said my intentions and actions sometimes stray from one another.

You might ask why I addressed this to you "girls" and not all three of my kids. Baby boy, if you're reading this, all the love and reverence definitely applies to you. However, a few of the messages would vary. I am hoping to find time to write down the differences: lessons on consent, how to be an awesome ally (since right now is thankfully NOT the heyday of the white male), and how to share the mental load. So many aspects of fatherhood are changing that maybe I won't need to say much, but the messages the patriarchy have beaten us all down with for centuries need to be deprogrammed and I want to help that effort. When you kids role-play at home he simultaneously plays the dad and the baby, so you girls are literally breeding him to be a man-child. He would need a whole chapter on avoiding that! Also, he's still a co-sleeping three year old, so it's more difficult, conceptually, talking to him about serious topics.

I don't know many men who have super deep conversations with friends, but they definitely seem to have a tribe. I honestly can't fathom how that works: is it all good because they have buddies to do activities with, or would they benefit from talking about their feelings and getting more emotional and spiritual support from friends? These are the things I haven't yet thought through. But I love your brother unconditionally and want the same wonderful things for him as you girls. So, if I never figure out or write down my messages to him, feel free to have him read this since the love most certainly applies.

Professionally, I can easily relay science and maintain objectivity when giving advice, which allows clear and concise communication. The communications take place within a well-defined space, time, and relationship. People are coming for help or advice; I am the expert from whom they expect compassion and care; and I've got twenty minutes to make it all work. I feel self-assured in how I should act and what I should say. After all, I trained for seven years to learn how to fit that mold. In real life, especially with parenting, everything seems less black-and-white.

When I become emotionally charged about the subject, and there is no clear right or wrong answer, my communication is much less clear. In trying to explore nuances and quantify a situation, it becomes mottled, fuzzy, and confusing. Trust me, the irony is not lost on me that I can calmly and confidently tell someone that they have cancer and then guide them through their treatments, pains, sorrows, and even death, but I can't explain friendship to my own kid.

It is also possible that my narcissism is leading me to spoon feed you all of my "wisdom". I don't claim to have it all figured out, but since I'm older I assume I'm wiser. Maybe it comes from a more benevolent place, knowing that I fumbled so hard through so many phases of life and I could possibly make it easier for you by sharing what I've learned along the way. Your dad also says I should "work on" my tendency to "monologue", or speak uninterrupted for long periods of time. Sooooo, you can tell how my progress in that area is going: I'm write-monologuing instead of speaking it out loud! Progress!?

For what it's worth, I am under no pretense that I have a talent for writing. I don't know if anyone will ever read this. I am not delusional. I am neither super interesting, nor eloquent, nor wise. But I am your mother and I see the way that your young eyes look at me, as if I have all the answers. Part of the reason for writing this book is to let you know that I do not have all the answers, and I will never have it all figured out, and that that's OK. When you are older, and you are lacking answers, I want you to know I was there once, too.

Part of me hopes that writing this will help me to shut up. When my impulse is to give you the answer, problem solve, offer input and "help" you through it, I need to bite my tongue and let you figure things out on your own. I want to support you so badly that sometimes I am not letting you do it on your own, even though I know how smart and capable you are. I am learning, slowly, that often the best thing I can do is STOP talking. Observe more, listen more, and stop interfering in the name of love. By getting these ideas out of my head, I can hopefully keep at least some of them out of my mouth.

I have been trying to exercise more control over what I say, biting my tongue, and allowing space to ensure my actions align with my intentions. Sometimes, I lose sleep over having said the wrong thing at the wrong time, and worry it will damage you forever or generally make things worse instead of better. I'm hoping to spare you my stream-of-consciousness lectures and uber flawed monologues. I tend to fumble my words in real life, but do better when I have thought prior to speaking. Unfortunately, thinking before speaking isn't really my jam. I figure if I carefully consider what I actually want to say and then write it down coherently (note I did NOT claim to be concise), then maybe I can make some sort of sense. Even if you never read this, it has spared you the original, more terrible versions of these lectures.

By fleshing out my message, perhaps it will translate into better day-to-day parenting NOW. In clarifying what I want to say on paper, I might ACTUALLY be able to articulate it clearly. I hope my efforts are not too preachy or trite or obnoxious. I hope I don't come across as judgemental or cliche or out of touch. I want you to know how much THOUGHT has gone into being your parent, why certain conscious choices were made, and where my actions did not align with my values. My ultimate goal is to help, love, and support you forever into eternity.

I intend this to be a gift to you, a tribute of sorts and a series of apologies and admittance of mistakes. I desire to take myself off any possible pedestal, speak my truth, and reinforce the lessons I want to share with you. My hope is that this book is the semi-complete narrative from the best, highest version of myself and can cancel out the noise from my lesser, lower days.

Growth: Evolution & Authenticity

9. Never ending metamorphosis

Buckle up, girls, this stream of consciousness book-journal is going to be all over the damn place. And imagine, these are my organized thoughts.

You are a beautiful butterfly, ever changing. But before you can flutter your wings, you must take the time to eat the leaves as a little caterpillar. Then, find a strong and comfy branch to weave a seriously awesome cocoon for yourself. Each stage has a purpose. You can't rush to the end, it simply won't work. Ultimately butterflies only fly after a lot of work and time.

Revel in your caterpillar stage, even when you yearn to get to the flying part. Being a kid only happens for a short time and once it's gone you can never get it back. Childhood is the BEST and it can be HARD. I fear that growing up in modern times is TOO hard. With social media, pandemics, wars, the political divide, and the pressures of parenting, it seems the world is not safe for a child. But here we are, doing our damn best and all we can do is keep trying. As your mom, I hope I can create an internal family life that is sheltered enough to allow joy and peace, but connected enough to nurture compassion and engagement.

Knowing the sour parts of the world, savor the sweetness of youth. You'll miss the times when you were naive, when you didn't know what you didn't know, and when you lacked a fully formed prefrontal cortex. There will be times when you make lackluster decisions for all the wrong reasons, but it turns out OK. In college, while stumbling home semi-drunk after karaoke, I asked a police officer to give my friends and I a ride home because my feet hurt. When he agreed, I convinced him to run the siren the whole way; it was glorious! Those are the types of adventures you just can't have as a working mother. They have a certain time and place and if you miss them they are gone forever. So be stupid in the best ways, be brave, and have fun! Date a hot mimbo, get kicked out of the library for being too loud, and laugh at a horribly inappropriate time. Unfortunately, with maturity comes responsibility. Childhood is too short, so make it last.

I guarantee that you will grow with time, and the big changes will occur so slowly that you may not notice them. You may look back and wonder what happened. You may miss the past. But while missing older versions of yourself, you can also embrace and be proud of the present version of yourself, and look forward to future versions that will be even better and more evolved. Perhaps, even, you will circle back to who you once were. Having children brings back playful parts that were previously lost. Hopefully, we will each continue rediscovering parts of ourselves that are lost and meeting new versions that are yet to be known.

10. March To The Beat Of Your Own Drummer

Quirks, weirdness, and being different are wonderful traits! Wear the dork and goof-ball label with pride! Going with the crowd and fitting in have never carried much appeal for me. As a teenager, it was difficult to accept the parts of me that stuck out, but now I know that they made me interesting and special.

I hope that you can embrace your inner weirdo and be proud of who you are. Feel free to dye your hair a neon color, get random piercings, and maybe even try bangs. I always had a sense of dread about trying new things and I regret that a bit. Teenage-hood is the time to experiment, follow your heart, and pursue your passions. When else can you have neon pink hair or wear glitter eyeshadow? Be warned, since I missed out I will likely be the seventy year-old grandma with rainbow hair. Being a teen can be hard with puberty, raging hormones, first loves, first heartbreaks, and finding your tribe, so be sure to balance that out with ridiculous amounts of fun.

I fully expect that sometime between ages 13 and 20 you will hate me for a bit. Your job, developmentally, during that time is to form a unique and separate identity from your parents. That involves pushing us away, so that you can differentiate yourself. This is normal. This is healthy. I will never resent you for doing this, though I'm sure it will be difficult. You should anticipate that you will hate me and want nothing to do with me, but please know that I will always be there, loving and supporting you on the other side of your slammed door.

A teenage girl hating their mom is a right of passage. I remember screaming and yelling at my mom and telling her that I hated her, though I cannot recall for what reason. She and I were always pretty close and I doubt there were any egregious errors on her part. But, I remember being mad at her and thinking she was extremely uncool. When you reach that stage, no worries. Afterall, I already know I'm extremely uncool!

As they say, you do you. Part of the journey is going alone for a brief period of time, knowing that you can always fall back for support. Hopefully, you'll have a solid group of friends going through the same things to commiserate. Remember that you are unique and different, and those differences should be cultivated and celebrated, not squashed. Listen to the little inner voice that loves and accepts who you are at the core, and not the voice that questions if conforming would be the easier route. The easy way is almost never the right way. Lean in to your quirks, take pride in what separates you from the pack. You are so, so special.

Look at Drew Barrymore, who is so unapologetically quirky and hilarious and beautiful. We all thank the heavens that she is herself and not trying to be some tiny, blond, boring, lifeless clone of all the other Hollywood actresses. Her energy is so pure, whimsical, goofy, and different. One of the many magical things about her is that the entire world not only accepts her, but embraces her. She is a poster child for resilience and proof that the world can love you just the way you are, if you are brave enough to be authentic and vulnerable. She gives each of us women permission to cry, to make fun of ourselves, to get emotional, to reminisce about our past, to admit shortcomings, and acknowledge that personal growth is a continual journey and not a trip from A to B. When you're busy hating me, maybe watch some episodes of her talk show. She's the cooler-than-me maternal loving energy you might need.

Embrace your own unique look and energy, don't get caught up in what everyone else is thinking or doing. Usually, people are not sitting around judging you as much as you worry they are, and those who are talking behind your back are not worth your time. Their negativity belongs to THEM and has little to do with you. They say confidence is quiet, while insecurity is loud. Your teen years are dedicated to the process of individuality, so use them to find out who you are and don't suppress your growth in favor of fitting in. Emulating those around you will postpone the joyous journey of self discovery. You have to go into your cocoon to become the butterfly that you are meant to be. Whenever you do come out the other side, I will be waiting with open arms.

11. Grow At Your Own Rate

Sometimes, when you are little, it is hard to see the forest through the trees; it can be impossible to get perspective. When you are lacking fully developed complex cognitive skills, you don't have the ability to zoom out. Little slights or inadequacies may consume your thoughts.

For example, right now, one of you is six years old and has not lost her first tooth yet. You are upset on a daily basis, because all of your classmates have lost their first tooth, except for you. You eagerly await the tooth fairy and what she brings. You are anxious, thinking a tooth may never fall out. I keep trying to reassure you that it will come when it is ready, but to no avail.

In life, everyone will lose that first tooth at some point, if we are lucky enough to live another day. It is important to keep perspective on whether you should expend time, energy, and worry on the wiggly tooth. It will come, I promise. There are so many times when I, even as an adult, will worry or stress about things that are beyond my control. I have to remind myself to take a deep breath, relax, and trust the process. Once I have taken all of the action steps possible, I have to relinquish control to a higher power, knowing my efforts will fail or succeed based on the will of the universe.

So, when your metaphoric tooth is not loose yet, don't fret. Try your best not to be consumed with worry, but rather look forward to the process. When you are eight or nine, and everyone has lost all of their baby teeth, you will not even remember who was the first and who was the last in your kindergarten class to lose their tooth. Your timeline says little about who you are and rarely anything about who you will become.

Ready for another metaphor? If humanity is a beautiful garden, various flowers will bloom at different times. Do we revere the flower that blooms first, that lasts longer, that grows tallest, or that is most beautiful? Beauty is in the eye of the beholder, anyhow. Know that you will grow at your own rate, so don't worry about what others are doing. If you are able to do this, it will release you from the cage of jealousy that I sometimes become stuck in. Instead, admire others and talk to them about their experiences, to prepare you for your own. Use them as guideposts of what's ahead, but do not get their journey and growth tangled up into your own. Each person will bloom when they are ready, as they are able.

A wise woman once asked me in a time of stress, "do you think this will matter in one year?" At the time, I stopped to think about it and answered yes. Even though, in retrospect, it did not matter at all. She then asked, "do you think this will matter in 10 years?". I answered no, which helped me to let go of the stress. She then added, "if it's not something that you will be thinking about on your deathbed, is it really worth any thought at all?". I think this is a valuable frame of reference and have realized that most topics of worry are not worthy of the time I give them. Stressing about having the right shoes for your soccer game or the right gift for your birthday party in the long run will not matter.

So let your teeth do what they are going to do. You can't force them to hurry up and you will be consumed with misery if you try. Some things that you wait for (meeting your life partner, having children, getting married, graduating college) are wonderful, but you should enjoy the process as it is happening instead of anxiously awaiting its conclusion. I graduated college in four years but wish I had taken a fifth to enjoy that precious time, which you can never reclaim after it is over. You will miss childhood, even being a teen, once it is gone. You will have a gaping hole in your mouth for a while once that tooth falls out and wonder why you wanted that so badly in the first place. Don't fret the small stuff. Once you have taken any action required on your part, relinquish control of your timeline to the universe. Letting go of the illusion of control will allow you to be more present and appreciate growth when it comes.

12. Know Your Strengths

Knowing your strengths is important because during struggles or self-doubt, you can remember the good parts of you and use them to help lift you up. At the ages of six and eight, I can already see some of your strengths developing, but I want you to find those yourself and not be defined by what I or anyone else says. I will say that you are smart and funny and brave and kind, but you get to write your own story about who you are and why you are awesome.

The stories we are told about ourselves can define us and become our internal dialogue. That was certainly the case for me. I appreciate that I was told positive things about myself growing up, but I question if I contorted and twisted myself to fit a mold that was presented but not 100% natural. I wonder who I would be if I had thought I was gifted in art and not science; if I had leaned-in to my love of animals; and if I had pursued my passion for music rather than sports. In a way, my strengths were pre-determined via frequent praise and positive reinforcement. I can't quite decide if that is a smart way to parent, or manipulative.

While my jury is out, though, I'm making an effort to praise your processes rather than the products of your efforts. I'm hoping you will feel like a confident, loved, accepted blank canvas and be empowered to tap into your natural abilities. I do believe that our inner voice as an adult is the echo of what our parents said to us as a child. So, I will work to make sure that that voice is loving and positive, open-minded, discerning, nonjudgmental, and kind.

Since I am discussing my mistakes and shortcomings, I'll also mention the things that I take pride in. I believe, at my core, that I am a kind person. I want to help others and I want what is best for them, hence becoming a doctor. I managed to find a career that suits my odd social skills. I enjoy hearing people's stories and engaging one-on-one, but am terrible at small talk and large group situations. In patient-doctor visits, I know appropriate topics and expectations and have a clearly defined role as listener and problem solver. I can curate a space where people feel safe to dive deep and open up. Once you know your own strengths, hopefully you can find good uses for them.

I am also leaning into my toxic positivity. I am an eternal optimist, the glass is always half full. Sometimes, I even convince myself it is 2/3 full, since we typically do not fill it all the way to the top. Your dad is a pessimist by contrast and I feel sad about that sometimes, like he is missing out. When I see the world through rose-colored glasses, he sees it through a gray cloud. I prefer my outlook and believe both were embedded in us at a young age by our parents and cannot really be adjusted or changed.

As you grow, I promise I won't always point out the silver lining and I vow to allow you to wallow in the clouds. I now see how my tangled web of toxic positivity + people pleasing + emotional immaturity + delayed self realization all weaved together to form a devastating tapestry. I refuse to let you fall into that same societal trap for girls to be shiny and happy all the time. I will encourage you to inconvenience me and society in general by being a full person with a variety of needs, wants, and feelings. Just because I'm OK with my toxic positivity, does not mean I will encourage it for you girls. I will bite my tongue until it bleeds, if need be, to let you feel all the feels.

One trait that I do hope you inherit from me and your dad is humor. When things are going terribly wrong, a well placed joke can reframe the whole situation. Your dad is even better at this than I am, with a seriously dark and twisted take on some things. But it gives me immense joy when he can poke fun at something that I am taking too seriously. His mom is pretty funny too: when I was near-stalking my sister trying to repair our relationship and was lamenting about all the unreturned calls and texts, she said "Take a hint!". It was hilarious, and painfully true. The funny comment actually helped me step back a bit from my desperate attempts to repair that relationship. It helped me to think about the fact that my sister's silence WAS her reply; that for reasons beyond my control and knowledge, she was not ready or willing to talk. Humor always makes everything better; use it wisely my young Padawan.

I also pride myself on being a very hard worker. I believe that results are often, though not always, proportional to effort. As a child, on my sports teams, there was always an end-of-season awards ceremony. Awards included: coaches' favorite, MVP, most improved, sportsmanship, spirit, etc. The award I got was the "workhorse" and I would not have wanted any of the other awards over the one that I got. I took immense pride in knowing that the coach recognized how hard I was working, even if I was not the MVP nor improving more than others. The fact that my hard work was acknowledged was enough for me. Sometimes you work tirelessly and you might not get recognition for that, but I hope you will develop an internal sense of pride at knowing your efforts.

Leadership and organization come naturally to me, but I minimize leadership roles because I don't think they bring out the best in me or add to my life in a positive way. Just because you CAN do something, does not mean you must or should. I dedicated a lot of time and energy to leadership as a medical student, and in retrospect I regret it. I could have used that time and energy for studying or exercise or developing and maintaining friendships. Being in a leadership position added stress to my life, and I don't think it really helped others that much. It brought out the worst in me: being controlling, micromanaging, and not focusing on what truly mattered. So, carefully evaluate how your strengths will add or detract from your life and feel free to say "no thank you" to opportunities for OTHERS to get the best parts of you. Sometimes an activity presented as an "honor" is actually a drain. Unfortunately, you may only know this in retrospect. Your time and energy are your most valuable resources; you must invest them wisely and hopefully in a way that will give back to you, others, or the world.

So, know your strengths, so that you can fall back on them when you need a boost. If you fail a test and are too ashamed to tell anyone, remember that you are smart. If you stumble awkwardly through a social situation, remember that you are kind. If someone attacks your personality, remember that you are funny. If you fall flat despite your best efforts, remember that you can still be proud of the hard work you invested. Know the forces of good in your life and use them to your advantage, to become the best version of yourself.

13. Know your weaknesses

As with all things, you must take the good with the bad, your weaknesses with your strengths. Over time, I have become pretty good at admitting my weaknesses and working to improve them. But they remain a core part of my humanity and I have learned to accept them and maybe even embrace them from time to time.

As a part of baring my soul to you, I'll lay out my perceived weaknesses here, in hopes that my vulnerability will help you to see that it's OK to admit imperfections. Everybody, including me, has hang ups, baggage, or "issues" (whatever you want to call them).

People pleasing has always been my Achilles' heel. I know I already reviewed this, but it deserves even more attention. It contributed to my perfectionism (wanting to earn my parents' love); it contributed to my inability to express emotions (wanting to avoid being difficult to those around me); and it contributed to not fully knowing myself (being who I thought others would like, rather than who I was or who I actually liked). Now that I know myself better, I am still learning about my own likes and dislikes. I hope that you will be so in touch with your inner wants and desires, that you will never have to question what your favorite color is, what food you like, what restaurant you would like to go to, or what movie you would like to watch. I hope you will know those things easily and believe in your decisions, without hesitation.

Taking feedback used to be a weakness, that I have now turned neutral. I am now able to hear feedback given in a neutral or loving/compassionate way. It's been a while since I've heard harsh or unloving feedback, but I think I would do better now than I did in the past. If someone provides feedback about a mistake I have made, I am able to acknowledge it and vow to do better in the future. I can admit wrong-doing without letting the knowledge that I "made an oopsy" destroy me. In the past, I had trouble admitting mistakes and taking responsibility, instead defending myself, making excuses, or trying to shift blame or subjects.

Previously, I would take any little critique extremely personally, thinking that the critic must hate me or that they are an evil person for attacking me. My fragile ego forced me to play the victim in my own life story any time I was not clearly in the heroine role. Such was my limited, black and white thinking. I didn't appreciate back then that being secure in myself did NOT mean never making mistakes, it meant owning them and knowing I was still worthy of love and respect despite errors. Hopefully, you will be confident enough and open minded enough to hear feedback without becoming defensive. Feedback is often correct and can always be an opportunity for learning, if you are willing to be vulnerable.

I've got some weaknesses that I am working on, but can't seem to make much progress toward expelling. Some of these tendencies that I am hoping not to pass down to you are: being uptight, oversharing, and monologuing. How am I doing with cutting down on the monologues? I am trying so hard not to lecture you in person, but it is not lost on me that I am now pseudo lecturing you in a book, and in no less than 300 pages. The irony actually hurts a little bit, as this book will be a literal/physical manifestation of my inability to control this tendency. However, at least I am getting all my thoughts and feelings out into the void, rather than depositing them directly into your ears. Just skip this entire book, if you want.

Sometimes I question whether aspects I attributed to high self-esteem are actually weaknesses. For example, I never wear makeup and am a fashion disaster. In contrast, my mom will not leave the house without a full face of makeup and prides herself on a colorful wardrobe. As a teen, my rebellion was to wear a T-shirt, baggy shorts and zero makeup. At the time, I took pride in not caring about my looks and not deriving any self-worth from "superficial" packaging.

A big part of me still believes that that was the right choice for me and served me well at that time in my life. But recently, I have been trying to up my style game and I am finding it incredibly hard! I am a newborn baby when it comes to fashion sense. I have begun to wonder if my earlier rejection of all things related to my physical appearance was actually a protective mechanism because I lacked confidence in my looks. I have never believed I was pretty. "Cute"? Sometimes! "Girl-Next-Door"? Sure! "Has an awesome personality"? Hopefully! "Hot or Sexy"? Absolutely not! If I had opted for full makeup and the cutest outfit I could muster, but still felt yucky, it would have stung much more.

So, maybe refusing to try was strategic. I could convince myself that not being pretty was a CHOICE. Perhaps frumpiness was my way of feeling control over something that I was not proud of and could not change, without plastic surgery of course. So my jury is still out on whether I was awesomely rejecting society's expectations for girls and protesting the patriarchy, or I was trying to be a wallflower and too scared to put myself out there. Was I failing to try or trying to fail?

Generationally, things I inherited from my mom and am hoping NOT to pass down are gossiping about other women, interrupting in conversations, and being judgemental. I heard somebody say that gossip is a cheap way to bond, but you can't truly befriend a gossip because they will talk about anyone negatively behind their back, including you. Too true. While it might feel fun for a minute, it's not who you want to be. If someone initiates a negative conversation about someone not there to defend themselves, the best option is to change the subject to a kinder one or walk away. That person will either learn to be kind and positive around you, or trash talk you as soon as you're gone. I am hoping you girls will be the kind of women who support other women, help them up when they fall, and cheer them on ferociously. Turn jealousy and envy into admiration.

Interrupting is just rude. While I can blame my role models, my ADHD tendencies, or my enthusiasm, I am working on ending this behavior. I pray it will end with me and not be passed to you. Grandma interrupts frequently and it was remarkable when you, at age 5, called her out. You were mid-sentence and she started talking about a totally unrelated topic. It struck me that she wasn't interested in your cute little story and thought her words trumped yours. The pride I felt when you said "hey! You interrupted me! I was TALKING!" was immense. Her scoff and rolled eyes, followed by continuing her words and ignoring your protest, were not just disappointing but triggering to my inner child. But I, in my adult power, walked toward you to physically tune her out and focused intently and enthusiastically on what you were saying. I hope you noticed, I hope she noticed, and I hope little me noticed.

14. Find Yourself, Repeatedly

The process of finding yourself can be joyful, scary, difficult, tedious, and a million other things. Sometimes you will revel in the moments of growth and others you will wish to regress to easier days. Growth is continual like a tree, not a point A to B sort of journey. You are a towering redwood in complex communion with your forest world, not a singular fruit that will one day be ripe for plucking. You'll always be discovering new parts of yourself and letting go of parts that no longer serve you.

You may be incredibly religious for a time and then not religious at all. You may be fully immersed in an activity and then no longer do those things in the future. That's all OK. That's all part of the process. Changes might be rapid or happen more insidiously over time. You may take tiny indiscernible baby steps toward putting yourself out there or a giant leap of faith. One morning you may wake up to look at yourself in the mirror and barely recognize what you see.

Over time, you will be able to recognize the good and the bad: what you want to flourish and what needs pruning. The key to growth is to know who you are and to see yourself clearly. Until you fully know and subsequently love yourself, you will be unable to love or be loved by others.

It took me until my mid 20s to really love myself, even though I always liked myself. I didn't really know who I was until after college, despite all of the soul-searching and deep inner work I had done. Self acceptance and embracing your shadow parts does not happen overnight, unfortunately. There is too much work to be done and it is never ending. I say that not to discourage you, but to let you know that there is no rush to "finish" the work. We all start as whole, worthy, perfectly imperfect humans.

You may feel that seeking and evolving make you incomplete, that you need to change yourself; but, in reality you are polishing and chiseling a beautifully unbroken core. Have no shame in your imperfections, your scars, or your propensity to evolve over time. No one would shame a butterfly for undergoing metamorphosis. In fact, few recognize that their wings hide inside their caterpillar embryo, ever present just waiting for the right circumstances to flourish.

After medical school, I was introduced to the idea of a values deck. Have I had the chance to tell you about these, yet? Gosh, I hope so. If not: it is a deck of cards, with each card stating a personal value, such as Truth, Discipline, Friendship, Justice, Peace, Health, etc. I first 'did the deck' as a group exercise, which I highly recommend. It goes like this:

First, go through the deck to sort values that matter to you and values that do not (set aside the values that do not matter to you)

Next, go through the values that matter to you and select your top 10

Then, narrow the top 10 down to your top 3

Finally, narrow down to the single most important value to you at that time in your life.

Does it sound too hippie-dippie? Good! I have since done this exercise almost every year on my own and the value that matters most changes over time. I have never once had a #1 value repeat itself. Sometimes, the value that was most important to me was authenticity; others it was respect; others it was kindness. In general, values I hope to instill in you are: being honest, respectful, responsible, compassionate, and hard-working.

Taking a few minutes to 'do the deck' can help you gain perspective and focus. As a group, the cards should be done with people you trust, since the discussions are uber vulnerable. If done with the right people, it is an enlightening and bonding experience where you expose and nurture your deepest self. Hopefully, we can do them as a family one day.

In the continuous journey to find yourself, loneliness and boredom can be your best teachers. When you are alone, your thoughts become companions. You might see the world more clearly and gain perspective on your greater place in the universe. Loneliness may come with sorrow, but in it you may also find joy. It is easier getting to know yourself with no one else in the way, clouding the picture. As I have said, and will say again, difficult and dark times are the ones in which you grow the most.

Boredom is another wonderful teacher. I was not allowed much boredom as a child. I was kept very busy, perhaps overscheduled, likely because I had so much ADHD energy that my parents needed to tire me out to help me focus. I can't say it didn't work for me, but I wonder if I would be a more creative person or my personal evolution would have happened more quickly if I had had more time to be bored. They say boredom is the first step for creativity. Creativity is something that I feel I may be lacking, but it's something that I hope you children will maintain as you age. There is such power and opportunity in thinking outside the box. Being able to see things from different perspectives, imagining a new way of doing something, and blazing your own path is a beautiful way to approach the world. I hope that your eyes stay open, and I do not lead you to squander the imagination that you've developed during childhood.

It was only recently that I realized in order to "find" yourself you first have to be a little lost. On your path in life, go off trail once in a while. Develop a wander lust and an ease in uncertainty, knowing that you can always come back to yourself. Longing for the past is part of moving forward. We all go through periods where we long for comfort or security from our past: to be more childlike, to return to a prior relationship, or to unburden ourselves with the pressures of the present. It would be lovely to transport back in time, to a place where all of our needs were met by a parent figure, our worries were few, and our future was unwritten. Who wouldn't want to go there? Don't let the nostalgia keep you stagnant or from moving into unknown territory; growth can be scary but don't let that hold you back.

Aim to find yourself over and over and over and over again. Know yourself fully and feel the consistent push and pull of adjusting who you are, what you believe, and what you want out of life. It will change. At different stages in life, you may want different things, have different friends, or vary your style or interests, and that is all OK. You may be more or less close with me or your siblings at certain times and that is OK, too. Know that you are fluid and changing, with deep roots, a solid trunk, and branches that sway and move with the winds. Growth is beautiful, brave, and beneficial.

15. Seek Transformative Experiences

Transformative experiences are one of the things that you should seek throughout your life. Have as many "life changing experiences" as possible! Give yourself opportunities for self discovery when you are young. Don't wait for a mid-life eat-pray-love situation. These experiences are times of exponential, rapid personal growth. The hallmark of these times is that they are immersive; they force you to dive head-first into uncharted waters all alone.

Usually this involves a change in scenery, where you can reinvent yourself and live more authentically. At home, where everyone knows the old you and has expectations for who you are and how you will act, it can be hard to introduce or integrate newer versions of yourself. But transformative experiences offer an opportunity to be whoever you want to be, right away. These could include: going away to summer camp, going away to college, pretty much any travel, or immersive group endeavors. These experiences help you to find yourself, to recalibrate who you want to be, and pluck you from your existence to show the world's possibilities. They might illuminate parts of you that you don't know are there.

My own transformative experiences have included going away to college and attending a month-long integrative medicine retreat in the redwoods. There have been other little ones along the way, but these are the two where I can recognize that the person who arrived and the person who departed were DIFFERENT.

College was the first time that I was outside of my hometown, on my own, and forming a new friend group from scratch. It was my first chance to really find myself. So cliche, I know, but I can't deny the truth. When I went to college, I walked-on to the cross country team and found a built-in social network amongst teammates; as discussed, this turned out to be a flawed social system for me.

My life pattern, up to that point, had been falling into friend groups due to convenience: neighbors, teammates, friends of friends. I had never consciously thought about what I wanted in a friend and then sought out those people. The process of questioning who I was, what I wanted, and then taking decisive action to get it was still a few years away.

Despite that area of stagnation, college catapulted me into a brilliant clear-blue ocean from my murky little pond of existence prior. I reveled in the newness of the college town: exploring local running trails, rummaging through used CD bins to discover new music, watching street performers or passionate protestors, and seeing vibrant life being lived around every corner. I even auditioned for MTV's the Real World one day because I literally saw a line, asked "what's this line for?", and then decided to stand in it. College times! Nearly every conversation was exciting and interesting because everyone spoke with such passion and enthusiasm. Everyone is coming of age together, as if all of the flowers in the garden are blooming on the same day. College is simply sublime.

College consisted of listening to Bob Dylan, studying while laying in the grass and staring at the clouds, and in general embracing open mindedness. I took a series of liberal arts classes about social justice, racism, non-violence, and women's rights. I became passionate about Gandhi and was inspired to become a vegetarian during my junior year.

My spirituality also blossomed while in college. As a child, I enjoyed church and the community that it provided, but didn't click with the people in my hometown congregation. When I got to college, a friend introduced me to a little church near campus. The members attended protests, supported homeless youth in the church basement, and were passionate about social justice activities. I felt I had found my people.

I attended church groups during the week and experienced a sense of fellowship while singing songs and sharing dinner. During lent, we sang "Holden Village Evening Prayer". Every time I hear those songs, I am nearly brought to tears because they take me back to a time when I felt embraced by a family that was not my own, fully accepted for who I was, and eager to enter into the future. In college, there is excitement because nothing is locked in yet. You have not chosen your major, your career, your eventual home base. The world is completely open to you to meet new friends, find the love of your life, travel to far off lands, re-settle in a new town, and change your mind as many times as you want.

That is the value of transformative experiences, they give you freedom to explore who you are in a safe way. It's possible to do that from home, though difficult if people already know you and have certain expectations about your behavior. You may be known as someone who is funny, but you want to stop using humor as a defense mechanism. There may be expectations that you will be a caretaker or helper, but you want to stop people-pleasing and start taking better care of yourself instead. You might tend to be dramatic or difficult or stubborn and want to change, but people maintain their preconceived notions of you. When you get plucked out of your comfort zone, all of that changes. You get a chance to present a new or better version of yourself and leave old baggage behind.

I believe seeking these experiences is why many people move jobs, cities, and friend groups on a rotating basis. They are hungry to move forward and feel unable to do so while staying put. All people are seeking chances for growth and it can be hard to recognize your own progress unless you change scenery. I think that being intentional with your choices, especially education, travel, and group excursions, can allow the growth that you seek without leaving your past in ruins.

My next transformative experience was at a month-long integrative medicine elective, which I have already mentioned. It was an amazing time: co-op living in the redwoods with a group of like-minded medical students. The tribe was pre-selected for me and I genuinely liked all of the people there. I had the space and time I needed to work through my residency match disappointment. There was singing with guitars around the campfire, dancing while hand-washing the dishes, group jogs through the forest, wandering aimlessly among the towering trees, and walking a labyrinth any time I wanted.

While there, I wrote daily in my journal for the first time in years. I had lost a sense of connection to myself during all the years of studying and relentlessly pursuing my higher education. That time among the trees helped to center my thoughts, lighten my heart, and bring me back to parts of myself that may have otherwise been lost.

Transformative experiences have to be sought out and they are an extreme privilege. They typically involve travel and being immersed in new groups of people. This goes without saying, but travel requires money and being immersed in new groups of people requires a sense of safety that some may not have due to their life experiences. I hope that you will be lucky enough to have both of those things, to make these experiences a reality.

Slightly less expensive options might include: volunteer experiences; joining the Peace Corps or Teach for America; studying abroad; backpacking through Europe; hiking the Pacific Crest or Appalachian trails; living in a van and traveling for a few weeks. More expensive options include: silent meditation retreats, yoga retreats, or Eco tourism. When I was traveling in Guatemala, I was boating down the Rio Dulce river when I saw on the banks an Eco-commune with hammocks overhanging the water, monkeys crawling through the treetops, and a group of young people passionately discussing politics on the dock. I stared in awe, because I knew that they were all having a life-changing experience right before my eyes. I was so happy for them.

So, do all that you can to foster these experiences, have them as often as possible, and always bring back what you have learned about yourself to your prior life. The process of reentry after one of these experiences can be difficult, because you are a changed person, returning to people who know the previous version of you. Have open discussions about things that you would like them to know, but feel free to keep parts of the magic to yourself. Self reflection and spiritual journeys are gifts that you share with a select few. You will be very vulnerable when you try to re-integrate into your past life, and some people may not understand because they have not had the opportunity for those experiences themselves. Choose carefully who you share the delicate new parts of yourself with, and treasure those who gladly greet the new you. Hopefully I will be one of those who gently embraces your fragile newness at each homecoming.

16. You Are Your Words

You are only as good as your word, and therefore, your words are one of the most powerful things that you possess. I hope to raise you with a great deal of integrity and kindness. Please choose your words wisely, think before you speak, and turn your words into action. I am not always the best at thinking before I speak, but I strive to do the others.

In our house, we have a saying to "make it right". We don't force apologies when we have offended one another, but we try to find a way to remedy the injustice. If someone hits or steals a toy, an empty apology is worth nothing. When you are not genuine with your words, people can sense it. Speak only your truth, anything short of that cheapens all of the other words you use. Learning the repair process with a sibling is extremely valuable and can be applied to all future relationships. That repair may involve no words at all, but they are your most readily available and easy to master tool. Words are free and when used wisely they are persuasive, eloquent, and concise. Obviously I struggle with the latter.

Never use your words as weapons. Though easy to do, it is not noble. While physical assaults create bruises that fade overtime, verbal assault can leave deeper wounds that echo in your mind forever. Know when to bite your tongue. When you COULD say something mean or callous, don't. Hold it in. You will regret every mean thing you ever say and sometimes the wrong words will haunt you by destroying relationships. When I get fired up about something, your dad is always telling me that my best response is to "say nothing". It's super annoying, but he is always right. The few instances where I ignore him and unleash a rant on someone, I immediately regret it, lose hours of sleep worrying about the consequences of my words, and wish I had just listened to him. Trust me, it is best to keep any harsh messages in your head and out of your mouth. Write them in your journal, if you must, but don't click send on any texts or emails.

Understand that listening is often more important than speaking, and that the less you say and the quieter you say it, the more people will have to lean in and pay attention. When you speak ad nauseam and loudly (like I do, unfortunately), people learn to tune you out, to spare their ears the trauma, and essentially to ignore your diatribes. Your words lose value the more you throw them around. Like all commodities, rarity increases worth. So, choose your words wisely. When you realize that words carry power and represent who you are, you will pay them their due respect. Always be genuine and sincere when speaking; if you are not, it erodes the respect and trust of those around you.

Your words also hold you accountable. When you say you will do something, please follow through and "keep your word". Those who are all talk and no action are pretty damn lame. Don't be lame! While passionate dialogue and intellectual discourse have definite value, turning your words into actions puts your money where your mouth is. If you're going to 'talk the talk', please my dear, 'walk the walk' as well.

I am acutely aware that as a mom my words carry even more power. They say one's inner voice is simply an echo of what they heard as a child. Therefore, the language and vocabulary that I choose as your parent are vitally important. I can choose to say that you are a daredevil, or that you are adventurous; that you are fearful, or that you are brave; that you are struggling, or that you're progressing via hard work. I try to stick with positive language, in line with my toxic positivity, because I want your inner voice to be one that is cheering for you, giving good advice, and above all loving and respecting you.

I have friends who, despite being amazing, sometimes look down on themselves, beat themselves up for mistakes, believe they are not worthy of good things, and make choices that are not in their best interest. I believe they do this because their inner voice is not kind to them, and I figure that's what they heard growing up. It makes me sad that I can't just hack into their brain and convince them of their beauty and worth. They are awesome people and would be better off if they believed that deep in their core. I hope that through the language I use and the attitudes I demonstrate, you will develop healthy self-esteem and avoid those pitfalls.

Words also comprise our stories. The stories that we tell and hear about ourselves come to define us. Therefore, always speak well of yourself and others. As I was growing up, my mom repeatedly told me that I marched to the beat of my own drum. It was a compliment and one that I appreciated. I took pride in knowing that I was different, and knowing that that was loved and treasured. Hearing that over and over embedded it deep into my consciousness, so that as a teen, I was very unlikely to submit to peer pressure. I hope that the stories I tell you help to build your confidence and not destroy it.

When you were afraid of diving into the pool or riding horses, I encouraged bravery and acknowledged that it was natural to be nervous or afraid. After you rode the horse, we talked about how brave you were and I hope that is the part of the story that sticks with you rather than the tears and hesitance. Hindsight and storytelling can change the memory of what happened; reality becomes trivial, because the story that lives on will bend the details to its will. They say if you tell a lie too many times, you begin to believe it. I will try to retell stories from your childhood truthfully, but in a positive light. Despite recall biases, we must tell our stories because those that we do not tell are forgotten and thus erased from our lives.

Your words represent who you are, what you think, and how you will be remembered. Despite my inability to decrease my own volume and verbosity, try to do as I say and not as I do by concentrating your words into thoughtful, intentional messages. I deeply respect those who can filter their thoughts, carefully choose their words, and only share them with a chosen few. Make your words a sacred gift to others and a testament to your character. Turn them into meaningful actions and a force for good in the world.

17. You Are Your Actions

The only things arguably more important than your words are your actions. They tell people everything that they need to know about you. How you spend your time and effort determines who you are as a person. Time is the greatest commodity on this earth. It cannot be bought or sold, you cannot get it back once it has been spent, and it is the one wish that cannot be granted. Spend your time wisely; fill it with purpose and adventure. Do not allow any discrepancy between your words and actions, your thoughts and intentions, your passion and your efforts.

I hope your actions will be guided by a strong moral compass. Some get their morals from their parents, some from their religion, some from their own conscience. Regardless of where you derive your ethical principles, I hope that you hold fast to them throughout your life. I hope that you will stick up for others, speak up when there is injustice, and consistently choose to do the right thing, which is never the easy thing.

A strong work ethic is held in high esteem in our family. Developing a work ethic includes trying and failing, repeatedly. You fall down and get back up again and again and again, until you no longer fall. That type of ethos can carry you through school, sports, your career, and parenting. Know the value of hard work: what it feels like to be exhausted and tired, and then to deliberately push on. There is satisfaction in putting forth your best effort. The self-respect that you can cultivate through dedication and determination is priceless.

Have caution that your self-respect does not turn into inordinate amounts of pride. Some pride is good, but too much is not. Stay humble and avoid an over-inflated ego. "Confident, not cocky" is a reasonable goal. Appreciate that sometimes despite your hard work things will not work out. Know when to call it quits or take a break to re-examine your approach. Hard work is excellent, but pointless effort is a fool's errand. Sometimes, you have to cut your losses.

The most important actions are the ones that you take when no one is watching. How do you treat yourself and others, when there is no risk of getting caught or consequences for bad judgment? How do you treat your body, when it is young and resilient and can withstand multiple stressors? How do you treat animals, children, and service workers, when you are in a position of power and there may be no repercussions for yucky behavior? When you reflect on your actions, can you rest easy because you are confident that you were the most kind, the most compassionate, or the most fair? I have lost sleep at night questioning my actions and wishing I had done things differently. That is inevitable to each of us perfectly imperfect humans, but when you are being your best self, you are less likely to suffer that fate. For that reason, aim for justice, work hard, and let your actions speak for themselves to show the world who you are.

18. Don't Outsource Validation

Your sense of worth, accomplishment, and pride must come from within. MUST! My own sense of worth came from outside of myself until quite recently, unfortunately. It's part of my people-pleaser tendency. I experienced pride from being a perfectionist: getting good grades, winning the race, and performing throughout my life. I never want you to feel that you must perform. You are a human, not a circus seal. I hope that you are building a strong sense of self, so that your wants will not waver with the changing tide.

The language that I use as your mother is so important to this. I often catch myself being proud of you and giving you praise, stating "I am so proud of you!". These are the things that my father said to me that gave me a sense of confidence as a child. But, I know that it is far better to say "wow, YOU should be so proud of yourself". That tiny shift in language is something that I am working on. It doesn't come as naturally to me as I wish it did.

Sometimes I see perfect "gentle" parents saying the perfect thing at the perfect time, and I am overcome with rage and jealousy. How does this stuff come so easily for them? It's ridiculously hard for me at times and my instincts seem at odds with the "right" choice. My heart agrees with my head (who has read all the parenting books), but then my big mouth grabs the wheel and drives that heart and head straight off a cliff into reactionary, manipulative parenting of the 80s. So, I am sorry when my words do not align with my intentions. I'm getting better little by little, and hope it's not too late to right our course.

Believe in yourself: what you are doing, what you are wearing, how you are feeling, and who you are deep in your core. The stakes are high, especially as a teenager. When someone is not confident in who they are, they are much more susceptible to peer pressure and doing things that they know are not in their best interest. If you do not feel good about yourself, from the inside, it can lead you down a path to ruin. It can lead to self-destructive behaviors and/or people-pleasing, which will make you feel even worse about yourself. It is a downward spiral that I hope you will be able to avoid. Many young girls look to their parents for approval, then as a teen to their friend group, then as a woman to their romantic partner. Just look in the mirror. Look yourself in the eye and do right by the little girl in front of you. You do not need anyone's approval, including mine. You have my love, forever and always, no matter what.

In our world, it is easy to look externally for positive comments and be eaten alive by comparing yourself to others, especially with social media. Social media worries me and I frankly hope it will be banned for kids before you get much older. If not, please remember that most people use their social platforms as a highlight reel, and it may not reflect their reality AT ALL. Liken posts to a make-believe movie; know it's not real life.

I remember feeling jealous of an acquaintance who had a huge wedding with, like, a dozen bridesmaids. She posted about her bridal shower, and I saw it on social media. My own wedding was small, 75 people, with just a best man and maid of honor. I don't think I KNOW 12 people I could ask to be bridesmaids. Realizing that triggered my feelings of social inadequacy. But I later learned that one of those dozen bridesmaids had slept with the groom, and the wedding was canceled. Yucky! I am not taking any delight in that poor bride-to-be's suffering, but I think of it often when I see posts-that-could-trigger-jealousy online. You never know what's happening behind the scenes. I can relax a little knowing that even though I don't have a BIG friend group to hang out with, the friends I *do* have would not sleep with my husband. Quality over quantity.

Don't get lost in comparison and envy, they lead nowhere worthwhile. Most clicks and validation from social media are EMPTY because the people don't know the real you. There are exceptions: groups or influencers who are dedicated to keeping it real and creating a supportive community online. That's super cool, but in general don't look to social media for any internal validation. Support, humor, and entertainment: sure! Self worth: absolutely not! Clicks and likes are empty; instead find fullness in genuine human interaction and the exchange of loving energy.

You never have to 'keep up' with anyone. You will be happier if you focus on your own well-being, desires and interests than if you chase what others have or value. Your dad and I have done that with our house: we live in a smaller house, in a less fancy neighborhood. It's enough for us and we like it, despite having some envy for those with bigger garages, extra bedrooms, and large yards. We chose this house to be more financially independent and also to avoid raising you in a mansion on a hill. We didn't like that life, conceptually. We also knew that if we lived in a fancier neighborhood, your friend pool would be wealthier and the expectations would flow from there.

My wish for you is that you can have a relatively normal childhood. Your dad and I were both raised middle class, and we hope to raise you similarly, even though technically you're a doctor's kid. You still have a lot of privilege, which I will address here, but in my humble opinion too much wealth leads to wanting more and more. Don't look to your friends to decide which jeans you want; instead try them on yourself to find what fits your body, your style, and your budget. Be bold, be original, and never fear if others don't get it. As long as you get it, that's the only opinion that matters.

When you have a friend with a new outfit or new boyfriend or new car, be happy for them without wanting for those things yourself. This is so much easier said than done, but I hope you have the confidence and internal stability to avoid being stirred up by comparison. They say comparison is the thief of joy, and I believe that to be true. Accept yourself, love yourself, choose yourself. Choose admiration over envy when it comes to others. Choose to appreciate differences, rather than become a copycat. Live your truth and write your own story, just like I am writing this one.

19. Embrace The Struggle-fest

The struggle is real! Struggling comes with being human and should never be a source of shame or embarrassment. Struggle often precedes growth. Remember, rainbows can only happen with rain.

In my childhood, I often conflated struggle with failure. It meant that I was unable to obtain perfection, and thus somehow less than. To struggle was shameful. Now, I know that we struggle when we are working hard at worthy endeavors; when we want to be better; when something does not come naturally, but we persevere anyways. The assumption that something is wrong when we are made to struggle is incorrect. I wish that I had embraced this concept from a younger age. Rather than feeling ashamed that I was having to stay up late to study for a test, I could have applauded my work ethic. I wish I could have been more proud of the effort that I was willing to put forth in order to achieve, instead of focusing only on the end product of those efforts.

When you try something new, embrace being a beginner. Accept that you will encounter the unknown, mess up or fall down, and it might feel hard. Try anyways. Be brave! Be willing to keep going even when it's not easy. This is the only way to learn, through not knowing. Revel in the progress you will make. If you refuse to be a beginner, you will hold yourself back from growth and adventures, which is no way to live.

I learned to ski in my late 20s and felt so discouraged and silly that I almost gave up. It felt ridiculous being passed by 4 and 5 year olds on the slopes, and falling every few feet not knowing how to stop or turn. As a former athlete, I was ashamed to struggle so much. Part of my initial issue was a too-advanced-for-me group lesson that ended in tears. After that, I hired a teacher who better evaluated my (lack of) skills and gave more specific tips. I finally started to learn. You've got to start where you ARE, not where you want to be. With more time and effort, I figured it out. I had to be willing to look silly. Now you are the tiny skiers passing the beginners, doing jumps and flying down the mountain. So, when you are the beginner, remember you can figure it out with the right attitude and the right teachers.

Sometimes the struggle can actually be fun, if you let it. Your dad and I were hiking in the rain the other day when cold blustering winds began to blow, making everything more cold. We were chilled to the bone and laughed about it all the way home, car heater blasting! There is a documentary called "Sufferfest" with Alex Honnold (the guy from the Free Solo movie), that your dad and I saw at an outdoorsy film festival. In the film, they discuss the concept of "Type-2 fun". Type-1 fun is when you are having fun in the moment and you recognize it as fun. Type 2 fun is when you are suffering in the moment, but you will remember it as being fun in retrospect. These are actually some of my favorite types of experiences. Medical school was Type-2 fun. Residency was Type-2 fun. Childbirth was Type-2 fun and sometimes parenting is Type-2 fun. When your diarrhea flew into my eyes and mouth, I wasn't laughing, but looking back it makes me smile. As they say "right now is the good 'ol days".

Many of the times that I look upon fondly NOW were not so great as they were happening. When my college boyfriend broke up with me, I was devastated; now I look back laughing and think what a silly relationship it was. I look back on miserable runs in the pouring rain as if they were the time of my life. During one particular run, we mud wrestled, rolled down a grassy hill, and ended the run filthy with mud in our ears, but in my memory it was bliss. I recall difficult hikes where your dad had to bribe me to reach the peak with a bag of cheetos, dangled in front of me like a horse with a carrot; but I recall seeing the view at the top and being proud of pressing on despite not feeling my feet. So, cry some ugly tears, get filthy and sticky, and embrace all of the challenges which will one day be your youthful type-2 fun!

Embrace struggle. Admit that you are not good at something, but willing to try anyway. Be ready to have delayed gratification; ready to ask for help and work with others; ready to take the path less traveled; ready to put in the work, even if there is no reward or it all falls flat. Failure is the best teacher. Frustration is the best motivator. Losing is the best coach. Suffering is the best counselor. Keep this in mind: the hardest times will almost always get easier. The hard times give us perspective, they build character, and they help us to become the best version of ourselves. The struggle is real, so keep on struggling!

Friendship: Kindness & Community

20. Find Your Tribe

There are important steps that you will take in life that will lead you toward great things. The first step is building your community outside of your born family. Some call it your chosen family, some call it your friend circle, others call it your tribe. I like the notion of tribe because part of what makes for good friendships is sharing a primal spirit, humor, and riding the same energetic wavelengths through the universe. Those are things that cannot be measured, but must be felt.

Finding your tribe does not happen in a day, or a week, or a year. We are lucky if it happens at all in our lifetime. First, you must find yourself, because you cannot find like-minded others until you know your own mind and know it well.

I have always appreciated humor and quirks and weirdness. Being funny requires intelligence, taking risks, and having confidence to put yourself out there and flop. Your dad has mastered dark humor and I deeply appreciate him for that. Making someone laugh is a gift and has the power to redirect the tone of a room toward levity and joy. When life is weighing heavily on me, your dad can shift my perspective or put a smile on my face with a well-timed joke. I spoke earlier about embracing your inner weirdo and finding a tribe of like-minded weirdos is a worthy goal. Do not be afraid to be loud (metaphorically), and do not ever shrink parts of yourself in order to fit in. If you are hiding parts of yourself or keeping quiet when you would otherwise speak up, you are not with your tribe. Be brave enough to make jokes and see who 'gets' them; it will be a helpful clue as to who 'gets' you, in general.

In order to attract the right friend circle, you not only have to know who you are, but you have to show who you are. I have always taught you that outward appearances are not important and that the insides matter more. However, many people will judge a book by its cover, so you should consider dressing accordingly.

You are your own billboard advertisement for friendship. By how you speak, how you dress, and how you act, you let people know your interests and overall vibe. If you dress like sporty spice (gosh, I hope you get that reference), you may attract athletic friends. If you love art and wear paint covered overalls, others who enjoy art may gravitate toward you. If you dress in goth clothes, you may find yourself a death metal concert buddy. There are so many different ways to be.

I have never dressed in a way that was meaningful, preferring to wear a T-shirt and jeans which say nothing about who I am. I wish I had been more BoHo or outdoorsy, and maybe it would have been easier to meet people. Being less of a fashion disaster is something I am working on, trying to match my facade to my insides. It is harder than it looks: I'm not confident in what I like, I'm picky about materials, and I don't have a creative vision that I'm aiming for. I finally understand and have profound respect for people who have taken more pride in their outward expression from a young age. I find it much easier to manage and treat life-threatening abnormal lab results than put together a cohesive outfit that actually makes a statement.

It is wonderful to be open to meeting all new people, because you never know when you will unexpectedly click with someone and who will invite you into their inner world. I sometimes listen to the Dax Shepard podcast, "Armchair Expert", and I'm always struck that he can find similarities with almost every single guest. Regardless of where someone grew up, what their background may be, and how they present themselves, deep down we all have a lot in common. We all share being imperfect humans, with difficult feelings, complicated families of origin, and deep desires for our future and the future of our children. If you dig deeper into who someone is at their core, you might find some connectedness, common values or interests, or a shared approach to life. If you are lucky enough to find those people, they can provide a sense that you are not traveling through the world alone.

Full disclosure: friendship is something I have struggled with. Until college, I chose the easy route rather than the more lonely, vulnerable, and difficult course. I made friends out of convenience: neighbors, teammates, or friends of friends. Anytime someone seemed to accept me, I would latch on and stick around without considering if they were a good fit. I found it much easier to have male friends than female friends. I never felt any competition with boys. I could ride my bike with them, play soccer, and laugh without overthinking everything. I wasn't comparing my outfit, my accomplishments, or my likeability because we were too different in my mind.

I had many male friends up until I started dating seriously. Once I began to have serious romantic relationships, the male friendships dissolved a bit, either out of respect for my new partner or a realization that the male friend wouldn't be morphing into something more. In retrospect, there was often a romantic interest from one or both sides in most of those friendships, so they were a bit doomed to begin with. I realize now that even though male friends may be easier to make, forming close relationships with other women is SACRED.

Find like-minded women whose behavior you would like to emulate. Find people who are on their own journey for personal growth, who allow you to be authentic and silly and complex. I was held hostage by my own jealousy toward other girls. My comparison and judgment alienated me from good people for too long. I wish I had been open minded and filled with love, so that I could have attracted others like that. People are truly magnets and tend to pull in what they put out. Once you have found your people, aim to stay inclusive and leave the door open for new group members.

At your school, they have a buddy bench for people who are looking for someone to play with. You yourselves have sat on that bench and no one has come. So, I'm trying to instill that if you see someone else sitting alone on that bench, you should offer to play with them. Putting yourself out there is a beautiful act, even if it all goes to hell in the end. If a person or group invites you to participate with them, but you are not interested, always decline politely. While you may not be interested in one moment, you may later realize that you have something in common or want to pursue a relationship. This has happened to me more than once: sometimes I have slammed the door in someone's face and they are no longer an option in the future, and other times I am pleased to get to know someone who I had previously discounted and realize that we are, in fact, kindred spirits.

Finding friends is a first step, but building the friendships and then maintaining them is where the main effort lies. I have had wonderful friends who were definitely tribe worthy, who I have let slip through my fingers. I didn't reach out to plan activities, I didn't wish them a happy birthday, and I may have failed to be there when they needed support. I wish I had done things differently, but when too much time passes between communication, it feels like it is too late. Currently, I have a treasured friend who I rarely speak with, but I keep reaching out in hopes that our connection is not lost. Sending a text or a call is a lifeline.

I remember when I was living in the redwoods for a month, with very little cell phone service, receiving two messages from home. I had had a difficult day and was feeling disconnected from the group. Early in the month, amidst our deep and meaningful conversations, I began to question if I really knew these people, if my feelings were really safe with them, and if our relationships were temporary. It was somewhat of an existential crisis. And on that day, I received two messages from the outside world. The first message was from a high school friend who lovingly teased me about my hippy-dippy redwoods experience, briefly updated me on their life, and said that they hoped I was having a good day. The second message, from a fellow hippy friend from medical school, expressed envy for the experience that I was having and stated that they could not wait until I returned, so that I could tell them all about it. Having those people reach out, especially the second one who expressed interest in knowing what I was going through, healed me that day. It helped me to know that even if the relationships in the redwoods were temporary, I had permanent relationships on the outside and I could carry the experience forward by sharing it there. Be the person who reaches out, you never know what it might mean to someone.

I'm still learning how to be a better friend, how to maintain friendships when life gets in the way, and how to meet new people. As a kid, you play with whoever is nearby and convenient. I failed to grow out of that mentality for far too long, opting for easy friendships even when I didn't feel they clicked well with me. I hope you will be brave enough to put yourself out there and try on different friends until you find those who truly fit. Gather your tribe early and hold them close; growing up is a bumpy ride and better as a group adventure.

21. Treasure your siblings

Siblings give us an opportunity to practice friendship from the time that we are born. We all have basic desires: taking a toy, crying for our mother, finding a friend, and engaging with people. Part of integrating into society is learning when to honor those desires and when to compromise them for the common good. If you have a sibling, you get daily practice in relationships, problem-solving, and sharing. That is a gift which some people do not have. I hope that you treasure your siblings.

Our siblings see us in our worst moments and know the darkest parts of ourselves. That does not mean that we turn them away or that we need to find friends who have never seen those parts in order to love us. It means that our siblings will have the absolute best understanding of who we are and how we became that way. If ever you have a falling out, try to mend the fence. Of course, you will have differences and go on your own separate paths at times. But the nice thing about siblings is that those paths will always intertwine again. Love your siblings, appreciate your siblings and cherish those relationships so that they flourish and are available to you when mom and dad are no longer there.

You may notice that I am not particularly close with my sister, and that is one of the great failures of my life. We were raised in the same household, but had two very different experiences. She was older, and unfortunately I think our parents divorce damaged her far worse than it did me. I assume her core childhood memories vary in tone from mine, though we have never discussed them. I was the baby and some would say the golden child. I was praised and loved, even when it took attention away from her. I was less kind, less understanding, and less gracious than I should have been toward her.

I was told growing up how different we were, and that is true. We were often pitted against each other and our differences were emphasized rather than appreciated. I wish that I could have been there to support her in times of need. However, I was not. I was often selfish, competitive, and petty. I deeply regret that.

My parents encouraged a competitive spirit and thus accidental sibling rivalry. I think they were trying to make us successful in the outside world, but within our own household it created a sort of war. I wish we had been encouraged to be teammates instead of opponents. I absolutely (secretly) LOVE when you three kids unite together as rascals against me; when you are partners in crime, even though I'm your victim. It makes me incredibly happy in the weirdest way and I hope some of your core childhood memories will be acting as accomplice for the big candy sneak of 2023, or hiding your sister so well during hide-and-seek that I had a panic attack thinking she was lost. I always want you to be united, even if that means united against me. When you're teens, I promise if you cover up for each other's mistakes or deception, I won't be mad but rather will be happy you've got somebody in your corner. Be each other's ride-or-die, bail each other out, and share your innermost thoughts and fears. I hope you'll be the type of sisters who share clothes, talk about your romantic interests, and are each other's travel buddy and maid-of-honor.

With my own sister, I had hoped at one point that we could evolve past our childhoods and become friends, but the reality is that we might be too different. We have grown further apart, rather than toward each other. Maybe we have always been too different and that is why we never forged a genuine friendship. As children, I was into sports and she was into theater. Now, we are on literal opposite sides of the country and opposite ends of the political spectrum. That makes it hard to have quality time and meaningful conversation. I don't think I will ever give up hope of being close with her, but I am currently processing my disappointment and accepting the estrangement.

Being apart from family feels WRONG to the core of my bones; I feel both shame and frustration, but am trying to come to a place of acceptance. After all, at times we need to "accept the things we cannot change, the courage to change the things we can, and the wisdom to know the difference"

(Serenity Prayer). I have called, texted, sent gifts, and apologized for some of my mistakes. At some point, I have to accept that I might be toxic in her mind, she might be holding a grudge or not value being close the way that I do. I may never know and it will probably haunt me forever, but grieving and letting go would be healthy, at this point.

So, with all my own sibling drama, I genuinely hope I am not putting too much pressure on your own siblinghood. My goal is to create a culture of mutual respect, teamwork, fair time and attention for each of you, and understanding the value in having siblings. Your sister can be a friend who will always be there no matter what. She can be an opportunity to learn how to play, fight, and resolve conflict. She is the first person you'll likely "need space from", and hopefully you are learning to kindly ask for that space, then eventually come together again. On a daily basis, I fight my urge to intervene in your conflicts and problem-solve, knowing I should stay silent and not rob you of learning opportunities. Unfortunately, you might have noticed that I'm not great at staying silent.

Hopefully you have enough room to stumble through being a sister, learning to be a friend, and using each other for fun, support, and personal discovery. I can't promise I'll say all the right things, and I know I won't be able to model any of this for you, but I do know I'll approach siblinghood with a positive attitude. Sisterhood will be viewed in our house with a distinguished reverence and held in high esteem. Fingers crossed I don't mess this subject up in your psyche, it really matters.

22. Take My Word For It, This Stuff's Hard!

As I have mentioned, friendship has been a struggle for me since childhood. My combination of ADHD impulsivity, the lack of friendship interactions I witnessed from my parents, and the breeding toward a competitive and gossiping nature were all to my detriment. Right now, I am trying to instill strong social skills in you girls, but it is a bit of the blind leading the blind. I have made some mom friends and have my few close, trusted friends scattered around the country, but I wish I could show you more. Literally, I am reading a social skills book for children and learning things myself.

I always admire how friendship comes so easily to some people. One of my best friends from high school is so gifted in their natural ability to approach people, make jokes with them, and feel kinship. I consider them one of my best friends, and I know at least 20 other people who feel similarly. One person with 20 best friends! I'm not sure I have anyone who would consider me their best friend, other than your dad. So, I am striving on a daily basis not to pass down my friendship challenges.

Despite my best efforts, friendship can still be a triggering topic. When you came home crying one day and said your friend wouldn't play with you at school, I was rushed back to my own childhood, where I felt like the friendless third wheel. I wasn't sure what to say or what to do, other than comfort you. My mind was racing, wondering if the other kid was at fault or if you had unknowingly said or done something unfriendly to them. My mind went into problem-solving mode, wanting to dissect the situation and figure out what happened and how to prevent it from happening again. Your dad said to let you work through it on your own and not worry about it, unless you explicitly asked for help. I see now that you were both just children, figuring stuff out, and likely no one was at fault. Part of me worries about bullying or having your hurt feelings go deeper to form a lasting wound. But, I am trying to trust the universe that you will learn through time, experience and mistakes.

Maybe I failed so miserably at childhood friendship because when I had conflicts, my mom would say it was the other child's fault. She failed to help me analyze how I contributed to or had agency in the situation. She would gossip and badmouth other moms, and when I mentioned a conflict with another child, she would badmouth them, too. It led to me having an early internal cancel culture. If I had one negative incident with one peer, I would mentally mark them off my list of potential friends, writing them off forever and never trying again. There are only so many children in one school and neighborhood. Therefore, I am encouraging you to do the exact opposite, to give people second and maybe third chances. I explain that everyone has bad days and other people's actions are rarely personal, and may have nothing at all to do with you.

Sometimes, I wonder if this is the right approach, because I want you to know that I am on your side, think you are wonderful, and will defend you. I don't want to put all of the responsibility for friendship on you and I never want you to give a bully a second chance. The line between an evil bully who you should stand up to and a misguided kid who is struggling internally and unleashing their stress on others can be murky. I want you to say no to verbal or other abuse, but also be reflective when something shouldn't be taken personally. I want you to take responsibility for your actions that may have contributed to the situation, without blaming yourself for every friendship struggle. Overall, to be a good friend and expect others to be good to you, in return, while understanding that no one is perfect and mistakes can be forgiven. See how complicated this stuff is?

Once you have made close friendships, we are then left with the next step of evaluating if you have chosen those friends wisely. I can already see some peers wearing crop tops and make up, who I do not think would be a great influence on you. But I shouldn't tell you to stay away from them, right? I'm not sure what I will do if you have a friend who is a negative influence in the future. Will I let you ride it out and learn for yourself, or should I say something and intervene by limiting contact? I don't know and thankfully we haven't had to cross that bridge yet. Once you do find friends that you love, who are tribe members, how can you maintain those friendships moving forward? When you go to different colleges, or they move away, or they are temporarily occupied by their first love, or an intense activity that demands their time away from you. What then?

Sometimes we subconsciously seek out those who have strengths where we have perceived weaknesses. Making assumptions about people based on your own projections is unwise. I always admired and made positive assumptions about people who were quiet. Because I was so loud and verbose, I assumed that those who were quiet had an inner strength that I lacked, that they were in command of their bodies, and incredibly thoughtful and careful with their words. I didn't recognize that they may have had social anxiety, been too nervous to contribute to conversation, or been keeping quiet for other reasons. I mistakenly assumed all quiet people were socially and morally superior to myself. I longed to get them to open up, to see what wise and carefully crafted words they would say.

In college, I became roommates with someone who was incredibly quiet and I was so excited to get to know her better. I put her on a pedestal despite not knowing her very well, projecting my assumptions based on my longing to have more control over my lack of brain-to-mouth filter. But, when she finally started talking, I learned that she was incredibly judgmental, though shy. She was…um…what's a nice way to say selfish? She was not too concerned with kindness nor justice, and was actually somewhat angry all the time. It was a difficult learning experience, because I had to continue living with her for the rest of the year, but it was incredibly educational. Let people show and tell you who they are, and until they do, avoid assumptions and let them be a blank canvas.

Like sisterhood, any lasting friendship will have its ups and downs; it won't always be rainbows and butterflies. When someone has done you wrong, please don't assume that they are a bad person or that they dislike you. Don't write them off and block their number forever. Consider that there were other factors at play: maybe they are unleashing difficult feelings in your direction; maybe they didn't sleep well or are hangry. Whatever the cause, don't jump to conclusions. Give them a chance to explain and apologize. I usually say give people a few chances to demonstrate their character, but once their behavior has clearly established a pattern and they have shown you who they are, believe them.

Also know that relationships are give-and-take. One in which you are always giving is not fair, and one in which you are always taking is not right. Look for people who choose to spend time with you for the pleasure of your company, not because you are being used for any other purpose. Do not choose to spend your time or participate in relationships that bring stress or drama. You have the power to walk away. We can only control your own behaviors, and while it may be well intentioned to provide constructive feedback or necessary to speak up for your boundaries, if you are sensing disrespect or someone causes your Spidey-senses to tingle, go with your gut. You cannot control how someone else treats you, you only control which treatments you will tolerate long-term.

When I was younger, I wanted everyone to like me and I wanted to be able to resolve all conflicts in all relationships to make them work. As I have aged, I realize some people were not meant for me, I am not everyone's cup of tea, and it is more important that I like myself than twist and bend for others' approval.

If or when you encounter mean-girls, know that mean people are typically very unhappy on the inside and are projecting their negative internal feelings onto other people. Do not tolerate it, do not take it personally, and do not let their tantrums and internal turmoil become your own internal turmoil. It is theirs, not yours. Their strife is not yours to manage or solve. Let them deal with it, you are under no obligation to make it right when you have done no wrong. Saying it again in case it needs re-hearing: you are under no obligation to make it right, when you have done no wrong.

If I had heard that a time or two growing up, it would have saved me a lot of stress and tears. I would not have taken every slight so personally or felt the impulse to fix others' problems. When other's dumped their doo-doo on me, I could have let it roll right off my back and carried on with my day. Aim to know what is for you and what is not, when to take constructive feedback and when to walk away from verbal abuse. Doing so will save you time and energy, and keep your healthy sense of self intact, rather than rattling your self-esteem cage too often.

Knowing who you are and being confident in your actions will save you from being the victim of those who are trying to bring you down to their level. As Michelle Obama says "when they go low, we go high". Always aim to be the bigger person: the more understanding one, the more compassionate one, the more forgiving one, the more respectful one. Seek out people who return those courtesies while calmly and confidently walking away from those who have not yet mastered those skills.

23. Jealousy Isn't Cute On Anyone

I believe jealousy is at the root of many of my struggles. I'm not sure if it was innately in me when I was born or was nurtured through my parents, but the force was strong in me. It contributed to my competitive spirit, friendship struggles, and sometimes threatened to chip away at my self confidence.

In elementary school, a group of us were learning a dance and one girl picked it up much faster than the rest. I felt it was unfair, since I was working hard and trying my best, but the moves did not come naturally for me. Looking back it all seems so silly, but at the time I became cranky, irritated, and unpleasant toward all of the other dance participants. I would have been better off either not caring as much, or transforming the jealousy into action, such as practicing more on my own. It was unfair to be so upset with this gifted dancer, who had done nothing wrong, and it was unfair to myself to get caught in a web of comparison. Like many things, I wish I had handled that differently.

As I have matured, I have realized that the core drivers behind my jealousy can be transformed into admiration. Instead of comparing myself to others and feeling less than, I can look at others and admire what they have. If I want to take it one step further, I can learn from and emulate them. It is a choice to always look for the good in others, and a choice that I hope you will make. Being "green with envy" is to recognize positive things in others, begrudgingly; being inspired is to recognize positive things in others, with admiration. Why not choose the latter? You will be happier and feel more whole.

Celebrating others is a key to healthy friendships. You want people in your corner who are cheering for you and hoping for the best, not hoping you trip nor laughing when you fall. In the age of social media, there are comparison traps laid out in a row, just taunting your ego to spiral into a crisis of confidence. But as I have said, social media rarely shows the full truth; it is a curated snapshot, not a complete picture of what someone is really going through.

Your dad and I always reflect that we don't have any ideal models for marriage or parenthood. The people who *seem* perfect only appear so because we don't know them well enough, yet. The importance of the word "yet". When someone seems perfect from the outside, you would likely think differently if you got to know them better. Your fantasy of who someone could be is always very different from the reality of who they actually are. That applies to romance as well. Keep that in mind, as I have found it a comforting thought when envy creeps up.

They say comparison is the thief of joy, and being jealous is a punishment to yourself. It drives a wedge between you and the person that you are jealous of, and the result is feeling worse not better. We rarely compare ourselves to others when we are feeling at our best. We start to look outside of ourselves and the comparison monkey jumps on our back when we are feeling low. They say the moon could be jealous of the stars, and I try to keep that in mind when I get a little green. Do not let jealousy consume you, instead use it as a tool to recognize what is important to you, what may be missing from your life, and what your deepest self desires. If you let it, jealousy can be illuminating. This is easier said than done, since it takes mental fortitude to recognize a difficult feeling, acknowledge which feeling it is, and then thoughtfully process it without getting swept away. My hope is that you will have the tools to do that, so that you can experience your emotions without falling victim to them, process your emotions without neglecting them, and express your emotions without unleashing them violently.

In conclusion, jealousy is never a good look, not even on you who I think are the most gorgeous, adorable, amazing little humans. Instead, look inward to process that feeling. It is normal and healthy to experience jealousy and it will happen throughout your life, just move through it so that it can illuminate your inner longings rather than letting it pull you down like quicksand. How you move through the feeling says a lot about you: choose to be inspired, to appreciate others, to celebrate differences, to be motivated for change if that's what's right for you. Fight the urge to let what others have affect how you feel about yourself. You are worthy, loved, and whole and no one should be able to convince you otherwise.

24. Tone and Intent

Tone and intent are important considerations, in addition to your words and actions. Sometimes, you can say the right words, but if spoken with the wrong tone, it changes everything. Similarly, if you are acting out of obligation and not passion or choice, your actions lose value.

I'll offer a particularly painful personal example: feedback that my college roommates gave me. In my final two years of college, I lived with three girls who were definitely not my tribe. I had met them in the dorms and though they seemed nice, we did not have much in common. We all did our best: we would watch TV together, talk about cute boys, and discuss interesting classes we were taking. I believe the three of them started to form deep tribe-like bonds, but I did not. Perhaps I could have tried harder to find commonalities and appreciate who they were. But I did not, and instead distanced myself and sought other friends.

We had weekly roommate's dinners and at one of those dinners they had a sort of intervention for my personality. At that time in my life, I would sometimes nervously monologue when I was not sure what to say, my ADHD impulsive tendencies would cause me to interrupt people, and my social skills were lacking in general. The three girls sat me down at dinner and stated that they did not like my interrupting and that I was not a good listener or friend. While they were absolutely correct about the interrupting and listening, at that time, they delivered the message as a firing squad. The weapons were their words, and their tone was one of disapproval, loathing and borderline mean-spirited. It caused me to become defensive, cry, and question myself as I tolerated their tirade. They had clearly discussed this in my absence. It was a very hurtful day for me, but illuminating nonetheless.

At the time, I had a pretty limited range of emotions, so the only one I could muster was anger. If I had been more evolved, as I hope I am now, I would have felt sadness and guilt, and perhaps would have been able to hear their words with more openness. But, at that time, I felt attacked and unloved, which is honestly how it came across to me. The same exact conversation could have been had with the intention of helping me and discussed in a loving way. They could have given me a feedback sandwich, with some positives about my personality, such that I was funny or kind or that they could see I was making an effort, despite not having much in common.

Instead, it was all negative and spoken with less than kind tone and words. Hopefully sharing that vulnerable story helps you to see the importance of tone and intent. The same conversation can be had two ways: one way is mean-spirited, without regard for someone's feelings and the other way is thoughtful and kind, in an attempt to help another person.

Obviously, if I could go back, I would have remained calm and listened intently. Perhaps if I had been less defensive, they would have been less aggressive, in return. Maybe I could have stuck up for myself, pointing out that although I lacked social skills, I was a kind person and would work hard to be more polite in conversation. I take full responsibility for my past mistakes, but how I handled that dinner is a big regret. I wish I had been less reactive, less hurt by people who clearly were not friends and did not like me, and more willing to hear hard truths. After that, I distanced myself from them and found my own tribe outside of the apartment we shared. I guess it ended up OK.

I have thought often about their deeper reasoning and can't fathom why they went about the conversation the way that they did. If you are providing feedback to someone, make it constructive. When you speak your truth, do so in a way that feels authentic to you, with no intent to cause harm to others.

After that personality intervention, I called a close friend. I was crying and explaining what had happened and they laughed. They said that while the feedback might have been true, the roommates were missing out on the wonderful parts of my personality. They noted that my listening was probably better when I was more interested or passionate about the topic of conversation. They told me that I was kind and funny, and that my social awkwardness was a lovable quirk to those who liked me. They reassured me that I was an excellent friend, just not a friend to those girls. Their exact words were: "f*$# those girls, they don't know what they're talking about".

And while, in retrospect, they did know what they were talking about, the friend's reassurances were just what I needed to hear. This friend reminded me that I was kind, even if my social skills were lacking and sometimes came across as rude. My intentions were pure-hearted and never malicious, and had we bonded on a deeper level, perhaps they would have been willing to look past my shortcomings and see the good stuff buried a little deeper. Even with all of my missteps in my relationships with those college roommates, I can hold my head up high knowing that while I was annoying, immature, unevolved, and impulsive, I was never cruel, uncaring, or evil. I can live with being clueless and awkward, but wouldn't sleep if my heart was filled with hate or I set out to hurt someone. Surely, I could have done better with being vulnerable and forging friendships, but that's a two way street and in retrospect, forcing something that feels unnatural seems inauthentic.

I am doing much better now with taking feedback. The person I most often take feedback from is your dad, who does love me. Even though his tone could sometimes be better, I know that he is coming from a good place. Often, he is encouraging me to stand up for myself in my workplace, or give you kids the opportunity to figure things out without me interfering. When he approaches me, he looks for opportune timing, when we can discuss calmly and quietly without interruption. When you know that someone is providing feedback with loving intent, it helps you to be more open to hearing what they have to say and set down your defenses.

Two people can leave the same conversation with totally different takeaways based on their assumptions and their preconceived notion of the other person. Pro tip: if someone begins to get defensive while they are speaking with you, the conversation is not going well. Learn to recalibrate your approach, or abandon it all together for a better time or place. If someone uses words as a weapon to attack you or their intention is to hurt you, feel free to press pause and walk away. Not everyone deserves your ear and while my college roommate's feedback did end up being valuable, I think I would have figured it out in my own time, less painfully. So, watch your tone and intent, because they paint the color to your otherwise gray words and actions.

25. Beware the Friendship Cliff

Friendships, like all things, may eventually end. We typically enter into a new friendship with the hope that it will last forever, but that is not always the case. As the great song (and Bible verse) says "to every thing there is a season, and a time to every purpose under heaven". Some friendships will stand the test of time, while others will fade from view. You will mourn the loss of some friends, while they are still living. They may choose to exit your life, lose contact, or you may be the one walking away. Either way, it will not be easy.

Some friends will slip silently into the night and you will barely notice their absence. Those are the easier ones, as the moving on is typically mutual. But, there will be others that you cling to who escape your grasp. When this happens, try not to take it personally. Their path is simply diverging and you are not meant to continue the journey with them. Perhaps, it is a time for reflection, in case you have said or done anything that led them to part ways. If that is the case, you still have to let them go, but at least you can learn from your mistakes. If you have not said or done anything to turn them away, then trust that the universe knows what it is doing. Sometimes people need space and will come back to you. This phrase is usually spoken about romance, but I think it applies even more to friendship: "If you love someone, set them free; if they come back to you, it was meant to be."

I think that the grief over loss of a friendship can sometimes be even more overwhelming than the loss of romance. After all, we expect that most romantic relationships are temporary, and only one or maybe two will lead to marriage and lifelong companionship. But the expectation that 'friendships are forever' can be unfair and unrealistic.

Which brings me to: beware the friendship cliff! The cliff is a point of no return: when you could go to great lengths to reconcile OR you could cut the ties and watch the friendship sail away; when you are at a fork in the road and can work to build a bridge or burn the union to the ground; when you are embroiled in conflict and could say hurtful words that you can never take back, or bite your tongue. In those moments, I hope you will mend fences and bite your tongue. It is always best to take the highroad and refrain from intentionally hurting others, or twisting the knife, so to speak. It is OK to close doors on friendships, but rarely is it necessary to slam them shut, lock them, and throw away the key. Part amicably.

If standing at the edge of the cliff, I say make the choice not to jump. People may change and want to come back to you, if you don't put any nails in their proverbial coffin. If you take the leap by doing or saying something that you can't take back, you may live to regret it. Friends evolve and feelings change over time, so even when you are certain about ending a friendship, do so kindly, with care and respect for the time you have spent together, the positive memories, and the ways the friend has influenced your life.

My perception of my role in relationships has changed greatly with age and maturity. I wish I had not slammed the door on certain friendships over the years, because there are people whose company I think I would enjoy at this age and stage. Besides, no one ever complains about having too many friends or too many options.

This reminds me of my own sister and our current estrangement. We can exchange small pleasantries and be in the same room for the sake of our aging parents, but we do not communicate on our own. Your dad thinks it is permanent and I should let go of any hope for reconciliation, but I hold out hope. There is a difference between estrangement and death. I refuse to let the relationship fully die. Someone has mentioned to me that perhaps she needs space, so I am trying to give her that. I am trying not to stalk her with texts and phone calls, as I used to. I am accepting that she has a right to cut off communication. Perhaps she will see that I respect her and potentially reconsider a relationship in the future. Maybe when we are in our 80s, and she needs someone to be there for her, I can be that person. If I allowed my frustration and anger to boil over, and communicated that to her, it would be the final nail in the coffin of our relationship.

One caveat: there ARE toxic people, or OK people with toxic traits, who you will encounter in the world. Don't invite them into your life and don't allow them to overstay their welcome. They advertise themselves very nicely: they are always wronged but never wrong. You can gently move them toward the door without writing them off forever. Maybe they will learn, eventually. Perhaps you can contribute to their growth by showing them firm but kind boundaries. It is neither in your power nor in your job description to change other people, and you would be foolish to try. But it is your responsibility to be kind and considerate, even to those who return your love with hate. Let their energy roll right off your back and don't waste your time or energy on them. Put out positive vibes to every living thing in the universe, regardless of what they send back.

Allow and even encourage others to continue their journey without you, but do so kindly. I encourage you to move on from negative situations or relationships that are not in your best interest, but just do it with grace. If you're standing at a friendship cliff, choose to walk away calmly and confidently rather than dive off into the deep end and throw away any chance at reconciliation in the future. You will evolve, friends will evolve, and the universe has a funny way of circling back to people or places who can help us learn and grow. Keep an open mind and heart.

26. Quality Over Quantity

Quality friends are hard to find. We talked about finding your tribe, and while you are waiting to meet those rare individuals in your life, there will be other groups of friends. I have never been one for large groups, I am better one on one. When there are three people, I automatically feel like the third wheel. When there are two people, I know I am in the group. It's pretty small minded and I'm sure it could provide a fun conversation topic if I ever find time for therapy, but it's how I feel. Luckily, you do not need large groups to feel accepted; one or two key individuals are the key to sisterhood and unlock all the benefits that friendship provides.

Always choose one amazing friend over ten subpar friends. Find the person who you can call at any hour, will be there to laugh or cry with you, and embrace your best and worst parts. If you find yourself with someone where you don't feel quite safe to be your full self, that's a red flag. I call those fluff friends, physically present but without much substance to sustain a real relationship. Fluff friends will not be there when you need them; fluff friends don't know or accept your authentic self; fluff friends look good in pictures, but do not amplify your human connectedness. Avoid fluff friends, they can actually make you feel more lonely than being alone.

Quality over quantity applies in many aspects of life, not just friendship. As an aspiring but failed minimalist, I have tried to simplify our home to only the things that matter. This is much easier said than done. When it comes to clothing, a few quality pieces will always win out over the trendy fast fashion which will fade, fall apart, and be out of style sooner than your next menstrual cycle. Obviously I do NOT apply this to writing, though I know it would be best to choose a few thoughtful words to encapsulate my message, I just can't resist a 300 page disquisition. I do see the humor in this statement, as I rant on and on. Being overly verbose is something that I am working on, and perhaps I can make my words and thoughts more concise during the editing process. Don't hold your breath, though.

Minimalism is a concept that I encourage you to explore. There is beauty in simplicity, and I hope you will be able to appreciate that one day. As a child, I was overscheduled with a different activity every night and not much time for free play nor boredom. So, when we have a quiet afternoon at home and you complain about being bored, it is music to my ears. Boredom is a gift to your sibling relationships and creativity, and the antidote to the hurried, overstimulated, fast paced rat-race that society has created for children. We don't want pressure on your childhood to be in many places and do many things. Being a child is enough. I sincerely believe that simplicity is one of the keys to staying calm and being happy. If you are content with less, you will avoid the pitfalls of consumerism. You'll be less vulnerable to sales tactics, peer pressure, and becoming a victim of capitalism.

While I want to give you the world and offer you every opportunity, I don't want to rob you of the opportunity to just be. Hopefully, you will have the space to learn relationships through trial and error, to discover your passions, to revel in nature, and to develop a strong sense of self. Accordingly, if life ever seems too complicated or too busy, or your world feels too messy or too big, the answer is to simplify. Give yourself the gift of untangling yourself from society's expectations, streamlining your obligations, and removing unnecessary complexity from your life. You won't regret it.

Quality friends will always welcome you. You will feel included and invited. You won't feel the need to tip-toe up to them and ask if they're free to chat. You can barge right in and enthusiastically join them without worry. Some wise person said "don't sit at tables where you have to bring your own chair" and that resonates with me. If you feel unwelcome, explore that and reconsider the friend group.

Of course, the exact opposite is true when it comes to employment and the patriarchy; there you must claim and sometimes demand your rightful seat at the table. Shirley Chisholm, the first African American woman elected to Congress, said, "If they don't give you a seat at the table, bring a folding chair." But in friendship, true soul mates will sit cross-legged with you on the floor, if there are not enough chairs. Find those people and hold onto them tightly.

27. Sparkly Peeps

If you are lucky in life, you'll come across people who absolutely light up your world, not in a romantic way, but who make you feel seen, special, or cared for. I call these angels on earth "sparkly people".

I can name the sparkly people I have had the pleasure to know on one hand, that's how rare they are. One example is a former co-worker, who was a nurse. One day, she knew that I was sick (pre-Covid, when everyone would go to work sick and power through it). On the second day that I was sick, she showed up with a special sickness tea for me (Starbucks Medicine Ball Tea). It made me feel so loved to know that she thought of me and brought me something to help me feel better. She always had a way of doing that. She knew what people were going through and brought a sensitivity to all of her conversations that made her a wonderful nurse and person to work with. We worked together for years and there are countless tiny little words or actions that she did that made me feel cared for. The super soft pink blanket that you, my oldest, sleep with every night was a Christmas gift from her.

There are also sparkly people who bring groups together. The person who, when camping in a large group, brings their guitar and starts strumming it around the fire to start a sing-along. The person who brings everyone in for a group hug in celebration. The person who organizes the neighborhood parties and makes sure that everyone feels invited. Those types of inclusive people are wonderful to have in your life.

Sometimes, the sparkly person is not as obvious. It may be someone in a grocery store who pays you a compliment or a small action that makes you feel that people in the world are looking out for you. Cling to those moments, because they help show the good of humanity and give hope for the world, when at times everything seems bleak.

Another sparkly person is a friend I met at the redwoods retreat. She has the most amazing energy and smile. It seems that light oozes out of her pores and she is eternally surrounded by a halo of glowing energy. She is so genuinely kind; I have never heard her speak badly about anyone or anything. Being with her feels incredibly safe and warm, both invigorating and calming. If you meet someone who gives you non-romantic butterflies, do everything possible to keep them in your life. She now lives on the other side of the country, but we text and facetime on occasion, as much as two working moms with little kids are able. It is a joy having people like that in your life, even if sporadically, because knowing that they exist in the world helps to foster hope and positivity.

I never felt that I was a sparkly person. I didn't think that I added much to others' existence. I either saw myself socially as blending in or being in the way, but not standing out as a magnetic, shiny personality. I was talking with one of my good friends once and explaining that I felt a mutual friend was incredibly sparkly. I was trying to put sparkli-ness into words. The friend I was talking to then stated that I was HER sparkly person. It still baffles me, and maybe she was just saying it to be nice, but hearing that has stuck with me.

In reflecting on that comment, I browsed through my high school yearbook. If I would have guessed, there would have been a dozen generic "have a nice summer" comments. Instead, I found closer to 100 comments that repeatedly used the words "kind", "fun", and "smart". There were dozens of people who wrote their phone numbers and asked to hang out over the summer, even cute boys. I never called any of them, because in my head none of them were interested in being my friend, despite their written proof to the contrary in that yearbook. So, keep in mind that even when you don't know it, you may be sparkling for someone else. While you may only be able to see the light that is shining toward you from others, your light is also shining outward.

I happen to find each of you girls incredibly sparkly and you each add a lot of sparkle to my life. Keep sparkling, seek out the sparkles, and journal or create core memories from those sparkly moments to carry you through the more difficult ones.

Love: Lust & Vulnerability

28. Kiss Some Frogs

Kiss all the frogs! I hope I don't regret saying this, and your dad would be absolutely enraged if he read this, but I fully encourage you to kiss all the people you desire. With consent, of course. Spoiler alert: None of them will become princes, but you will have fun anyways.

In my youth, grandma convinced me early on that sex was a very big deal and should not be taken lightly. In fact, all things sexual were strongly discouraged. I want to take a different approach with you girls: I want you to feel empowered and not afraid or ashamed of any sexual curiosity or desires. I want you to be open-minded and comfortable to explore all parts of yourself, including romantic interests. Disclaimer: your dad one thousand percent disagrees with this approach.

So, with the above in mind, I will tell you that kissing is 100% harmless, is typically fun, and can be a wonderful outlet for young hormones. My mom's scary sex talk explained that our family was incredibly fertile and that her sister had become pregnant during her very first sexual encounter at the age of 15. I lived in fear that as soon as I had sex I would become pregnant. I'm not sure if this was a genius marketing plan to guarantee my virginity, or a factual truth. In reality, I did become pregnant the first time that I had unprotected sex, but luckily due to my mothers warnings, I was married and trying to conceive at the time. I mention that because sex can have unintended consequences, whereas kissing does not.

I will review some of my own frogs now. Both for comic relief, and to share what I learned.

<u>Boyfriend #1</u>: Junior year in high school. I met my first boyfriend when I was 16. He was cute and that was all I needed to be deeply "in like" with him. We were on the same cross country team and got to know each other over the summer during team practices. He didn't have a car or a job, so "dates" consisted of watching movies at each other's house or hanging out with friends. I'm not sure if kids really go on dates nowadays, either.

He was incredibly sweet and absolutely adored me. However, we never had any 'real' conversations during our year-long relationship. When we talked on the phone, it was plagued by awkward silences. I still have no idea what he thought of politics, social justice, or any issues that actually mattered. I knew his favorite Saturday Night Live skits, his favorite movies, and which church he attended, but never went into deeper detail about his beliefs in God. That's the funny thing about high school, when you are immature and not thinking of the bigger picture, you don't bother to ask big questions.

I broke up with him when I got bored of not having much to talk about. I have kept some of his love notes, which always enraged me due to all of the grammar and spelling errors. If you ever write someone love letters, make sure to proofread! You can still find his adoringly and poorly written epic love note in my junior year yearbook, if you're interested. Ugh, I sound like such a heartless biznatch....am I? I guess I was, once upon a time. When we lacked conversation topics, sometimes he would fill the void with adoring compliments. The words of affirmation were nice to hear, for a while, but began to wear on me when I realized they were a substitute for substance.

<u>Boyfriend #2</u>: Freshman year of college. For my next big relationship, I dated someone who started as a friend, which I think is a great place to start a romantic relationship. We had a lot in common, but still failed to dive deep into our innermost thoughts and fears. It was puppy love from the start and probably should have stayed a friendship. We dated for a year, but both recognized that passion was lacking and it was probably just a friendship sans sparks. I genuinely liked him and was unwilling to admit defeat, so he finally pulled the plug and broke up with me. I was devastated, but in retrospect it was a good thing.

In fact, in retrospect he was a bit clingy. At one point, he suggested joining a club I attended to "spend more time together" and I recall thinking "More?!?". I felt a little suffocated and didn't want to share every single activity. I was acutely aware of the necessity to have my own identity outside of a romantic partnership, but he believed couples should share everything and be together all the time. Looking back, it's a bit hilarious that I clung so tightly to that union when it was so clearly wrong for me in multiple ways. Hindsight, AmIRight? I went on a few dates in college, but nothing else stuck.

I was then single from sophomore year of college until third year of medical school. That's right, seven years of being single. At the time, I felt frustrated because I was seeing friends meet their life partner or have multiple boyfriends while I was solo. In retrospect, that period was my time of greatest personal growth. I had the space and loneliness and time to reflect on who I was, what I needed to work on, and what I wanted. Which brings me to:

Boyfriend #3: Last year of medical school and my last boyfriend before I met your dad. At a medical school party, I stumbled upon a very nice guy who was a friend-of-a-friend and we dated for six months. We connected on our love of music, being outdoorsy, and he was the very handsome hippy-dippy type that I had always been interested in. We spent a lot of time together and dated exclusively, but never expected it to go anywhere long-term.

One day, he casually mentioned to his friends that he never wanted to get married or have children. My mouth dropped open and my internal monologue began yelling at me in overdrive. What was I doing? Why was I with him? I realize that the six months I had spent with him were a colossal waste of time. I was at the age where I was seeking to meet my long-term life partner and could not think of any reasons to continue spending time with him. So, later that night I explained we shouldn't date anymore and, being the laid-back dude he was, he seemingly didn't really care. It was done.

Maybe I was living out my younger self fantasy of dating around aimlessly and being casual without intention, but the reality was that I desperately wanted to find my special person and every minute I spent with anyone else was potentially prolonging or misdirecting me away from my ultimate fate..

Maybe it was good to wander, however briefly and late in the game. Perhaps, #3 helped me to focus on what really mattered to me and start pursuing that more purposefully. I met your dad about a year later, via my very targeted internet dating search, lol.

The final frog was your dad, who I guess for the sake of storytelling, turned out to be the prince. I already told you how we met. There is a part of me that wishes I had kissed more frogs along the way and there were certainly kisses with others not worth mentioning. Maybe I would've learned more about myself, or maybe it would've delayed my inevitable self realization. Who knows.

There is importance in dating around to know what you like. My high school boyfriend treasured me and was full of empty praise, which turned out to be an inadequate replacement for genuine conversation. My college boyfriend wanted to be together every second, which I found absolutely suffocating. My last boyfriend was TOO laid-back and aimless. When I get frustrated with your dad for not offering words of affirmation as a love language, I remember that I once had those words of affirmation and was incredibly annoyed by them in the end. When your dad does his own thing, I remember how lucky I am to have time to myself and that I find independence very attractive. When your dad is less hippy-dippy than I wish he were, I remember that I wasted some months with a totally direction-less, passive, lovely person and that was plenty for me.

The frogs will help to clarify what is really important. If someone is incredibly cute, but also shallow and void of substance, you'll be able to value another person's depth. If someone is smart and successful, but cannot make you laugh, you will revel in the dark humor of your future spouse. If someone is suffocating and wants to spend every waking moment with you, you will value the person who gives you space. All of the latter apply to your dad: he's got the depth, the hysterical dark humor, and the independence. The others taught me what I didn't want and helped me appreciate what I eventually would have. Treasure all the frogs: the annoying ones, the bad kissers, the video-game obsessed losers, and the nearly-right-but-not-quite. They all serve a greater purpose in the universe, which is to lead you to your eventual partners or solo destiny.

29. They Might Be Into You If...

Figuring out the playbook for dating is really tricky. I would like to recount to you all the times I have been a bumbling idiot, for the dual purpose of helping you avoid my mistakes and showing you that even when you stumble repeatedly, it will probably all work out in the end, regardless.

Below I will recount why, when a person that you like puts their arm around you, you should lean in for heaven's sake. I never did this and there are too many examples to count. I always had friends of the opposite sex (please change pronouns to same sex, if you're into that; I fully support you whoever you love!). More often than not, I was interested in those male friends romantically, but did not know how to say so or act in a way that led them to draw that conclusion. In fact, I would often act aloof, accidentally misleading them in order to avoid vulnerability.

In high school, there was a boy who gave me butterflies in my stomach every single time I saw him or talked with him. Those 16-year-old hormone induced butterflies are the absolute best! Cherish those feelings, because as life gets more complicated and you get more mature, they are harder to come by. You'll think more with your mind than your hormones, which is no fun at all. Anyways, there was this gorgeous boy and I had a major crush on him. We were acquaintances in high school, and then reconnected after college and became very close friends. We would talk on the phone for hours, go running together, go out to eat, hang out at his house, and one time he invited me to the movies.

It was a silly movie, but I was very excited to sit so close. We had watched movies many times at his house, but on separate couches (cue sad violin music). While watching the movie at the theater, he put his arm around me. I was so excited that I completely froze. I did not lean into it AT ALL. In fact, I might have leaned forward, being nervous. He casually left it there for 5 to 10 minutes, giving me plenty of time to respond. But, I did not. I have very few regrets in life, but not leaning into that arm is a big one. I should have indulged my 16 year old self by not effectively rejecting her dream guy. Instead, I sat there. He waited patiently as I did nothing, until he finally put his arm back in his lap.

Maybe he just needed to stretch? Maybe he wasn't interested but was just seeing if I would take the bait? Maybe he always likes to put his arm on the seat next to him and I just happened to be sitting there? These are the ridiculous, stupid thoughts that went through my head in those ten minutes. He wasn't dumb. He made a very small move and I was a coward to not respond. Don't be me! Take the bait! But who knows, maybe the universe knew what it was doing by paralyzing me. Life could have been very different if I had leaned into that arm; he was all sorts of trouble. A beautiful, genius, narcissistic, selfish, floundering trainwreck. A ridiculously gorgeous six-pack-abs trainwreck, but a trainwreck. But, it probably would have been fun for a while if I had given it a chance!

Another story of another boy. This time I was in college. I remember it clearly, as one does with things that do not go well. You would think I had learned something by then about romantic interests, but you would be wrong! In college, one of my best friends happened to be male. When we met freshman year, we were both in relationships, so it was platonic. However, over the course of four years, we both became single and I became interested romantically. I would always try to dress slightly cuter when we met up but otherwise sent no messages of interest. Neither of us ever discussed the possibility of dating nor made any "moves". So we were stuck in a platonic-yet-interested phase for over a year.

Then, I was devastated after a terrible day (the college roommate personality intervention) and up all night crying, so I called this guy friend the next day. He gave me the best pep talk (see previous story), and told me he would pick me up later to take me out, to ignore those mean roommates, and that I was awesome! It was just what I needed to hear and from just the right person. However, I didn't want to go home to get dressed cute, because I didn't want to see those roommates. So I stayed in an old ratty T-shirt and jeans, hair in a ponytail, and with unbrushed teeth.

Fast forward to that evening: he picked me up and took me to a bar where he met up with a bunch of his friends. The night ended with him and I talking in the parking lot. He had really cheered me up, I was laughing, and he went in for a kiss. What did I do? The girl who's been wanting him to kiss me for more than a year? The girl who really thought he could be the person I was supposed to marry? Obviously, I pushed him away. I was self-conscious because I had not brushed my teeth and I didn't want our first kiss to be bad. I was worried that he would think I was gross and he would throw away any feelings he had for me, because my breath was terrible! (Granted, this still rings true as a possibility. This guy is now a dentist.)

However, it was a stupid move. I could've kissed him and then apologized for my breath and explained the hygiene faux pas. That's what any normal person would have done. However, I'm an idiot! So, I pushed him away and then explained that it was bad timing because I had had such a rough day. And, in my infinite wisdom to make it less awkward and cover my story, explained I wasn't sure I wanted to "ruin the friendship". I definitely wanted to ruin that friendship! Burn that Sh*# to the ground! I would've been fine! That's not all true, but added for emphasis on how stupid my reaction and explanation was. So I got in my car and drove away. I didn't go to the store, buy a toothbrush, and then show up at his house for a re-do, which would have been another alternative option. The next time I saw him, we discussed the failed kiss and he agreed that we should not ruin the friendship. I, trying to save face and not seem desperate or overly interested (despite being super interested), emphatically agreed. Another failed attempt at love by yours truly.

I wish I could stop the stories, but I've been an idiot more than twice.

I will spare you the details of these other stories, but suffice to say that if someone goes into great detail to tell you how good they are at sex, how regular condoms are too small for them, or how highly desirable they are to women, you should probably take that as a hint that they are advertising themselves and hoping you will be interested. Otherwise, you should probably reevaluate the friendship because they are extremely awkward.

So, take the hints; maybe even make some wrong assumptions and definitely consider making a huge fool of yourself in the name of love. Put yourself out there in ridiculous, embarrassing, and courageous ways. In this day and age, with boys being instructed on consent, it is more likely that you will be making the first moves or putting out the vibes (Unless you date girls, which I hope you know I fully support). Either way, lean in to the arm, go for the kiss, lay your feelings out on the table and see what happens. Vulnerability is beautiful and rejection can be character building.

30. Teenage Lust, The Ultimate High

The best "love" is 16-year-old lust for someone you barely know. Behold, the delightful metaphoric bursting of your loins when you hold hands with someone for the first time. When I was young, cuteness and a goofy sense of humor were enough to make me fall head over heels. I suppose I was shallow and unevolved, but I never discussed politics, religion, or anything that actually mattered with young loves. The irony is painful, because now I can barely stand superficial small talk, instead constantly oversharing and seeking out deep conversation. Perhaps I spent so much time on those superficialities as an angsty teen that I reached a BS threshold and can no longer tolerate it at all? Nevertheless, there's something nostalgic and enchanting about how easy and meaningless teenage love can be. Have fun with those butterflies, as they tend to taper off in long-term relationships. High school is partly for periods of unabashed indulgence with temporary people, who make your present day pretty magical.

Few feelings will ever be as strong and pure as those butterflies that you get in high school, and maybe college. The raging hormones help with that. But, be clear not to confuse lust for love. Sure, some people marry their high school sweethearts, and that's great, but don't put all of your eggs in your first-love's basket. I know some of those people, and I wonder if they were extremely emotionally mature and evolved as teenagers, or if they've never evolved past their teenage self. Were they light years ahead of where I was at that time, or permanently stagnant and emotionally stunted?

Among friends, I saw some be genuinely devastated after breakups where they put too much pressure on their high school partner to be "the one (forever)". Instead, try to think of any high school partners as "the one (right now)". They are there to help you learn, have fun, and make memories. Never be afraid to love because it might not last, instead let yourself savor the good times and get caught up in the feelings. First heartbreak is a right of passage, after all.

Part of early relationships is learning to balance who you are as an individual with who you are in relationships. It is so easy to get sucked into your partnership and want to spend all of your time with them, but don't forget your own interests and your own friends. Your friendships will likely outlast any high school relationship. And if you do have a teenage relationship that outlasts high school, hopefully you will have friends in addition to the partner. Never sacrifice breadth of relationships for depth of relationship; ie you need girlfriends just as much as you need your boyfriend (switch pronouns if applies). Maintain your own social outings, your own hobbies, and a strongly rooted sense of self.

When you enter an adult partnership, sometimes couples begin to morph into one blob of a person, but fight that with all your might! Know who you are separate from a partner, and choose partners who support your independence and individuality. If someone loves and respects you, they will want the best for you and encourage you to pursue passions and friendships outside of them.

Don't be a victim of momentum; just because a relationship has forward motion, does not mean that it should continue. Evaluate if someone is the right person at the right time. Treasure your youth and the freedom it allows; do not squander it devoted to some cute dude (or dudette) at the expense of living fully. Romance when you're young can be super fun and add to your life, but if you find yourself better off as a free-agent, then cut ties and go on your own merry way. I myself have fallen victim to relationship momentum: staying with the wrong guy for too long because I was having fun, it was convenient, and it seemed like a lot of WORK to end things. It was easier to just let it roll. But, in retrospect, wasting other people's time and your own time is disrespectful. If freedom beckons you, oblige the universe and liberate yourself.

If you prefer not to concern yourself with romance, that is a wonderful choice and you are probably far more mature and evolved than I was at your age. You do you. But if you do date, don't expect the relationships to last; don't take them too seriously; don't lose yourself in the partnership; don't let your first heartache get the best of you. Do let yourself fall head over heels; let yourself camouflage some hickies; let yourself read and write terrible love notes; let yourself have hushed phone calls in the middle of the night; and let yourself be consumed by thoughts of a person you may barely know but somewhat love. That's what teenage dreams are made of!

31. Have (Some) Sex!

If you are reading this, it means I am alive!! Woohoo! I know this because I told your dad about this journal entry and he said that if he ever needed to give you your hardcover copy of the journals (ie, if I die), he would rip this chapter out. So, if it's here, yay!

Sexual intercourse. Might as well make this as awkward as humanly possible, eh? I know, I know, I know. Stop talking, mom! This is weird and gross! Nevertheless, she persisted! I have internally debated writing this, then re-written it a few times, and edited the poop out of it. I am lucky you're young and I have many years before we have to have "the talk", because I'm not certain how or when that should happen.

I didn't have a super open dialogue about sex with my own mother, who mostly discouraged me from having any until I was married. Of course, she told me about the birds and bees, named the body parts, and explained how babies are made. She emphasized our family's fertility and that I WOULD become pregnant immediately if I had unprotected sex. And darn it, she was actually right (luckily I was married at the time and trying to get pregnant, so I suppose I should thank her).

But I wish I hadn't been so afraid of sex for such a long time. So, I want to say out loud (without having to say to your face) that I expect and actually encourage you to have (some) sex. By all means, I would like you to do so responsibly, but I do not think there should be any guilt or shame or hesitance to express yourself in that way if you feel moved to do so. If you decide to be asexual and completely avoid sex, that is fine as well. Your dad would be so happy.

My mother's scare tactics worked like a charm; they scared me into avoiding sex until after college. You don't have to wait THAT long, but mine was a thought-out, intentional decision with someone I had known for years, trusted, and treated me well. I hope your first encounter will be similarly premeditated and safe.

While teenage hormones are great for lust, I'm not sure a 15 or 16 year old should be responsible for such a big decision and I would hate for you to have any regrets. Maybe I'm old fashioned or up tight and shouldn't make such a big deal about it. Who knows. What I do know is that sex requires some level of maturity and, as a woman, can have consequences if you don't plan ahead. You probably won't be sorry for deferring a bit, to make sure the person and the moment are right, but if you rush into it you might wish you had waited.

I believe my mom's approach stemmed from not wanting to worry about unwanted pregnancies or STI's or what I was doing in my free time with people of the opposite sex. And I understand that, since her sister was a mom at 15 and that rapidly redirected the course of my aunt's life. My mom believed in me and my ability to accomplish great things in life, so she saw sex as a threat to my future. Perhaps I would not have been as focused on school and sports, if I had discovered sex in high school. So maybe her approach worked well for me and was well-intentioned, but I hope to be more open-minded and not deny that that part of you exists.

I wonder if my mom had been less sex-negative and more birth-control-positive, if I would have felt less awkward and left out. I remember feeling left behind in college, when everyone but me was extremely sexually active. There was a certain lighthearted attitude and experimental/exploratory time in my early 20s that I completely missed out on. I want to give you permission to live that part of your life fully, though responsibly.

One thing about sex is that I believe it gets better with the more experience that you have. You may think that the person you are with is wonderful, until you meet the next person who is much better. Funny thing is, you won't know what you're missing while you're missing it. This is not to say that I am encouraging a ton of partners, but it is worth noting that a little variety can be beneficial, just like in dating.

I grew up in a generation where girls were slut-shamed and there was still a lot of stigma surrounding sexual activity. I sincerely hope that the world has evolved past that for you girls. Obviously, I want you to be safe and emotionally ready, but once you feel that you are, I hope there is no guilt or shame surrounding sex. Unfortunately, I have to add the caveat to stay safe. Be cautious with your vulnerability, be vocal with your consent, and be certain that potential partners are worthy of your trust. Hopefully, we will have a relationship that allows you to ask me questions and discuss sex openly, without fear nor judgment. That seems like enough awkwardness for one chapter, you're welcome for stopping here!

32. What We Give Is What You'll Seek

Generational cycles are inevitable, but hopefully your dad and I can spare you from most of our generational trauma. I know we are both trying our damnedest. One would think that being aware of what we would like to change would be enough to just DO that, but it isn't so easy. There are parts of me that act with intention and pride, and then more feral parts that fall back on repeating my own experiences. All of my gut reactions are verbatim words that my mother said, or knee-jerk reactions that are identical to what my parents did. I'm not happy about that and it is something I continue to work on.

Your dad and I both hope to create new family dynamics and traditions. We know that despite our best efforts, we will both be carrying forward small bits of our generational traumas and creating new, fresh generational traumas for you kids. We know that we are your models for marriage, parenthood, friendship, and physical well-being. It's a lot of pressure, and I am acutely aware of my shortcomings and mistakes as they are happening, despite my best efforts. I also know that many girls marry a version of their fathers. This was very true of my sister, and less so for myself. However, when my dad and your dad sit down and discuss finances, or both order plain vanilla ice cream when there are '31 Flavors' available, I wonder how far I strayed from the model.

My dad is eternally optimistic, funny, and quite extroverted. Your dad is a pessimist, also very funny, but much darker than my dad, and a definite introvert. My dad is a consummate people pleaser and desires approval from all directions. One of the most attractive qualities about your dad is his confidence; I do not believe he has one single people pleasing bone in his body nor any need for outside approval. He knows who he is, what he wants, and does not seek to please others above himself. It's a great model for me to see and definitely one I hope you girls will emulate rather than my people pleasing ways.

We know, as your models, that you will be handed down some of our quirks and hopefully strengths, as well. We don't expect you to completely erase the blueprint, but hope that you will deviate from it enough to feel independent and unique. We recognize that our interpersonal dynamic as husband and wife will be emulated, likely subconsciously, and it will become your instinct to act how we act. Even if you partner with someone very different than your dad, you may fall into the dynamic that he and I have.

We hope to show you a relationship of respect and humor, support and teamwork, and how to resolve conflicts lovingly. Communication is one of our strengths, and so vitally important to a lasting relationship. We want you to know the type of love that you deserve as an adult; that you will expect compassion and demand someone who treats you well as you treat them.

Hopefully, you will find a partnership that helps you grow. Someone who helps heal your childhood and familial wounds, through their unwavering support and love. You wouldn't be wrong to choose someone like your dad as your partner: loyal, intelligent, funny, adventurous, and pretty cute too. He is working on a more positive tone, which does not come naturally to him, but otherwise I think you've got a good man to demonstrate the type of love you deserve in the future (be it from a man or woman).

33. Love Languages Exist

Love languages are definitely a thing and can give you insight into how to express your love. They are, per the book "The 5 Love Languages": quality time, words of affirmation, gifts, acts of service, and physical touch. I'm not 100% certain what my love language is, but I can clearly see the love language of those around me. As a child, I hope that you will be surrounded by so many people who love you, that you will experience all five languages and more. You deserve every expression of love because you are magnificent.

My mom's love language is gift giving. She grew up middle class, but has somewhat of a shopping habit and enjoys buying things. Sometimes, I think that her gift giving is just an excuse to buy more and not an act of love at all. Nevertheless, she gives gifts and brings toys and clothes for you grandchildren. It lets me know that she is always thinking of you and keeping an eye out for things that she believes you may enjoy.

My dad's love language is words of affirmation. He grew up in the midwest and from what I could see his mother dangled approval like a carrot in front of him. I think she did give affirmations, but never completely. In my opinion, he spent much of his adult life trying to win her approval. His father (my grandfather) died when I was very young and was reportedly a great dad but in typical 1950s midwest fashion the words of affirmation didn't flow freely.

So, in response, my dad expresses his love multiple times per day and is full of praise and compliments. Hearing his positive words growing up helped to give me confidence and security. I would not trade that for anything. Now that my relationship with my dad is slightly strained, the words seem almost knee-jerk. Sometimes, I doubt their sincerity. Sometimes, I wonder if he is using them to heal his own inner child more than to communicate to me. Regardless, it is nice to hear them and those words helped shape me as a young adult. I do try to emulate words of affirmation with you, but also am trying NOT to mold you into someone who seeks constant approval and praise. I would much prefer that your validation comes from a strong sense of self and is found internally, rather than externally from others.

Your dad's love language is acts of service, especially cooking. I believe his mom's daily act of love was cooking dinner for the family. He was raised in the country, when children would go outside and play all day, then come back for dinner. Therefore, dinner time was an important time of connection with parents, who may not have been as present during the day.

Compare this to parents now, who are expected to know every detail about their child and watch over them every minute of the day. We are expected to get down on the floor and play with children, which is wonderful in many ways, but also adds more pressure to raising kids. The free range method was the law of the land when I was a child, and I do think that your dad and I both benefited from that. So, following in the steps of his mom, your dad is passionate about cooking a gourmet level meal at night and us all sitting down at the table. It is a wonderful family time, to discuss your day and reconnect after being apart at work and school. Sometimes, there is yelling or frustration leading up to the meal, because people are not respecting that time as he believes it should be respected. So we are finding the sweet spot between respecting the effort and act of service, and not putting too much pressure on the outcome of that act.

Every evening after you go to bed, I prepare a small dessert for your dad. It may be a small bowl of ice cream with hot fudge, heating up cinnamon rolls, or pouring a small bowl of cinnamon toast crunch with milk. He said to me once that making him dessert every night is the only way that he knows that I love him. I rolled my eyes at the time, because it seemed ridiculous with all of the other ways I show my love, both large and small. But now, I see that it was his way of expressing how important that small act was to him. It was me reflecting the motherly love that his inner child might miss. I sometimes cook dinner, but he gets frustrated with the way that I do things, the mess of dishes afterwards, and though he enjoys my food, he prefers to cook himself.

There are probably one million love languages, and definitely more than five. No one will have the exact same love language as their partner, but it is important to know what helps them feel cared for.

I would like to think that my love language is quality time. I am trying to be a minimalist, and not focus as much on material things, and rather focus on experiences. I do my best to be present when I am with you, though I know I stare at my phone too much. We blast music and dance when I am cooking in the kitchen, we go for walks around the pond and feed the ducks, we rummage through books at the library bookstore (I love the smell of used books and wandering through libraries), and just generally enjoy time together. Every morning, when you wake at the crack of dawn, we snuggle under the covers. After dinner, we try to make a habit of going for a walk around the neighborhood, and that is where most of our best chats happen. For bedtime, I read the same two books every night (Spot Goes Shopping by Eric Hill, and Baby Animals on the Farm by Rebecca Heller), sing the same song (Wheels on the Bus), and rub your back for a few minutes before you fall asleep. I love all of our little rituals and hope that they make you feel treasured and adored, as you are.

I think when it comes to the sustainability of relationships, you can consider love languages as a way to understand your partner's wants and needs, and what you want and need. As we discuss all the time, there is a difference between wants and needs. Sometimes I think that I want someone to listen, but what I actually need is to process the feelings that are happening within my body. Sometimes, I think your dad wants me to problem-solve for him, but what he actually needs is attentive and active listening without any input. Tease out the difference between the want and the need, and you will strengthen your partnership and expend your energy where it will be most appreciated.

34. Relationship Red Flags

While I want you to be open and vulnerable with the world, some people do not deserve your company. While I do not believe that anyone is bad at their core, some people need a great deal of growth before you can allow them to be a part of your life. Personally, I needed a lot of growth to be in a place to meet the right person. I had to love and respect myself, fully, before I could expect anyone else to be able to do that.

On the importance of little things, I have another metaphor. This time: baking (Yum!). When I was in high school, cookie and cupcake making was always a disaster. At that time, I didn't understand the importance of miniscule ingredients like baking powder and baking soda, salt, vanilla, nutmeg. I would use them interchangeably, not measure exactly, or leave them out altogether, since they were always in small amounts. I should've known better (afterall, I did well in organic chemistry), but I was hell-bent on seeing food as art and not science. I cooked like a cartoon character: flour poofs in the air, egg shells lost in the bowl, and recklessly (though joyfully) sprinkling this-or-that here-or-there. But, now I realize how little things can really impact the overall product. The same goes for relationships in both good and bad ways: add a little humor, a well-timed show of support, or a commonality that runs deep, and that seemingly small stuff may contribute to a relationship going the distance. Likewise, a pinch of disrespect, a tiny misplaced comment, or one ill-intentioned action can snowball out of control and lead to total destruction of a seemingly good union.

I have discussed loss of friendships and that it is OK to move on. There are phases in life where some people may be very prominent and then may fade to the background later on. When it comes to romance, a romantic partner tends to be at the forefront of your day-to-day life, so you have to be pretty choosy with who you let in. They end up affecting your attitude and will be a main character in your memories from that stage, since they consume more of your time and energy than others. Giving someone such a big role in your life is a precious gift; allowing them to be a part of your chosen family is a high honor. Please choose your partners very carefully and look out for some traits that I consider to be red flags.

#1 Being Controlling: Being controlling can come from a number of places, such as being the older sibling or having a difficult childhood. Everyone is controlling to some degree. However, when someone takes it to extremes, they start to stamp out parts of who you are, your interests, your hopes, and your livelihood. That type of controlling behavior is absolutely toxic and it's not sustainable. If someone makes you feel small or that you cannot fully be yourself, run! Run fast and far in the opposite direction!

#2 Lack of Authenticity and Vulnerability: One of the things that immediately clicked with your dad was his complete honesty. He made me feel safe to be myself and that I would not be rejected or judged. I felt my quirks were embraced and that the parts of myself that were a work in progress were recognized without being discouraged. The openness allowed an immediate trust, which has never been broken. If you are unable to trust someone or fully be yourself, that's a no go. If you are unable to show parts of yourself around them, then the relationship is not likely to succeed in the long term. You've got to be able to let it all out, show your demons, and not hide the shadow parts. Never compromise who you are or what you want out of life and never ask someone else to do the same.

#3 Disagreeing on Big Items: Big items would include religion, politics, and finances. I know couples who disagree on religion or politics, and I worry that it could be the deciding factor in a breakup. Nowadays, politics seems to have seeped into most corners of our world: whether or not someone is vaccinated or cares about the environment seems to depend on whether they lean to the left or the right. I believe there is great value in political discourse and having friends on opposite sides of the fence, but potentially being married to someone with an opposite political affiliation could be insurmountable. Entering into a union with a known long-term source of conflict is OK, as long as it can be discussed calmly and respectfully. Differing religions, I suppose, is not as big of a deal, but may lead to difficult extended family dynamics. Perhaps, even, if you approach religion and spirituality with an open mind, it would be an interesting area for growth and exploration. Finances are a different beast. We are teaching you to be savers and live within your means, and if someone has been raised to 'keep up with the Joneses', that is a deeply ingrained psychological trait that would need to be worked on prior to combining assets. Unless someone has demonstrated a desire and ability to change their financial habits, differing approaches to money could be the ruin of your relationship (and your credit score!)

#4 Ultimate Lifestyle Goals: Lifestyle goals include where you want to live and if you want to have children. Where to live and whether to have children are two of the biggest choices a person will make in their lifetime. If two people disagree at their core, perhaps they are just not the right match. Perhaps it is better to move on and live another life with another person. You can never keep someone from having children, if that is in their heart. It would not be fair. Similarly, it would not be fair to force someone to have children who does not want them. Children change your life forever, in ways that you could never imagine and should not be entered into lightly. Please do not compromise who you are or what you want out of life, and never ask someone else to do the same.

#5 Abuse: This one seems obvious when it is physical or sexual, but more subtle forms of abuse can confound you. Verbal and emotional abuse can have gray areas. Someone can be a bit controlling, and then cross a line into emotional abuse. Someone can fight with you and yell, but if it happens too often, it becomes verbal abuse. It can happen slowly over time until one day you wake up, realizing that the person who is supposed to love you is making you feel terrible. If the abuse is unbeknownst to the perpetrator, talk about it, work with them, go to therapy. But make sure that you stay safe and protect your psyche. Feel free to leave, if you need to. If you do find yourself in a gray zone, speak with a trusted friend or go to individual therapy to work out what is happening and why.

#6 How They Treat People: On our first date, I noticed your dad nodded or greeted every hiker on the trail. It was a very good sign, a green flag. Notice how someone treats people in the service industry; how they speak to them and how they tip can give you insight into their innermost thoughts and values. Notice how they speak of others: are they hopeful and positive about their siblings, or making fun of them or complaining about them? Are they close with their mother? Are they able to be analytical and loving at the same time? Are they able to see a relationship from multiple perspectives, or from their side only? Are they still in a childlike state of putting their parents on a pedestal? How do they address their boss and coworkers behind closed doors? Do they gossip or badmouth, or are they kind? Are their expectations for a romantic relationship realistic or idealistic? These answers are important to notice, because they signify respect and foreshadow problems down the road. Also, that old adage that 'if someone is speaking ill about others, they will also speak ill about you' is true. As the closest person to your partner, you will eventually bear the brunt of all their inter-personal habits; a partner will most likely treat you worse than others, so don't expect to be the exception to their bad behavior.

<u>**#7 Bad Sex**</u>: As long as you feel that you fully know every part of someone and genuinely like and respect them, most things can be worked on. Maybe bad sex can be worked on, but where's the fun in that? Sex is supposed to be one of the good parts of the relationship, even when someone is being a total pain in the a$$ otherwise. When someone is being obnoxious or annoying, you should at least know that you still enjoy their company in other ways. For this reason, I do not recommend prolonged long distance relationships, because you are missing very important aspects of the relationship. You can enjoy someone's company on the phone as a friend, but in my experience being in a romantic relationship involves getting a hug when you need it, having someone to cook dinner with, and sharing life's little to do lists. Maybe long-distance can work, temporarily, but if there is no end in sight, what kind of life is that? I know there is excitement in seeing someone, when you have not been together, but that's no way to live perpetually. Just my two cents and maybe you find someone who is worth the trouble, but make sure that at least the sex is good.

Loss: Despair & Redemption

35. Embrace Your Shadow Self

Ah, the shadow self. It would be lovely if we could eradicate all the parts we are not proud of, toss them to the curb, be rid of them forever, and proceed through life being wonderful and happy and proud all the time. But, instead, we are humans and we live on earth. Despite trying to be our best selves, make good choices, and treat others with respect and kindness, we will falter. We will make mistakes, hurt people, and stumble again and again. Perhaps we will do so less frequently as we age, but we will never cease to fumble the ball. Just like professional athletes, regardless of how much we practice, there is no such thing as a perfect game.

Herein enters the concept of our shadow self. There are parts of us that may be shrouded in darkness. These are the parts that we are not proud of and we wish would just go away. But, alas, they will not. They are equally important to the parts of ourselves that we like. They are the yin to our yang (or the yang to our yin, I'm not actually sure which). It is important to acknowledge their existence and aim to understand them. Without them, we would frankly be quite boring. There are those who say that you can only experience true joy if you have experienced true suffering, so the shadow parts exist because there is light illuminating them. There would be no shadows if there were no light, only a sea of gray clouds.

My shadow parts are jealous, competitive, and sometimes over-thinking. But, having those parts is what makes me who I am today. Without those parts, I would likely not be a doctor. Without those parts, your dad may not have fallen in love with me. Without those parts, I wouldn't be driven to write all this nonsense down for you. The parts of yourself that cause you to feel shame, doubt, or even self hatred deserve to be closely examined and not rejected nor suppressed. Sit with them until you come to a place of acceptance, peace, and understanding.

Once you have recognized your shadow parts, the REAL inner work, ie the good stuff, can begin. They may be your most base desires or parts of your wounded inner child that are still screaming out for healing. They may be the result of many micro traumas or repressed major traumas (that I hope you never experience). Regardless of their cause, they exist. Just as your kindness and awesomeness permeate every cell of your being, the shadows are right there, too. By embracing them, you will fully love yourself. By knowing them, you will allow others to fully know who you are. By accepting them, you can move forward with more peace than you would if you rejected those parts of yourself. To attempt to extinguish them is futile. So roll with it, journal about them, and examine them under the microscope, until you fully understand them and can appreciate how they contribute to your wholeness.

36. Hard Times/ Defining Moments

I've said it before, and I apologize, but I am about to say it again. It is not the victories that define you, but the defeats.

When you are older, you will be filled with memories. The ones that stick with you no matter how much time has passed are typically the ones that were the most difficult. What strikes me is the reverence that I have for those hard times. They helped to shape me far more than the good times did. I barely remember my best running race, but I remember every detail of my worst: I tripped at the start of the race and cut open my knee, trampled by the other runners. I got up and ran the whole race with blood dripping down my leg and onto my competitors. I finished the race much slower than usual and was very disappointed. I collapsed at the finish line into a puddle of tears and my mom rushed over to comfort me. I was equal parts angry that I had tripped and disappointed that I had not been able to push through with a faster time.

I kept a Band-Aid over that knee's abrasion for a month as a reminder of my disappointment. Now, I have a scar there (though small) and it doesn't remind me of the disappointment; instead, it evokes pride that I actually got up and finished the race. I remember my moms embrace and my blood stained running shoes. My friend took a picture of that moment and I still have it somewhere. It's a moment I recall fondly. It doesn't matter that the race didn't go as planned; the way that I handled it says a lot about me and I tap into that memory when I need to persevere now. I wish I knew back then how much that race would mean to me and how it would be viewed so positively in retrospect.

So as a parent, I know how important it is to allow you to struggle. I know that coddling you and child-proofing every life experience so that you don't get hurt will not serve you well. When the hard times come, as they inevitably will, know that they are an opportunity to make you stronger.

They are your chance to practice and build resilience. Of course, this doesn't apply to big-time childhood trauma, which I hope to help you avoid. But the games that you lose, rejections from friends or foes, and the seemingly large disappointments that you will face will make you better. They will teach you about yourself and others.

When everything is going perfectly, it doesn't SAY much about who you are. If you've gotten to that place through grit, determination, and hard work, then those are the stepping stones that you revel in, not being at the top. When the poop hits the fan and you are alone, soaking wet and freezing cold, that is when your true self has a chance to shine. That is when the jokes start flowing, you get creative to problem-solve, and you find out who you can lean on for support. My goal as your mother is not to celebrate victory after victory with you, but rather to quietly and confidently watch from the sidelines as you move through difficult experiences. They will carry you from childhood into your teens and finally into adulthood. They are the true measure by which you will grow.

You may not handle all disappointments with grace, and that's OK, too. They are opportunities to learn and sometimes we learn through mistakes. Sometimes you might react with big, negative emotions instead of handling something with sportsmanship and a positive attitude. Hopefully those moments do not speak to who you are in a larger sense, but they are important in moving forward. Everyone does and says things that they are not proud of, so don't be too hard on yourself. Simply learn from the error of your ways and vow to do better next time. If I had quit that race, the lifelong regret would have kept me from ever quitting again in the future. The fact that I pushed through helps me to know that I can persevere. Both reactions can serve as learning experiences, one cautionary tale and one unexpected inspiration.

Just like core memories from your childhood, we do not get to pick our defining moments. Instead, they happen when you least expect it and stick with you forever. While you think your defining moments will be some of your proudest, the exact opposite is true. My defining moments were getting cut from the college cross-country team, not matching to the residency of my choice, and my first few heart breaks.

I barely remember when I got into the college of my dreams, got into medical school or graduated, or had my first date. Those moments didn't define me, because they were the culmination of hard work and I expected that work to pay off. I suppose I took them for granted and saw them as a given, in a way. But, the unexpected hard times that came out of left field when I was forced to roll with the punches, I remember vividly. I can recall songs that were playing in the background, what I was wearing, where I was, and who I reached out to. I remember specific things that those people said to me: that it didn't matter in the long run (they were right, but I wasn't ready to hear it), that it was all for the best, and that they supported and loved me.

It is hard to hear in the moment of disappointment that something is for the best, but it is usually true. I have chosen to believe that the universe sometimes has greater plans for us. Of course, big traumas or deep tragedies are the exception. If I die suddenly, and you are left motherless, I would hope no one says it's all for the best. But, when you fail a test or lose the game, and it seems like the biggest, baddest thing that could possibly happen, those are peak learning experiences.

That awesome Rolling Stones song, "You can't always get what you want" says it better than I can. It is impossible to see in the moment, and even years later, but when you look back on your life, you will see how small ripples led to changes in the current and swept your life in a new direction. If my life had been different in getting into the residency of my choice, I would never have met your dad and you would cease to exist. That would be the greatest tragedy I can imagine. If I had made the college cross country team, instead of being cut, I likely would not have studied harder and gotten into med school. Even though running was fun, I think being a doctor was part of my calling in life. It is something I feel that I am good at and I can contribute to the universe and help people on a daily basis. If my silly college boyfriend had not dumped me, I could have off and married someone who was completely wrong for me. So, when you are a puddle of tears, I hope I am there to embrace you and I promise I will refrain from saying "it's all for the best" until I think you are ready to hear it.

37. Don't Fight The Feelings!

All feelings should be fully felt, respected, processed, and accepted. This is not the message that I was taught growing up, but I think I would be a better person if I had been allowed and encouraged to feel my feelings. I understand why I was given an alternative message that encouraged only positive emotions and shut down negative ones. As a parent, it is incredibly difficult to watch your child suffer. To see their sadness, know that you could cheer them up, but not do so is near impossible. But I firmly believe it is important to experience sadness; feeling it will enrich your humanity, increase your resilience, and actually make the sweet moments even sweeter.

Up until recently, I found it difficult to express any negative emotions. As a child, my mom would say "don't cry" or bribe me to be happy with treats. Any hint of negativity was shushed, so I stuffed it deep down into my little self, believing those feelings could be dead and buried. I was praised for being a happy and easy child. As your mom, I am trying to send the message to you that it is OK to cry. Tears can be therapeutic, they are important, and they should be given a place in your emotional repertoire.

I have been putting on a happy face since before I can remember and it's still my default. Once, an advisor in medical school who knew me well complimented that I was "smooth waters". He meant that I stayed calm under pressure, nothing seemed to phase me, and I came off as self assured and serene. At the time I was extremely flattered, because I wanted to be 'smooth waters'. But little did he know that I am a rip current. I am calm on the surface, composed, and seemingly have it all together, but underneath there are times when I am tumultuous and brimming with all of my repressed feelings. As a doctor, it serves me well having a calm exterior. I believe patients want to see that. But for my own personal well-being, masking my emotions and not wearing my heart on my sleeve is probably unhealthy. Now, I laugh that I was flattered to be smooth waters, when I am secretly a riptide.

My youthful emotional range was either happy or mad. I would not allow myself to feel sad. When that feeling occurred within my body, I was unable to identify it and instead would become angry. Anger was an accepted emotion, but not a productive one. Eventually, as I mentioned before, a close friend suggested that I keep a feelings journal. That friend noticed during a conversation about feelings that I didn't understand what they were describing and couldn't name many emotional states. Keeping the feelings journal was immensely helpful, and I encourage you to do so. I had to use a feelings wheel that I found online, in order to name and identify exactly what I was experiencing. I highly recommend having one on hand, as it can help you label what is happening in your body.

Naming the feeling was only my first step, because after that, I felt a responsibility to experience the feeling, which was quite uncomfortable. I hope that you will never have the experience of feeling something yucky and not being able to understand or accept it within your body. At my Redwood retreat, a wonderful doctor named Lee Lipsenthal (RIP) taught us a method for processing our thoughts and feelings. I used it then as a journaling prompt and I use it to this day. It goes something like this:

1) "What is bugging you?" Write down a list of all the things that are bothering you/on your mind

2) "Why does it bug me?" List why you think it is bothering you. For example, did it bruise your ego, did you feel it was unfair, did you feel like your efforts were not worthwhile, did you fear judgment or rejection, did it cause harsh realizations?

3) "What emotion does it evoke?" Think about what emotions it causes in your gut. The feelings wheel can be helpful here. Distill all of the thoughts from #2 into one-word feelings. It may be bitterness, shame, regret, anger, sadness, gratitude, etc. Usually more than one feeling is present surrounding the topic.

4) "How might you shift perspective?" What is a more efficient/ effective attitude? What do my feelings really say about me? For example, if feeling disappointment, it really says that this subject matters to you or that you care deeply.

5) Resolutions. What actions could you or should you take? What positive things can this reflection bring about for you?

I'm not sure that made any sense at all, so maybe an example would be helpful here.

1) "What is bugging you?" I was disappointed about not matching to my 1st choice residency.

2) "Why does it bug me?" I felt like all of my hard word in medical school had not paid off; I felt rejected; I felt I was being denied a change of scenery, which I was yearning for; I was angry that I had not tried harder during my interview or said something different; I was ashamed about not getting top choice; my ego was bruised; I wasn't sure WHY I was not chosen, so it shook my confidence a bit; I had imagined a new life for myself in a new place and then felt the rug pulled out from under me

3) "What emotion does it evoke?" Shame, Anger, Surprise, Confusion, Embarrassment, Powerless, Resentful

4) "How might you shift perspective?" I can parlay being surprised and confused into being open-minded about the future. I could recognize that the people who rejected me didn't KNOW me personally. They rejected me on paper and in an awkward interview, not with full access to the core of who I was. I didn't tell people my top choice wish, so no need to feel ashamed or embarrassed; my match was still a great one and many would be proud of it. I WAS powerless since the match is a binding placement, so I needed to roll with it and not live in regret and resentment. I needed to make the most of it: move apartments, give myself as fresh of a start as I could in the same town I was already living in. It was OK to be disappointed and mad, sit with it and don't bury the feelings in denial. Match is the culmination of four grueling years of work, so it is reasonable and rational to feel upset.

5) Resolutions. I could trust in the universe that this plan was best for me. I could be grateful to be closer to my aging parents than I would have been at my top choice. I can be happy that some good friends from medical school were also staying local, so I would have friends outside of residency. I could remain hopeful in finding a new tribe, discovering new parts of an already cool town, and being my best, most authentic self moving forward.

Another example, this one more trivial:

1) "What is bugging you?" There was a long group car ride where I was the driver and became frustrated with the people around me. They wanted to read some poems about death and then have deep conversations about them the whole drive, and I stated I preferred NOT to read those poems, but they did it anyway.

2) "Why does it bug me?" It bothered me because I felt no control during the situation. I felt it was an intimate subject and I was not wanting to open up with this particular group of people. The poem book was something that I had been planning to read on my own and create a meaningful experience from, alone. They robbed me of that. At that time, I had a lot of fear surrounding death and my grandmother had died somewhat recently, which I was still secretly processing.

3) "What emotion does it evoke?" Anger. Powerless. Helpless. Excluded. Vulnerable.

4) "How might you shift perspective?" Shifting perspective, I could have allowed myself to be vulnerable with a new group of people. What's the worst that could have happened? If I had not been so resistant and hostile, it may have created a bonding experience. Perhaps those were possible tribe-mates, in retrospect. Once they started reading, despite my wishes, I tried to block them out and went silent, which created weird energy and probably made it less enjoyable for the rest of the group. I wish I had been more mature and not rained on their parade. I wanted to bond by listening to music, my love language, and then felt trapped in a multiple-hour car ride against my will. I could have been stronger in speaking up for myself, stating my desires and needs, and perhaps they would have been more respectful. Or maybe they were jerks, who knows?

5) Resolutions. I resolve in the future, if I'm in a similar situation, that I will speak up and calmly and respectfully state my needs and preferences. I will be more open to vulnerability. I will recognize that I may have some inner work to do surrounding death, and work on processing the grief over my grandmother's death. I will applaud myself that I am experiencing difficult emotions and that I have the capacity to feel things deeply.

Gosh I hope that made some kind of sense. I have found it really helpful over the years. Maybe more emotionally mature people can do all of that in their head, but I have to actually write it down and follow the prompts. Any time that I take a moment to run through it, I always come away with a better understanding of myself and a plan for action moving forward. It helps me not stuff down the feelings and put on my people-pleasing happy face, but rather notice why the emotions are there and how they might be serving me, however difficult it is to feel them.

If it makes no sense and is of no use to you, that is OK too. As long as you feel safe to experience and express your full range of emotions, you will be OK. I love the concept of screaming into the void; it can be liberating and therapeutic. Feel free to furiously rage into the nothingness, allow your body to melt into a puddle of tears, feel the fullness of the pits of despair, observe the dizzying elation of surprise, discern the subtle difference between anxiety and excitement, the optimism of hope, the shame of regret, and ultimately the euphoria of pure unconditional love. All emotions are worthy. And, you may feel multiple emotions at that same time: sadness with relief, anxiety with excitement, or anger with resentment.

Recognize that while I encourage you to experience the full range of feelings, society does not. Certain feelings need to be expressed in a safe space. You will need enough self-care techniques and self control that you can unleash your feelings at the right time and with the right people. They call that emotional intelligence, or EQ, defined as: the ability to understand, use, and manage your own emotions in positive ways to relieve stress, communicate effectively, empathize with others, overcome challenges and defuse conflict. I have always found journaling to be a wonderful outlet to express and process my feelings. Reading through past journals helps me to see how far I've come. I can both laugh at my younger self, and hold space for her and what she was going through at the time.

Take caution in finding a balance between the light and the dark. If the darkness seems to be prevalent throughout the day, be sure to talk to someone about that. If depression and anxiety are impacting your ability to function in the world, to see your friends and family, to do your job, or to experience life, then they have crossed the line from normal feelings into possible pathology. Seek help, talk to me or someone else that you trust, because sometimes feelings are more than feelings. Do not pathologize all tough feelings, but do pay attention and recognize when they are overpowering you and the feelings are taking control of your actions.

I hope that you discover the joy in sitting and crying your eyes out to a good song. Know your internal rhythm in moving through your feelings, learn to expect how long they will last, and how they may cloud your judgment. Learn to know what parts of you are crying out from the inside: is it your inner child? your prideful ego? your wounded partnership? your feared rejection? Knowing the origin of the feeling can help you work through them. What you feel is important, valid, and deserves your time and attention. Please never forget that.

Don't let emotions be contagious, ie don't catch other people's feelings. Be empathic without diving into someone else's sorrow. Their feelings belong to them, have nothing to do with you, and you can better support them from outside of their emotional bubble. This is something I am having to learn as a parent. When you are irrationally upset, I have to stay calm and be the steady rock that your waves can crash upon. If I started metaphorically violently thrashing about with you, we would both suffer more. So, I try to be a source of stability rather than a reflection of your inner turmoil. A cup you can pour into, to hold space for your emotions without giving them power over me; to be a funnel, not a sponge.

38. Grace and Grit For The Win!

Resilience is the current hotword in parenting. They say it is what we should instill in our children to help them be successful, independent, and happy. I have firmly jumped on that bandwagon. The definition of resilience is: "the capacity to withstand or to recover quickly from difficulties"; alternate definition is "the ability of a substance to spring back into shape". Synonyms are toughness, elasticity, flexibility, durability, strength, adaptability. These are all qualities that I wish for you.

But how does one become resilient? Unfortunately, it is through withstanding difficulties, repeatedly, and learning how to navigate through them over time. When life gives you lemons, you make the lemonade, over and over and over again until you can easily balance the sour with the sweet. It involves being the bigger person, sometimes biting your tongue, and always trying to do the right thing.

Sometimes resilience involves being stubborn, persevering when others would quit, and approaching an obstacle with tenacity. I consider myself stubborn and I'm proud of it. It is the quality that allowed me to have unmedicated childbirth, that made me continue breast-feeding even when I was cracked and bleeding, and that got me through medical school. It has probably helped sustain our marriage and has led me to stick with gentle parenting, even when it feels like it is not working. Stubbornness can be a gift, if you let it. I'm not actually sure if there's a difference between stubbornness and perseverance, other than negative and positive connotations that people attribute to the words.

The attitude with which you approach difficulties is the key to the outcome, in my humble opinion. When you know that the road will be hard and long, you can move forward with hope or fear. You can confidently brace for the bumps ahead or clench your teeth and close your eyes for them. Manifestation is real. Sometimes, what you put out into the universe will come to be, so hoping and planning for the best is wise.

Hard things will happen and, as I have discussed, they will come to be defining moments. The outcome of those moments is less important than how you handle them; focus on the process not the product. Have some grit, be willing to put in the work and get dirty.

Grace is a word often associated with the Lutheran faith, in which I was raised. I almost named you girls "Grace", because I love the concept so much. Grace synonyms are elegance, courteousness, poise, respect, dignity, and honor. To 'handle something with grace' means to withstand adversity, bounce back, conquer obstacles, face challenges head on and then rise above. Grace is when everything is going wrong, but you maintain a positive attitude. Grace is when you could act out or be enraged, but instead choose to maintain your composure. Grace is being a good sport and turning the other cheek.

I hope I give you enough opportunity to become resilient. I am continually amazed by how you girls seem to be resilient at your core. When you fall down, you immediately get back up. When you have a disagreement with a sibling, there may be tension for one minute that can quickly fade into laughter and resuming play. If resilience comes naturally to you, then my job is to not mess it up. Your natural kindness, propensity to forgive, ability to move on, and inclination to find joy must be preserved at all costs. I promise that I will do my best.

39. Crisis Mode Rituals

Crisis mode rituals can be awesome. I will tell you about some of mine and I trust that you will form your own based on your unique needs, interests, and what you find soothing. Please continuously develop and tweak them, knowing they may shift with time or lose their effect if used repeatedly.

I am including a list of songs and shows, because those have been important factors in my rituals. Music is my go-to method; there are few things as profound as sitting alone in my teenage bedroom, on the floor with my head in my hands, puddle of tears in my lap, listening to Fiona Apple. Back then, I couldn't always name my feelings and was pretty limited in processing them, but when I would give in and let the tears flow, I always felt immensely better afterwards.

After my mom's mom died, I compartmentalized my feelings and failed to honor my grief until one day I could no longer hold it in. It scratched its way to the surface and uncontrollably began to flood out of my eyeballs. Once the tears arrived, they would not stop. They were unrelenting. I drove to a lookout point and watched the ocean waves crash and dissipate as the tide moved out. I'm not sure how long I sat there, probably hours. I finally allowed the tears to come (not that I could have stopped them). By the end, it was dark and I could see the moon's reflection on an otherwise calm ocean. I finally ran out of tears and was able to breathe deeply, imagining that if my grandma could see me, she would be happy. Watching the waves in those moments felt like I was honoring the dead. Since then, I have considered large bodies of water healing spaces and make a pilgrimage to them in times of need. I figure I must have been a sea turtle in a past life.

Exercise has been another healing ritual, specifically running. When my head is awash with thoughts and I cannot make sense of them, I go for a run. Something about being breathless helps me ponder bigger uncertainties. I think, physiologically, that when our bodies are moving and fatigue sets in, it provides mental clarity. You are unable to distract yourself in those moments; you just breathe in and out, put one foot in front of the other, and repeat. There is no space for doubt and uncertainty. Thoughts will coalesce and little lightbulbs might go off.

I am also aware that you can't have 'ritual' without spirituality. When I attended church regularly in college, I would often find solace there. I wish that I had a church community now but have not been able to find a local group that is a good fit. If you end up being someone who goes to church or praises a god, that can offer many outlets for crisis. Sometimes, even now, when I want to send positive energy to someone in the universe, I will pray for them. I start with the Lord's Prayer, say a few words, and then take a moment of silence. Prayer overlaps with mindfulness, meditation, holding space, and manifesting. Whatever you choose to call it, it involves putting your intentions out into the universe and then trusting that the universe will take care of them. One of the benefits of being religious or spiritual is that it provides a tried-and-true framework for processing challenging times. Typically, there is prayer and song; seeking counsel or confession with an elder; communion, where you partake in group customs; and stories, which are passed down and usually have a moral message. The benefits that organized religion can offer during difficult times should be cherished and if you find solace there, I applaud you.

Seeking community is something that I know I should do more often. I'm not sure why I avoid it, because I do have trusted friends but they are all busy working moms like me so I hate to burden them with my stressors. I also think there are still parts of me that have shame for feeling tough stuff and want to pretend to be perfect. I do have some online communities and Instagram Influencers who I follow, who oddly provide a sense of community. Online chat groups, while they may seem impersonal, are a great place to vent and ask for advice. They offer a level of separation, for me, that makes vulnerability easier. I feel a level of anonymity that allows me to verbalize my emotions and concerns, in a way that I may be hesitant to do in person. Worth a try, in my mind.

Whatever you do, be sure to recognize your patterns and evaluate them, to ensure they are working. Sometimes, I will eat sugar to help myself feel better. I am well aware that that is not wise, is my addiction, and something I need to work on. Avoid self destructive coping mechanisms.

When I have been in crisis mode, I have a checklist of options to try: start by listening to a song; if that doesn't work, get outside in nature and exercise; if that still doesn't work, phone a friend; if I prefer not sharing my feelings, then journal or vent in an online group. Your order and activities may be different from mine that I just listed. My hope is that I will be there to support you and I can be one of the people that you call. But in case I am not there, know that I love and support you, you will get through this, and I am putting out healing energy into the universe for you to feel in the future.

40. Music Therapy Options

When I was growing up, the biggest act of love you could display was making a playlist for someone. Sharing a unique mix of songs was a way to open up your heart. I remember those who have made them for me, both romantic and platonic. It is incredibly special discovering your new favorite song. For many songs, I can remember exactly where I was and who I was with when I heard them for the first time, or who introduced me to the song. When someone takes the time to hand-select art to share with you, cherish it. Listen to every lyric to fully appreciate their effort. I hope that by creating these playlists for you, I will give you the gift of absolute elation, when you hear an incredible song for the first time.

Before I had the language and vocabulary, and frankly maturity, to describe how I was feeling, I had music. Instead of saying I was sad or angry, I would describe my mood as being in "an Alt J mood" (creative), "a Fiona Apple mood" (sad), "an Eminem mood" (angry), or "an Avett brothers and Iron and Wine mood" (happy). Music was my only means to describe my internal state to someone outside myself. Hence, I divided my song recommendations into categories based on emotions.

Music has always been a vital part of my emotional stability. A song can bring me back to places I like to revisit, soothe me when I'm sad, and motivate me when I need support. Sharing music with others has been a quick and helpful way to identify members of my tribe. It is also a way to recognize when someone doesn't quite vibe with you in the way that you had hoped. Music is a free tool, available to you anywhere and anytime, because it lives rent free in your head. Use it to your advantage, let it carry you through hard times and be the soundtrack for good times.

As above, I have organized songs by feelings, so that if you are experiencing heartache or joy, you'll have your mom's soundtrack of what I listened to when I was having similar feelings. I look forward to you sharing your musical tastes with me, introducing me to new bands, and maybe attending some concerts together. Someone's list of favorite bands says a LOT about them (maybe all you ever need to know?), mine are: Iron and Wine, The Avett Brothers, Fiona Apple, Counting Crows, the Beatles, and Bob Dylan. Sharing music, to me, is intimate and vulnerable and profound.

I recall once post-college I was driving with my mom and decided to play an Iron and Wine song for her. I'm not sure where the vulnerable moment came from, but she listened willingly and, in my recollection, kind of shrugged and said it was "fine". I felt I had barred my soul to her and the response was lackluster. I should not have been so disappointed, as it wasn't her style of music, but it stung a bit. Even though she had no idea what sharing my music meant to me, it felt like she didn't "get" me. I'm certain if she had known, she would have responded differently. It's a memory I would rather forget, but one I have to keep in mind as your mom, as not to miss when you are discretely baring your soul to me. I promise to attempt to hold space for you, and to try to tease out the moments that might be bigger than they seem.

In college over Christmas break, my high school friends and I used to meet up at a bar in our hometown to hang out. We would usually eat something but the best part of the night was always heading back to the parking lot and all five of us would cram into someone's car and play music, singing along to songs from high school. It was the most joyful, dorky, bonding experience and I looked forward to it every year. Once we all went our separate directions after college and two of those friends moved abroad, we didn't meet up anymore, but I cherish the memories. Music has a magical way of connecting people and bringing them back together.

If you don't read any other part of this book, please read this list and consider checking out a song or two. Musicians can say all the things I want to say, but eloquently and in tune. I recognize my messages may be out-of-tune and stuttered, so these artists capture the sentiment better than I ever can. I've added little notes or favorite lines to some and bolded ones that speak for themselves in the best possible way. Playlist made with extreme amounts of love. - Mom

<u>Inspiration:</u>

• Marty Haugen "Holden Village Evening Prayer" (esp "Let My Prayers Rise Up", sung in a round)

• Bjork **"Alarm Call"** (lines 11-20/49)

• Tracy Chapman "Talkin' Bout A Revolution" (watch the Wembley music video of her single voice with only a guitar, then panning out to the huge crowd. She is so beautiful and so brave)

• Tupac "Changes"

• Eminem **"Lose Yourself"**

• Marvin Gaye/ Tammy Terrell "Ain't No Mountain High Enough"

• The Chicks "Wide Open Spaces", "Sin Wagon"

• Avicii "Wake Me Up"

• Beatles "Let It Be", "We Can Work It Out", "Across The Universe" "Yesterday"

• Bob Marley "Redemption Song", **"Satisfy My Soul"**

• Macklemore & Ryan Lewis "Same Love"

• Jolie Holland **"Goodbye, California"** (lines 18-21/32, I think about the concept of "immaculate calm" often)

• Hinda Hicks "Our Destiny"

• Alt J "Fitzpleasure", **"Something Good"** (Your dad and I used to listen to their album "An Awesome Wave" on road trips and saw them live when I was pregnant the first time, so they might be the first band you heard live, in womb)

• Des'ree "You Gotta Be"

• Pat Benetar **"We Belong"**

• Jessica Andrews "Who I Am/Rosemarys Granddaughter"

• Leann Womack "I Hope You Dance"

• Christina Aguilera "Cruz"

• Fleetwood Mac "Never Going Back Again"

• Kelly Clarkson "Breakaway"

• Destiny's Child **"Survivor"**

• Birdy **"Keeping Your Head Up"** (my re-discovering myself after motherhood anthem)

• Taylor Swift **"Shake It Off"**, "Karma","Invisible String" (I love all the comments about time and always listen with a broad concept of "you" as if it could be more than a person)

• Tom Petty **"Learning To Fly"**

• Foo Fighters "My Hero" (my old running anthem)

• Lion King, Carmen Twillie and Lebo M "The Circle Of Life"

- Debby Kerner and Ernie Rettino "This Little Light Of Mine"

Shame/Feeling Bad About Yourself:

- Coldplay "Lost"

- Jimmy Cliff "You Can Get It If You Really Want" (listen while fiercely dancing)

- Neil Young "Heart of Gold"

- The Shins "Saint Simon" (Line 19/26)

- Taylor Swift "Anti-Hero"

- Teitur **"All My Mistakes"**

- Simon and Garfunkel "I Am A Rock", **"Bridge Over Troubled Water"**, "The Only Living Boy In New York"

- U2 "Still Haven't Found What I'm Looking For", "Stuck In A Moment"

- Marconi Union "Weightless" (supposedly to help you chill out)

- Weezer "In The Garage"

- Oasis "Wonderwall", "Don't Look Back In Anger."

- Death Cab for Cutie "Soul Meets Body"

- Fiona Apple "A Mistake", **"Extraordinary Machine"**, "Every Single Night"

- Counting Crows "Mr. Jones", "All My Friends" (Lines 12-17/ 39)

● Tracy Chapman "First Try", "Unsung Psalm", **"At This Point In My Life"** (Lines 45-50/60; Sometimes I just NEED to hear "No matter if you find it" as only she can sing it)

● Bastille "Pompei"

● Sheryl Crow "Strong Enough", **"I Shall Believe"**

● Alanis Morissette **"That I Would Be Good"**

● Jewel "I'm Sensitive"

● John Mayer "My Stupid Mouth"

● Fleetwood Mac "Landslide"

Happiness:

● Colin Hay "Beautiful World"

● Fun. **"Some Nights"**

● Mungo Jerry "In The Summertime"

● Regina Spektor "Poor Little Rich Boy" (watch the Lollapalooza video where she plays drums with one hand and piano with the other. She is so kicka$$)

● U2 "Beautiful Day"

● Six Parts Seven (with Iron and Wine) "Sleeping Diagonally" (my alarm clock song in residency, a lovely way to wake-up)

● Counting Crows "Mrs.Potters Lullaby", "Omaha"

● The Foundations "Build Me Up Buttercup"

- Van Morrison "Brown Eyed Girl"

- Taylor Swift "Seven"

- Rihanna "Live Your Life" (our redwoods retreat dish-washing anthem)

- Iron and Wine "Boy With A Coin" (watch the video)

- Beatles "Here Comes The Sun"

- Mariah Carey **"Always Be My Baby"**

- Biz Markie "Just A Friend" (A guy serenaded me with this song Senior Year in high school... and based on that I chose to date him, oddly)

- Enigma "Return To Innocence"

- Big Country **"In A Big Country"** (Lines 9-14/36)

- The Proclaimers "I Would Walk 10,000 miles"

- Bon Jovi "Livin On A Prayer" (the chorus was screamed at the top of our lungs while swaying in the embrace of a large group hug at our wedding, HIGHLY recommend singing it that way)

- The Chicks "Goodbye Earl"

- Jack Johnson "Sitting, Waiting, Wishing"

- Foo Fighters **"Sky Is A Neighborhood"** (our favorite for family living room dance parties, or car rides where we can actually BANG on the ceiling)

<u>Love:</u>

- David Grey "This Years' Love" (personal goal to learn this song on the piano, if I ever learn to play the piano)

- Iron and Wine **"Naked As We Came"**

- Norah Jones "Not Too Late"

- Bright Eyes **"First Day of My Life"** (cried in the library the first time I heard it)

- Avett Brothers "November Blues"

- Edward Sharp **"Home"** (your dad shared this song with me, and it was our wedding day first dance)

- Josh Radin **"Today"**

- Joni Mitchell "Both Sides Now"

- Nick Drake "Northern Sky"

- The Beatles "I've Just Seen A Face"

- Dave Matthews Band "Crash Into Me"

- Jack Johnson "Do You Remember", "Banana Pancakes"

- Otis Redding **"These Arms of Mine"**, "I've Been Loving You Too Long"

- Smashing Pumpkins **"Thirty Three"**

- The Shins "Those To Come"

- Counting Crows "Colorblind"

- Leon Bridges "Take Me To The River"

- Dar Williams **"Iowa"** (All the lines, especially lines 7-8 and 15-17/19, I sang this as your brother's nightly lullaby)

- Tracy Chapman **"I Am Yours"**

- Cranberries **"Dreaming My Dreams"**

- Extreme "More Than Words"

- U2 **"All I Want Is You"**

- Adele "Make You Feel My Love"

- Hozier "Take Me To Church"

- Alanis Morisette "Head Over Feet"

- Desiree "Kissing You"

- Bare Naked Ladies **"Light Up My Room"**

- Gavin Degraw "Follow Through (stripped version)", **"Overrated (stripped version)"**

Loss/Breakup:

- Bob Dylan **"Boots of Spanish Leather"** (he is a musical genius, truly)

- India Arie (version of Don Henley's) **"Heart of the Matter"** (Lines 25-39/75)

- Ingrid Michaelson "How We Love"

- Adele "Rolling In The Deep", "Someone Like You" (Lines 17-20/43)

- Lizzo "Truth Hurts"

- Ani DiFranco **"Untouchable Face"**

- Mumford and Sons "White Blank Page"

- Sia "Elastic Heart"

- Wood Brothers **"Lovin Arms"**

- Taylor Swift **"The 1"**, "My Tears Ricochet" (live long pond studio session, not produced studio/official version)

- Fiona Apple "Carrion", "Fast As You Can", **"Parting Gift"**

- Cranberries **"No Need to Argue"**

- Tegan and Sara "Floorplan", "Call It Off"

- Annie Lennox **"Walking on Broken Glass"**

- Boys to Men "Water Runs Dry"

- Foo Fighters "Walking After You"

- The Chicks "Let Him Fly"

- Kelly Clarkson "Since U Been Gone"

- REM **"Country Feedback"** (the way he sings "I NEED this")

- Queen "Another One Bites the Dust"

- Supergrass "Low C"

<u>Loss/Sadness (pair well with crying):</u>

- Bob Dylan **"Hard Rain's A-Gonna Fall"** (Lines 52-53/57)

- U2 "Staring At The Sun"

- Vision Of A Dying World "Barges"

- Fiona Apple "I Know", "Never Is A Promise" (I have shed thousands of tears while listening to this song, so many good cries)

- Simon and Garfunkel "The Sound of Silence"

- Counting Crows **"Round Here"**

- Tracy Chapman "Paper and Ink" (Lines 21-26/46)

- The Shins "Young Pilgrims"

- Mirah (version of Bruce Springsteen's) **"Dancing In The Dark"** (obscure, can only be found on Youtube)

- Greenday "Time of Your Life" (Billie Joe Armstrong says his goal was to encapsulate "hurt feelings without hard feelings". In my mind, that's an ideal ending: sadness and feeling the loss without anger or regret.)

- Cranberries **"Ode To My Family"**

- Iron and Wine "Upward Over The Mountain"

- The Beatles "Hey Jude", "Because", "Golden Slumbers"

- Leann Rhimes **"What I Cannot Change"**

- Bright Eyes "Landlocked Blues"

<u>Anger:</u>

● Limp Bizkit "Break Stuff" (my go-to rage companion in high school and college)

● Fiona Apple "Limp", "Fetch The Bolt Cutters"

● Eminem "Real Slim Shady" (another musical genius, your dad and I bonded early on in our relationship over our shared love of him)

● Christina Aguilera **"Fighter"**

● Bright Eyes "Road to Joy"

● Britney Spears "Stronger"

<u>Dance/Rock Out (mostly 90s Teen Angst):</u>

● Weezer **"Undone (The Sweater Song)"**

● Yeah Yeah Yeahs "Maps" (I played this song on continuous loop for a week in college, and rocked out every single time)

● Right Said Fred "I'm Too Sexy"

● Sir Mix-a-lot "Baby Got Back"

● Janet Jackson "Love Will Never Do", "If"

● Michael Jackson "The Way You Make Me Feel", "Thriller"

● Madonna "Like A Virgin"

● Toni Basil "Mickey"

● Dion **"Runaround Sue"**

● Cyndi Lauper **"Girls Just Wanna Have Fun"** (another girls-only family dance favorite)

● Trisha Yearwood "She's In Love With The Boy"

● Lady Gaga "Just Dance"

● Queen "Somebody To Love", **"Bohemian Rhapsody"** (for karaoke and cooking in the kitchen)

● Prince "1999", "Kiss"

● Jimmy Eat World "A Praise Chorus", "The Middle"

● Duran Duran "Hungry Like The Wolf"

● 50 cent "In Da Club" (a birthday must)

● Flo Rida "Low" (your dad dancing to this is the funniest)

● 69 boyz "Tootsie roll"

● Shakira "Try Everything"

● Walk the Moon "Shut Up And Dance"(another living room dance party favorite)

Grief/ Play At My Funeral:

● The Flaming Lips "Do You Realize"

● Avett Brothers "Laundry Room", "No Hard Feelings", **"Murder In The City"** (maybe just listen to every single Avett Bros song, OK?)

- The Beatles "In My Life", "Blackbird"

- Counting Crows "Long December" (Lines 24-25/29)

- Edward Sharp **"All Wash Out"**

- Iron and Wine "Sodom, South Georgia", "Each Coming Night", "The Trapeze Swinger"

- David Pomeranz "It's In Every One Of Us"

- Mumford and Sons "Awake My Soul", **"Roll Away Your Stone"** (Lines 30-36/ 44)

- Nick Drake "From The Morning"

- Simple Minds "Don't You (Forget About Me)"

- Joe Cocker (Version of) "With A Little Help From My Friends"

- Imogen Heap "Hide and Seek"

- Pearl Jam "Just Breathe"

- Ani DiFranco **"Everest"** (Lines 25-32/43; a perfect description of what an awesome church will feel like)

- Bright Eyes "At The Bottom Of Everything" (Lines 34-36/44, excluding talking intro

41. Screentime Therapy Options

In the past, when I have wanted to escape my feelings (setting aside whether that's healthy or not for now), I have turned on a movie or show. I am, of course, trying to teach you NOT to deny your feelings and NOT to zone out in front of screens. However, once in a while flipping on the TV and flipping off your brain can be helpful. With that in mind, here's a watch list that I would recommend, in general. They might be watched for fun or as a form of escapism. I plan to watch many with you, once you're older.

<u>Shows/movies from my teens:</u>

"Buffy the Vampire Slayer": I know that the premise of this TV show sounds silly, but trust me it is amazing. You will laugh, you will cry, you will cheer both for and against vampires. The musical episode should have won an Emmy. Give it a try.

"The Sound Of Music": At my mom's house, we used to watch this movie on holidays with my aunts and grandma. Each of us knew all the songs and it reminds me of my childhood.

"West Side Story": As a kid, I didn't appreciate how unique this movie was. It was so beatnik and artsy and tragic. It could be skipped, but if you've got time, why not?

"Dawson's Creek": Like all teens who grew up in the 1990s/2000s, I watched it. I'm not super proud of that, but it is what it is. Pro-tip: fast forward to all the Joey-Pacey scenes (they are the only two worth watching), all of the other characters and storylines are insufferable and boring.

"Dirty Dancing": Not quite sure what grandma was thinking, who was otherwise trying to convince me to be a nun, but I watched this one all the time. A classic IMHO and a must watch so you'll get my frequent reference that "nobody puts baby in the corner" (since your dad refuses to watch it).

"Pretty Woman": Again, what was grandma thinking? An endearing story about a prostitute? Check! A semi-redeeming fairytale ending? Check! A scantily clad early Julia Roberts, who somehow makes the whole thing work? Check!

"Annie": We recently saw Annie the musical and now you know all the songs. Singing them with you brings me an inordinate amount of joy, so thank you for sharing and embracing this little sliver of my childhood. According to my parents, I watched this movie every day during their divorce. Was it a red flag that they missed, that I was obsessed with an orphan during my own parents separation? Yes, probably. But, I suppose the movie had a happy ending, and so did I, so it all worked out.

"Clueless": I still know every word to this movie and it is highly entertaining, endearing, and hilarious. One day, I hope when I say things like "as if!", " she could be a farmer in those clothes", "it was his 50th birthday!", and "that was way harsh, Tai", you will get it. Currently, when I say those things, I receive a blank stare from both you and your dad, which is incredibly unfulfilling. I will continue to say, at every stop sign, "I totally paused" regardless of if anyone ever understands.

"Legends of the Fall": I can and will happily cry from the opening credits until the last scene of this movie. It breaks my heart every single time, even though you are seeing Brad Pitt at his absolute most gorgeous. If you need a good, ugly cry, start here.

<u>Shows/Movies from College:</u>

I didn't have a TV for most of college and streaming wasn't a thing yet, so I actually didn't watch too many shows. There was a store, called Blockbuster, where one could rent movies, usually in a group with friends, because binge watching solo was not yet a pastime.

Sometimes, I enjoyed watching movies with the director's commentary. Knowing they spent hundreds of hours to make two hours of cinema is fascinating. Hearing their careful intention for seemingly small aspects of each shot gives an appreciation for all the little things that we can miss, if we are not looking carefully.

"My So-called Life": The tragedy is that this show only got one season, but perhaps that makes the episodes that do exist even more precious and treasured. It is a must watch. It so perfectly captures the innocence, naïveté, and stumbling that can happen as one comes of age. Many quotables here: "Yeah, we had a time." "Like, the way you are!!" "People alway say you should be yourself, like yourself is this definite thing, like a toaster or something. Like you can know what it is, even", "If only there was a button somewhere that I could push, to force me to stop talking", "It's good to get really dressed up once in a while, and admit the truth. That when you really look closely? People are so strange and so complicated that they're actually…. Beautiful. Possibly even me." I can quote almost every episode from start to finish here, because it is so eloquent and angst-y, timeless and specific, and just plain beautiful. But I will spare you and let you watch Claire Danes, in all her existential struggle and glory. Needless to say, Jared Leto is the epitome of everyone's teenage dreams.

"Sex and The City": (the TV show and definitely not the movie) I watched this show at a neighboring frat house with a big group of people. It may not have aged well, but I can appreciate the humor and female bonding that I experienced while watching this show. Not a must see, but frilly and easy to watch if you are ever bed-ridden after a surgery and need something to binge.

"Mean Girls": "On Wednesdays, we were pink!" Half fluffy teen comedy and half meaningful social commentary. All fun. They are remaking it, which I do not understand. Why is it that the only good movies nowadays are remakes of classics? Always go for the real deal and skip the updated imitation. It's like trying to cover a Beatles song; unless you are Joe Cocker at Woodstock, don't bother messing with perfection.

"Never Been Kissed": Drew Barrymore, chef's kiss.

"Saved": If you want to mindlessly binge something without having to think too hard, this is a good one.

"Catch and Release": Technically I was in between college and medical school when I watched this, but who's counting. In this movie, I fell in love with Jennifer Garner and loved her quiet maturity and overall vibe. I can still watch it anytime and enjoy the music, the style, and the story. Usually coming of age movies involve high school or college, so I appreciated that she was an adult who was still finding herself.

"Arrested Development": Hilarious all around. It's dry, it's sarcastic, and hopefully your brother and I do not turn into motherboy. I liked it so much that I re-watched it with your dad. Too many funny inside jokes to detail here, well worth a watch.

Shows/ Movies I Have Watched With Your Dad:

"The Office": Every character is perfect. Every scene is hilarious. Just watch it, you will thank me.

"Schitts Creek": Ditto what I said above. Dan Levy is a genius.

Other Shows Worth Watching:

"Survivor": I recently started watching and I'm a big fan. When you are older, I would love for us to watch together. It's a pretty family-friendly show, explores human-ness and can be inspiring. Maybe one day you will even play. It would be an opportunity for fun, adventure, and to learn about yourself.

"Girl, Interrupted": Depressing, beautiful, disturbing. Watch at your own risk.

"The Beach": I liked the concept and watched it when I was in my existential pondering phase, which made it a good fit.

Bluey, "Sleepytime" (Season 2, Episode 9)- If you ever become a mom, watch this to remind yourself that you are their sun.

42. Other Therapy Options

There are so many different ways to soothe ourselves and heal our inner child. Screen Time and music have been two of my go-tos, but there are others as well.

Pets! I had cats growing up, and while dogs are great and very friendly, I find cats more appealing because you have to win their affection. They are extremely discerning and choosy about who they give their love to. Therefore, when they do come snuggle up with you, it means more. If overcome with difficult feelings, petting a gentle animal or having them sit on your lap can be extremely soothing. The innocence of animals is unparalleled. They do not have ill will or harbor any negativity. They are vessels for pure joy and positive energy. So, if you are sad, gaze into a sweet animal's eyes, watch them go about their business with nothing but purpose and clarity, and feel the love that they can provide.

Art! I'm not the best artist, but I can see the calm and focus in you girls when you sit down to color or draw. Making or viewing art can be calming. Music is art, too, of course. Perhaps you will play an instrument or enjoy singing. Maybe you will be passionate about photography or sculpting. Adult coloring books are very cool and I know people who find them therapeutic. For many, cooking or baking is calming. I think the combination of being 100% in control of an outcome and having your creative juices flowing is very cool. Being "in flow" is a state I wish I could tap into more often, and one I hope you will master.

Special spots. I have had a few special spots in my life, where I can sit and ponder. In college, there was a stone bench in a remote corner of campus next to a trickling stream. I would sit there and read, and feel like I had a secret little refuge from the busy campus. Near my mom's house, there is a cul-de-sac with a huge mansion at the top of a hill. Sometimes, when I didn't want to go home and needed some time to think, I would park at the bottom of that house and do some inner work. I'm still looking for a local spot like that around our house, and I hope to find one for myself. I hope you find one for yourself.

Physical experiences. Floating in water, massage, energy work, toe tapping, and somatic therapy. Progressive muscle relaxation, belly breathing, and box breathing are some others. Literally changing your bodies' experience can help to sway your mind, as well. Your dad pretty much invented cold plunging. He will dive into ANY freezing body of water, even glacial temperatures. I am too chicken to do it and I'm always chilly, but it could be a useful way to hit the reset button on your physical and mental state.

Spiritual Rituals. I've done a few shamanic journeys in my time and those types of experiences can be really cool. Maybe try hypnosis, reiki, energy work, etc. I have already mentioned some transformative experiences while walking labyrinths. I hope one day we can walk one together. When my insides have felt messy, I will enter the labyrinth with the intention to clear my mind, meditate on my troubles in the center and "receive" whatever wisdom the universe has in store, then focus on mindfulness while walking out, feeling each toe touch the ground and each breath come and go from my body. It's always cool.

Nature! I saved the best for last. Luckily, I have often lived near the ocean, so when I am filled with despair, I drive to the beach and watch the waves. There is something extremely healing about the ocean. It is a literal representation that the world is so much bigger than us. What is happening in our life is a small drop in an otherwise massive body of water. There are so many ways the ocean can provide metaphors – the size of the ocean, the unpredictability of its waves, and the changing tides. All of those have been useful reflections at one point or another for me. If something is difficult, wait for the tides to change. If something feels too big or too important, remember, you are a speck of sand in the wider scheme of things. And finally, when you are enveloped in grief, remember that it is like the waves. You can learn to ride the waves, or let them pummel you; you can keep watch over your shoulder, so that you are not overcome; and you can look out for the undercurrent and learn to predict the tides to protect yourself. You know I love metaphors, and the ocean is a good one.

Nature has many beauties to offer: waterfalls, trickling streams, soaring redwoods, the shade of an oak tree, and seeing wildlife in their natural habitat. Mostly, nature can pull you out of yourself and into a different world. Even indoor living things like plants can provide a sense of serenity. I wouldn't know with my black thumb, but I can imagine. Sometimes, a change of scenery is all you need to change your mindset.

I also feel that nature is very accepting of all emotions. There are no good or bad trees, good or bad streams, or good or bad moons. There are large and small streams, there are healthy and sick trees, and there are full or half moons. Nothing in nature needs to be attributed positive or negative value, it just is. It exists in its own unique beauty, whether it may be destructive to things around it or symbiotic with its ecosystem. Feelings are like that, too.

For me, there has always been something incredibly healing about being outdoors. Hopefully I have instilled that love in you since an early age. I personally believe that hearing the trickling of the stream, the rush of a waterfall, or the slash of mud beneath your feet turns on the parasympathetic nervous system. It sends a deeply ingrained message through our DNA that things are OK, and we can breathe a deep sigh of relief. Nature programs our bodies to heal and relax, and often in crisis those are exactly the things we need to see past the stress and take action to move to a better place.

Lest not forget, actual freaking therapy. Try that ◈

Partnership: Teamwork & Harmony

43. Say No To The Dress

"Marriage, marriage is what bwings us togever". Hopefully, you get the Princess Bride reference. Honestly, weddings are great but they can easily cross a line into being too much. My unsolicited advice is to focus on the marriage and not the wedding.

If you are the type who loves party planning and getting groups of people together, then by all means have fun planning your wedding and enjoy the day. But, if you are more introverted and prefer a quiet private ceremony on the beach, please do not feel obligated to have a big wedding. There are certain societal pressures that make absolutely no sense, and in my mind marriage ceremonies are one of them.

I loved my wedding day with your dad and everything went as planned, but it was a lot of work and a lot of money. We did mostly DIY and had a smaller gathering, but it was still probably more than we needed. I believe we would be just as happy if we had eloped on a beach in Hawaii with just our parents. I do love having the wedding day photos, so if you elope make sure to take pictures, but otherwise the food, the flowers and the cake are forgettable. I loved my dress and have preserved it for you girls, but the marriage would be the same if I had been wearing a tank top and flip-flops.

Financially, weddings are not the smartest choice. They are extremely expensive and while it is wonderful for people to celebrate your love, does it require such overt outward expression? Could you send out an announcement and receive congratulatory calls and texts instead? If having a wedding means starting your life together in debt, then please skip it. Financially, you could spend the money on a trip of a lifetime, a down payment for a house, or your future possible children. When I was growing up, the assumption was that everyone would get married in a big wedding, buy a house, and have kids. I never questioned those inherent societal expectations, but perhaps I should have. Of course, not the kids and house part. I have already mentioned that I want you to blaze your own path and question societal norms, so perhaps start with the wedding industry.

Whatever you choose to do, know that you have my support. If you elope in Vegas and I am not invited, I will understand, though please take pictures. If you choose to partner without any official ceremony, I fully support that. Filing taxes jointly is no fun at all, anyways. Don't ever do anything because society tells you that you should. As a matter of fact, don't do anything because I tell you you should. Be open, be creative, be willing to do things differently, and I believe you will maximize your happiness.

44. Teamwork Makes The Dream Work

Ideally, teamwork is something you will have the opportunity to practice throughout your life. Whether that be on formal sports teams, family camping trips, playing with friends, or other endeavors, working with other people successfully is a necessary life skill. Part of being a good teammate is being able to regulate your emotions, expressing them at the right time and in the right way, and being considerate and conscientious. If you can master those skills, teamwork will come easily and be a source of joy. You will be able to genuinely celebrate your victories & comfort yourself and others in inevitable defeat. Fail to master them, and you will struggle like I did.

The most important team I've been on is in my marriage. The learning curve was steep, but so far your dad and I play well together.

Though I was sporty as a kid, I switched from a team sport (soccer) to individual sports (distance running and swimming) in high school. Right at the time when I would have benefited from camaraderie and team spirit, I delved deeper into my competitive nature. I never considered, as a kid, that my chosen sports revolved around competing AGAINST my own teammates rather than working with them to achieve a common goal. Practice was with my opponents, in my mind.

On most teams, each player would be seen as a valuable contributor; but in my sports, there was always a clear MVP, since the fastest time was known to all. I would have been better served in a true team sport like basketball, volleyball, or soccer. One in which the whole group wins or loses AS a team, rather than me winning at the expense of a teammate. My good days were, by definition, others' bad days and vice versa. And while I would love to say I handled wins and losses with grace, I won't lie. My sportsmanship was C minus at best. I didn't gloat outright, but I wasn't exactly wishing others well.

Not my proudest admissions, but I share to help you understand why I'm choosy about which sports you gravitate toward. I am hoping you will have true team spirit, true bonds with lifelong friends, and be competitive in a more positive light. Be just as happy with the assist, as with the goal.

I didn't know it at the time, but building skills as a team player would have parlayed into friendship, romantic relationships, and professional life. Too little, too late for me. I had to foster all of my teamwork skills much later in life and their absence ruined a friendship or five. So, it follows that as siblings, I strongly encourage cheering each other on. It is practice for the rest of your life in wishing well to those closest to you instead of feeling in opposition. If you can fight to understand rather than to win, you will resolve conflict productively. If you can lean into collaboration and understand its give-and-take nature, your creations will exceed what you can do alone.

Ready for a teamwork metaphor? Gospel choirs! Musical harmony requires different voices. There is beauty in the complexity that a chorus can offer, far exceeding the capabilities of a single voice. Listen to some gospel and notice how everyone contributes their unique abilities and it blends together beautifully. The choir is a team. Try not to be butt hurt when the most powerful moment in the song is sung in a round and not as a solo. Keeping with the metaphor, note that all good songs have both minor and major keys; the happy and sad tones blend together to generate highs and lows, giving a song texture and depth. Harmonizing is what makes for beautiful music.

Teamwork makes all things possible in marriage. All people are unique and partnership is about finding someone who compliments your differences, who fills in the gaps, who will work alongside you, and is the yin to your yang. You might have a lot in common or be polar opposites. Regardless, you should be able to expand and contract together to navigate difficulties. When you have a terrible day, something hilarious happens, or you've got an accomplishment to celebrate, your partner should be your go-to person. Call your mom second, of course.

I have struggled finding the delicate balance between self respect through personal boundaries and selflessly giving of myself to benefit the union. I am working on the gave-and-take of stating my limits without feeling selfish, and contributing joyfully without feelings like a doormat. Clear and respectful communication is the key. I am aiming to problem solve as a pair, work in tandem not opposition, and remember that teamwork takes practice.

Despite our differences and imperfections, I think your dad and I make a killer team. We've learned how to communicate, how to read each other's tone and body language, and how to time conversations. Nobody is perfect, so of course we have conflicts but we resolve them well and usually in front of you kids (that's what the parenting books recommend these days). Our family wins when we problem solve, have productive exchanges or conversations, and there is a mutual respect for what everyone is contributing.

Sometimes outside forces affect me and worm their way into our team life: a patient is dying or angry and I bring the difficult feelings home with me. Sometimes in conflicts with your dad, I will literally stop and ask myself: "Am I *looking* for a reason to justify my yucky feelings? Even if he said/did everything perfectly, would I still be pissed?" On occasion, when I've asked those questions, my answer is a resounding YEP! It helps me re-frame if he *did* something wrong or if I came into it *looking* for something wrong. Big difference. Reminding myself that we are on the same team, with the same goals, and mutual love and respect can usually snap me out of it. Usually.

Part of being a good team member and collaborator is listening. The goal is always to listen more than you speak; obviously in my case I absolutely suck at this, but it is good advice in general. I consider myself a fantastic listener at work and with you kids, and a decent listener with your dad. Sometimes, unfortunately, our partners get our left-overs. After we consistently give to others at an unsustainable rate, we might not have much left for them. I am trying not to do this and decreasing my work hours has helped.

Know that there might be roommate-like periods of your union, often postpartum. Don't despair, it won't last forever. All relationships shift and have some rough patches. No sports teams have winning seasons every year, right? Sometimes there are re-building years where you go back to the drawing board and work things out. There's no shame in rough patches, from what I've heard they are normal in any long-lasting marriage. Trod through that roommate phase, knowing it too shall pass; the romance isn't gone, it's hibernating.

Your life partner is your #1 ride or die, above all others. Do not speak ill of them, always champion them to others, and vehemently rebuke anyone who dares to speak badly about them. Shortly before I met your dad, I had made a new friend. She was tribe-like. We went to brunch, farmers markets, and poetry slams together. But, she was very attached to the idea that we were two single girls and was consistently encouraging me not to pursue the relationship with your dad. There was never an ultimatum, but I didn't like her negative take on my blossoming love. So, we gradually stopped seeing each other.

In contrast, another close friend from medical school was an active listener when I was talking about our burgeoning relationship. She was full of hope, support, and excitement, even though she was single at the time. Those are the types of friends you keep close; the ones who are rooting for you and your partner, not the ones who encourage or hope for the relationship to end. Surround yourself with people who are cheering on your union and supporting you as a couple. Of course, relationships can end and then you'll want friends who will be there to console you and be sad with you, not someone who will applaud the demise of your relationship and say 'I told you so'.

So, find a person who excites you, challenges you, and can roll with you. Expect wins and losses, remember that you're always on the same team, and be each others' biggest fans. Make sure those close to you are in your relationships' cheering section. I promise I will be there cheering you on, trusting in your decisions, and vow NOT to be the mother-in-law from hell. Or, at the very least I will try.

45. Hope For The Best, Plan For The Worst

Marriage can be hard. If you are expecting gentle kisses with rainbows and butterflies every day, you will surely be disappointed. Managing expectations is important in all aspects of life: friendships, romance, work, and parenting. Here I will discuss expectations for romantic partnership or marriage.

Spoiler alert: Expectations directly correlate to satisfaction. Of course we have dreams about what our union can be, but we also need to have a level of acceptance for reality. The two are typically quite different. Communication is your best tool for a long lasting and healthy union. Being able to talk openly and honestly was the number one deciding factor in me falling in love with your dad. I felt open and vulnerable, never judged, and was able to discuss difficult topics with him in a calm and respectful way. It felt empowering when we could weather difficult storms together. Indeed we have. Learn communication skills, if they do not come naturally to you. Do not make negative assumptions or take things personally, instead assume the best about your partner and that their intentions are loving and pure.

Expect fights and difficulties. Never keep score; afterall, you are not the referee, you are a teammate. Keeping score is basically harboring a negative list in your head, that you will use as a weapon during battle later on. How else would a scorecard be used? If you can think of a positive use for keeping score, great, but I can't so I avoid scorekeeping like the plague. You will each have your own roles in the relationship and household; hopefully over time you will be able to find a balance that feels fair to everyone. In fact, aim to happily give more than you take and if your partner does the same, you will both be content.

Having shared interests can keep your union strong, but you should also have things that are just yours. Perhaps a girl group, a coffee hour, a book club, or an interest that you do alone, or with a separate group. Keeping little parts of yourself outside of the union helps to keep you balanced and maintain a separate personality from your partner. Nothing is lamer than two people who become one giant, boring blob together and lose all hints of individuality. If you expect to be together 100% of the time, you might get bored or frustrated. I firmly believe that a bit of alone time and unique interests will strengthen your bond and make you happier than co-dependence ever can.

Appreciation and acknowledgment of each other go a long way to sustainability. While words of affirmation may not be your love language, they are important. When someone takes out the trash, does the dishes, or cooks dinner, those efforts should be recognized. Even if they burn something or their efforts do not turn out the way you had hoped, they still tried. If you want something done a particular way, you should do it yourself. I always laugh because your dad likes the dishwasher loaded in a very specific way. When I load the dishwasher myself and he critiques it, I will not load the dishwasher for many weeks moving forward. Criticize or comment to your own peril, lol. I figure he must love doing dishes his way more than he loves having them done by someone else. I'm OK with that.

Finally, to fart or not to fart? Certain expectations should be explored prior to marriage. Are you the kind of couple that will fart in front of each other? Will you poop with the door open or closed? Early on, we tend to put our partners on a pedestal. But if you live with someone, especially long-term, the yucky parts of their humanity will be living with you too. You have to consciously decide whether you are going to keep those parts as hidden as possible, or let them out in all their glory. Think about which type of union you want: one where you are an imperfect human, or one where you remain a tiny bit on that pedestal. Your dad strongly prefers the latter, which I guess is fine by me. But you may choose differently and it is an expectation that should be explored prior to cohabitation.

Basically, consider and discuss all of the things: finances, religion, children, dishes, childcare, and yes, farting and pooping. If you are willing to change and work together, nearly everything can be OK. But if there are certain aspects that are overly important to one or both people, and compromise cannot be reached, pause to consider what that means and if moving forward together is the right call. If you talk about all of these things, it will help to manage your expectations. When you set your expectations low, you will always be pleasantly surprised when things go better than you thought they would.

46. Partner As Catalyst To A Better Self

When people talk about their life partner, you will often hear them say that they "bring out the best in me". That is true in my case, but in a very complicated and surprising way. Your dad challenges me, he calls me on my BS, and he encourages me to be contemplative and better myself. While all of that is in my best interest and I do appreciate it, it is difficult. I somehow imagined that "bringing out the best in me" would be easy, like frolicking joyfully in a field of wildflowers. I assumed he would praise me, see me as perfect, and highlight my best features. Instead, your dad provides true but hard to hear feedback to me while I'm in the trenches. He loves and accepts all of me, but sees my humanity and pushes me to grow. It is super annoying sometimes. But I know that the alternative of being with someone who puts me on a pedestal and fails to see the parts that need work would leave me stagnant and stunt my growth long term.

When your dad knows that I am working on something, and I slip, he will gently remind me of my goals. Sometimes, there are things that I don't even recognize I need to work on that he will point out. Yes, it is helpful, but it is also hard. I believe he does this out of love. I believe he wants me to be my best self, and sees ways that he can help me achieve that. In essence, he is holding up a mirror and at times it is difficult to look into that mirror. I do hope that you find a partner who can hold up the mirror compassionately and consistently, and that you are vulnerable enough to open your eyes to what they are showing you. It's not fun, per se, but when I am older I can imagine myself saying that he brought out the best in me.

Finding a partner who can be a catalyst for your personal growth is valuable. Hopefully, you can grow with another person, in the same direction, at a similar rate. Having a partner who helps propel you along your path is a wonderful thing. However, as they are helping you to become your best self, they also may seemingly be critical about your current self. Take it with a grain of salt. Acknowledge when they are right (unfortunately your dad is usually right). Sometimes, I have to remind myself not to take his feedback as an insult and get defensive.

When I take it personally or feel attacked, I try to dig deeper and see the truths he might be telling. When I am unable to do so, I get defensive because I am sensitive and want him to like me. It sounds so silly, but by helping to bring out the best of me, sometimes he brings out the worst in me. However, it is a wonderful thing to have someone who fully accepts you, faults and all, and is loving, honest, and patient enough to hold up that mirror and encourage your growth. The mirror can be heavy and sharp and dangerous; some people are so scared to speak up that they avoid it and become complacent. Get good at taking feedback, make a personal goal for continuous self-improvement, maintain open dialogue, and appreciate your partner when they put themselves out there with hard-to-hear observations.

47. Fingers Crossed We Don't Mess You Up!

Marriage is hard; divorce rates are high. As I write this, I think we'll make it but I know statistically it comes down to the flip of a coin. To make matters worse, we have no models for a "good marriage" that we can emulate or go to for advice. We are blazing our own path and only have examples of what NOT to do and the types of relationship we do NOT want.

We are acutely aware that we are the model you will know and that our relationship is what you will normalize and possibly unconsciously copy. I am constantly considering: Is our tone toward one another disrespectful? Are we not affectionate enough? Do we resolve fights in a productive way, all the time? Can we continue being real and imperfect, or should we be more performative in front of you kids, which feels inauthentic? So far, we're keeping it real and hoping you see the love and understanding that we have.

I'm sorry that we are your only opportunity to see a marriage play out. All of the long-term married couples we know are imbalanced. Some are together out of co-dependence or convenience; some are more roommates than partners; and worse yet some are addicted to the drama of their union. It's all cautionary tales and red flags, no inspirational real-life rom-coms nor positive influences. I wish we had a few guiding lights, who we could ask advice or hear their stories, but we are making our own stories and hopefully they will be remembered fondly. Like I've said about people on pedestals, relationships that look amazing from the outside are usually just unknown to you. After a lot of living and learning, I assume no relationship is perfect.

So, if we ever divorce, I hope you will remember some good stuff. I hope it doesn't happen, but if it does then I hope it doesn't leave you kids with deep scars. If we divorce, I vow to give my all to peacefully co-parenting, never speak ill of your father, and exclude you from any separation drama. As I've said, being partnered, specifically to your dad, makes me the best version of myself, however annoying his constructive criticism may be at times. If divorced, I worry about not having anyone to hold me accountable, basically no one there to call me on my bullsh*t. I promise I will bite my tongue and not run wild with lectures and metaphors (I'm getting all of that out of my system on these pages, anyways). But I would miss not sharing the behind-the-scenes laughter and stressors of parenting. I would miss the inside jokes and watching shows together after you kids are asleep. Mostly, I would miss knowing I have a partner to ride through life with. Fingers crossed it never happens, but if it does I am sorry and we tried our best.

48. If You Choose Not To Partner

If you decide not to get married or stay entirely single, you have my support. Reject society's expectations, if that feels right to you. They say the happiest demographic is single, middle-aged women without children. I can't imagine my life without children, but you do you.

Marriage is not for everyone, so if you do not partner I hope you find a tribe for travel buddies, befriend your neighbors, volunteer in the community, and immerse yourself in a social group to create a family outside of your genetic ties.

I hope that you will form deep and meaningful relationships, even if they are not romantic. There are many benefits to having people in your life who care about you and who you care for. Being single should be a choice and not because you have not found the right person yet. If you want to be partnered, keep trying until you find someone who fits. If you do not want to be partnered, make sure you are doing it for the right reasons. Do it because you love your independence, because you want to be a nomad, or because it suits your goals and lifestyle. Do not do it because you have been hurt by relationships in the past, because you fear vulnerability, or because it is simply easier or more convenient.

I've now been married for a decade and I suppose many would consider that a success. Marriage is hard work, as I've mentioned above. In my opinion, being married for 10 years should not be defined as "success". For some of my friends, ending a marriage and walking away was the most positive and courageous thing to do. Some people married before they had a chance to know and love themselves. Some people married a person who was not right for them or who held them back. Other people married a person who was right for them at the moment, but grew apart over time. Prioritizing one's own happiness, even if it goes against societal norms, is the best thing you can do for yourself. It is a mark of true self love and confidence. It's something I have generally NOT done, but have great respect for. So, right now our marriage is good and I am grateful for that, but being married is not synonymous with being happy or whole.

Partnership provides benefits that you can find elsewhere. Having a strong friendship circle will give you people to talk with when you've had a bad day, an activity buddy, and someone to binge watch your favorite shows. You will need travel buddies, concert buddies, someone to text if you go for a hike alone (as a safety measure), and someone to get your mail when you are on trips.

My biggest hope is that you will find someone to hold up the mirror for you, as I mentioned your dad has done for me. That even if you're single, you will still have people in your life who love you and are close enough to give you meaningful and compassionate feedback. People who push you to be better and who know you well enough to tell you the truth. Those types of friends are hard to find, but if you come across them, do not let them go. It is easy to be complacent with who someone is, even when they let you in enough to see some of their weaknesses. It is much harder to clearly communicate with a friend about their shortcomings and how they might improve. Not everyone is able to verbalize that and many people are not able to hear it. But hearing it is important and productive. So have an open heart and open ears, and seek out those who will both lift you up and inspire you to rise.

Parenting: Leadership & Caretaking

49. Pregnancy and Birth Stories

How did you come into this world? Joyfully, in short. I was very lucky to conceive each of you kids quickly and to have relatively easy pregnancies. Physically, I felt good. Mentally, I felt anxious. Your dad was so anxious that he was unable to discuss your arrival or build your crib until a few weeks before you were born. My pregnancies were the elephant in the room: whenever I brought up the future, he would shut down the conversation. Later, he said that he was worried something bad would happen and he was trying not to jinx it. I tried to stay active and healthy while pregnant, to give you the best possible start in life. Given the paucity of scientific evidence supporting vegetarianism in pregnancy and my fear that you would miss some key micronutrient due to my choices, I started eating meat while pregnant after twelve years of proud and passionate vegetarianism. One day, I hope to return to that choice.

During my first pregnancy we took the "Bradley Method" course, which is "partner coached birthing". Basically, your dad learned to be a Doula. He empowered himself with all of the medical terms and possibilities of labor, with our ultimate goal being a natural, unmedicated childbirth. Our 8-week-long Bradley class was the one time every week that your dad was forced to acknowledge your imminent arrival. I absolutely loved those classes; they were part power-point lectures to teach your dad all things labor-and-delivery and part enhancing our connection through practicing different labor positions and massages. If those courses still exist if/when your time comes, I highly recommend them. It gave your dad enough information to feel a part of the birth process, rather than an uninvolved spectator. As you will hear, he was clutch in us having a great birth story.

I often analyze why natural birth was so important to me. I believe I was convinced by the science, but of course, I also think I was trying to prove something. I'm not sure what or to who, but I do think it was ultimately the right choice for me.

For my first delivery, you (my first wonderful daughter) arrived three days after your due date. It was the longest three days of waiting in my life (until your brother, of course). I had been taken off of work due to low amniotic fluid a few weeks prior and was anxiously awaiting your arrival. Like all pregnant women, I tried all of the things to get you to come out: spicy food, long walks, bouncing on a ball, etc. Finally, in the middle of the night, I got up to use the restroom and felt some fluid leakage. I was excited that something was happening, but nervous because the contractions hadn't started yet. I quietly left the bedroom where your dad was sleeping and started pacing around waiting for a contraction. Once they began, each contraction caused a little more leakage, so I labored alone in the bathroom while watching the show "Parenthood", of all things. I needed something to distract me from the gradually increasing pain.

I think I labored there for approximately three hours before I woke up your dad and informed him that it was finally, really happening. He got up and made a big breakfast of bagels, bacon, and eggs. I drank a bunch of orange juice through all three labors, as recommended in the Bradley Method. Our goal was to labor at home as long as possible and then go to the hospital when we thought it was time. We labored at home approximately three more hours, and then embarked on the 20 minute drive to the hospital.

When we arrived, I thought I would be close to delivering but I was only 4 cm (out of 10). I was devastated! I thought I could not possibly go on with natural birth and would need pain medication. However, the progression from 0 to 10 cm is never linear, as I was about to find out. I passed the time by bouncing on a birth ball and took my mind off the contractions by watching "Family Feud". After another hour or so, the contractions became extremely strong and I was 6 cm. At that point, I thought I might be able to proceed with the med-free plan. Next cervical check, I was 8 cm and finally felt ready to push. From the time my water broke to the time I began pushing was approximately ten hours, relatively short in the scheme of baby births.

During my transition period, we stuck to our plan. I had a few moments of weakness where I asked for pain medication and your dad calmly and quietly told the nurse to leave for about ten minutes. By the time she returned, I had regained my will and was no longer asking for medication. I pushed for maybe an hour until you finally arrived, screaming and healthy. Having never done any drugs and not having any labor augmentation with Pitocin or epidural medication, that first hit of Pitocin when I saw you was the greatest high of my life.

I asked your dad to review this for accuracy and add any details, and here are his additions. He stayed at the head of the bed and didn't want to view the scene, as he gets faint at the sight of blood. However, right after you were born a bucket full of my blood splashed across the floor onto his flip-flops, leading him to get woozy and leading me to move my oxygen mask from my face to his. Needless to say, he wore closed toed shoes for all future deliveries. All four of your grandparents were in the waiting room, eager to meet you. Everything went very smoothly with your birth, except of course my postpartum course and breast-feeding, which I will discuss later.

My second birth was equally joyous and less nerve-wracking. Another easy pregnancy, punctuated by an extremely excited two year old who was over the moon about having a sister on the way. She absolutely could not wait to meet you and there were many adorable conversations with my growing belly. You (my amazing second daughter) were again three or four days after your due date and I tried all the things to get you out, to no avail. Finally, the contractions started, again in the middle of the night but this time with no water leakage. We labored at home for 2 hours, while waiting for grandma to arrive to watch your older sister. I took a hot shower, which was fantastic for the contractions. Then I felt ready to go to the hospital. Your dad thought it seemed early, but I felt the strength of the contractions and didn't want to have a baby on the freeway or ruin the car's upholstery.

Again, when we arrived at the hospital, I was only 4 cm. But I knew from the last delivery that it didn't matter and things could progress relatively quickly. I was confident in being able to have a natural birth, but when I hit the transition point, I was surprised by my desperation for pain medication. The transition is approximately 10 to 15 minutes shortly before delivery, when there's a flood of horror, fear, anger, and typically the woman will say 'I can't go on'. It's a short but intense hormonally-driven roller coaster.

My transition with you was the most dramatic I could imagine. I started screaming at the nurse to give me pain medication. Our Bradley birth plan was to wait it out, which had worked well with the first delivery. But, I still had my wits about me and tried to use them to get an epidural. When your dad asked the nurse to be patient and give us some time, I SCREAMED across the room that: 1) I was a doctor, 2) I still had medical decision-making capacity as the patient, and 3) she had better get anesthesia in there, STAT!, or I would sue their a$$es. I knew exactly what to say to get her attention, thanks to all my years of medical training. Both your dad and the nurse looked at me stunned, as I had been very pleasant prior to those moments. Your dad, bless him, stuck with the Bradley plan. We had discussed that if I completely freaked out, he should hold strong. I told him before the delivery that my deepest, innermost want was for a natural childbirth, and that superseded any hormonally driven changes in a moment. I had told him prior to delivery that I would try to give in, but he should not. We discussed that I would be eternally grateful if he could hold that boundary for me in my moment of weakness. And he did! That poor nurse, though. She was paralyzed and uncertain what to do, especially with the legal threats. Oops! Your dad went over to her and convinced her to leave and give us 10 minutes.

As in the first delivery, when she returned I was better and the demons had left my body. In fact, shortly after that moment passed my water broke. The nurse had just checked me at 8 cm, then two minutes later my water broke and I began saying that I needed to push and I could feel the head. The nurse said there was no way that was possible, since she had checked me minutes prior. I opened my legs, she saw your hair, and everyone rushed to deliver you. I can't remember if the midwife made it into the room or if the nurse delivered you. I believe I only pushed two or three times and then you were here, healthy and beautiful. Another joyous, medication free delivery, approximately 6 hours from start to finish. Your postpartum course was as lovely as I had imagined the first would be: naps, snuggles, easy breastfeeding, walks in the park. I am so thankful that I got to experience the quintessential postpartum experience of my dreams with you.

When I went back to work after fourteen blissful weeks with you, you decided to sleep all day and waited to party overnight with me. They call it reverse cycling. You woke every two hours to eat from 14 weeks old to 18 months old. My mommy brain/ sleep deprivation got pretty intense. I say this not as a guilt trip, but as a perfect example of the universe's interesting sense of humor. Perfection doesn't exist, so after our joyful postpartum, it wanted to remind me of that. Your older sister's postpartum course was nightmarish, but at least she was a great sleeper.

Your brother's birth was a different story and the last time I will ever pass a human out of my body. Another easy pregnancy and another unmedicated delivery, but fraught with drama. Instead of being three days behind schedule and then kicking off labor on my own, I had a week of waiting and worry during pandemic lockdown. My contractions started and stopped a dozen times, but never persisted for more than an hour. I was exhausted, frustrated, nervous about leaving the house for the first time since lockdown (I hadn't left other than for doctor's appointments), and worried as to why labor was not starting naturally. He was a full week late and I had to be induced.

Typically, with induction, they use Pitocin and the contractions are so strong that no one can continue without pain medication. I was crying on the way to the hospital for the induction, thinking that my final delivery would be a disappointment. Your dad was supportive and reassuring, relishing his final role as an awesome birth support person. When we arrived, I declined Pitocin and instead asked for a gentler cervix softening medication. Again I was thankful for my years of medical training and knowing enough to make my own labor plan. Luckily, after softening my cervix, the contractions started on their own. We arrived at the hospital at 11am, the medication to soften the cervix was placed at noon, and your brother was born at midnight.

I guess, looking at the positives, I was confident that I did not need pain medication and stuck to that without any drama (my embarrassment about my transition fit during delivery #2 helped me be on my best behavior for birth #3). I assumed he would come as easily as my second delivery. But, when it came time to push, he was stuck and his heart rate began to decline. The doctor had a very worried look on her face; I was pushing to my best ability but he was not coming out.

I told the nurse that I needed to take a break and catch my breath between contractions. That lovely nurse grabbed me by the hospital gown, got 3 inches from my face, and looked me in the eye with a look that I will never forget. She was full of dread when she said, "you don't understand, you have to get this baby out NOW!" I knew from the way she said it that he was not going to survive much longer. Sans contraction, I took a deep breath and then pushed for his life.

He came out limp and blue, no crying. The NICU team was there and swiftly whisked him over to an incubator where they tried to get him breathing. We waited anxiously to hear a cry or whimper, anything. Those minutes of silence were the worst of my life. I looked over at your dad, who began to cry, and questioned how it all could've gone so wrong. I remember saying over and over to your dad, "It has to be OK, it has to be OK". Finally, we started to hear some whimpering. They had given your brother oxygen and his previously seemingly-lifeless body started to wake up. After about five minutes, he was crying loudly and they announced that he was OK. It was the longest three or four minutes of our lives.

He ended up being fine, thank the heavens. He was 10+ pounds and had had the cord wrapped around his neck while his shoulder was stuck. I felt and still feel so lucky that everything turned out OK: that the wonderful nurse shook me enough to push him out, that the OB popped his stuck shoulder free, and that the NICU team arrived to resuscitate him. I know other women who have not been so lucky and that in other countries things would have turned out very differently for both of us.

His postpartum course was difficult, too: re-admission for high bilirubin, another round of struggling with breastfeeding due to a tongue tie, an initial tongue tie release with too much bleeding to finish the procedure, followed by a second attempt by a different doctor ten days later that finally led to pain-free and satisfying breastfeeding. All-in-all, a roller coaster. And all during pandemic lock-down. Before I had kids, I used to say "save the drama for your mama" and I think your brother heard me and took it to heart. *shrug*

If you have children, I hope that your birth stories are more like yours and nothing like your brothers. The day of your child's birth will be one that you will remember forever. You will remember the things that your partner says to you, the things that you say, and the details of what goes right or wrong. I am glad that I had a natural birth, because I can recall my birth stories with pride and feel that everything went as planned. Many people suffer disappointment about their birth process. Perhaps they intended no medication, but got an epidural; perhaps they desired vaginal birth, but had a C-section; or perhaps they suffered a birth injury or something else went sideways. The ultimate goal is a healthy mom and baby. I am eternally grateful that we had that outcome three times.

If you embark upon pregnancy and birth, find a balance between having goals and seeing the bigger picture. If you have a healthy mom and baby when it is all over, then everything went splendidly. The pressure put on moms as to how someone gets born is unfair. Having an unmedicated birth is a common goal, but remember it is a want and not a need. I am so glad I birthed at a hospital and not at home, as your brother would not be with us if I had made that choice. As a hippie granola doctor, I have friends who have successfully done home births and I like the concept, but I preferred the safety net that a hospital provided. I also believe in science and think it's potentially a lifesaver to have the full arsenal of medicine in your pocket, on the off chance that you need it. As with all my advice, do what feels right to you and don't suffer from societies' expectations. You owe society nothing and your birth experience belongs to you, your partner, and your baby, no one else.

50. Expectations, Inversely Proportional To Joy

Nobody should tell you motherhood is easy. Joyous? Absolutely. Worth it? Most likely. All rainbows and butterflies, 100% of the time? Absolutely not! I think I felt a bit misled, and perhaps my whole generation did, about parenting. We were raised on the cusp of change. The feminist movement happened during our moms upbringing, so they were burgeoning career women who were convincing us that we could have it all. But I'm sorry to inform you that you can't. You have to know your priorities and pick your battles if you want to maintain your sanity.

Expect the worst and hope for the best. It's a smart approach in many situations, but especially when you enter into parenting. Hope for a natural vaginal birth, but accept if an epidural and/or C-section happens. Hope to be able to breast-feed, but do not despair if your baby eats some or all formula. Hope for a blissful and smooth postpartum course, but let go of guilt or shame if you have postpartum mood struggles or hormonal shifts cause some instability. If you set yourself up for the highest of highs, it will make the lows much more difficult. So, set yourself up for success by expecting a rough ride.

The initiation into parenting would be classified as hazing and outlawed if it were perpetuated by adults rather than adorable newborns. Sleep deprivation is a form of torture, after all. Being conditioned to rock and pace, because every time you sit down there is a shrill shrieking in your ear, is a Pavlovian response deemed too cruel by animal trainers. Motherhood is legit. I was lucky to be prepared for it in many ways by being a former endurance athlete, working 80 hours per week in residency, and being "on call" overnight as a doctor where we are forced to make life-saving decisions one minute after being woken from sleep by our pager. It could all be a funny joke if it weren't harsh reality. Despite all that prep and having cared for newborns in a medical capacity, my initiation into the club of motherhood was bumpy at best.

I think the crux of my postpartum disappointment was breast-feeding. Both grandmas told me what an easy and joyous experience it had been for them and how I would feel incredibly bonded to you through providing food. I had zero doubt that I would breast-feed; it wasn't even a question that I asked. I was adamant that my baby would never have formula, telling myself that it was chemical-filled evil and the worst thing I could possibly do to my child. Of course, none of that is true. It is baby food, period. But I was so stubborn and steadfast in my breast-feeding desire, that no alternatives were an option.

When you were born, the latch was pretty painful but the lactation consultant in the hospital told me it would get better. When it got worse, I visited another lactation consultant who stated everything looked good. I was not satisfied, so I went to yet another one through my insurance. She encouraged me to try formula supplementation, so I promptly disregarded every other thing she said. My nipples became so raw and cracked and bleeding, that you had a good amount of blood mixed in with your milk. Sweet little girl, you didn't seem to care, you kept trying despite the struggle.

Around two weeks of life, you became so frustrated at the feeding process that you went on a 24-hour nursing strike and refused to eat. I was frantic and didn't know what to do. I pumped, but there wasn't much milk supply. Finally, on a Sunday, I searched for a lactation consultant outside of my insurance. I found a wonderful woman who was able to see us that day in her home. She was an absolute pro, having many children and grandchildren of her own and having been a lactation consultant for thirty years. She knew exactly what to say: that I should be commended for my efforts, that breast-feeding was hard, and that struggling was no fault of mine nor yours. No one had said that to me over the previous two weeks. They had said it should be easier, that I should just keep trying, and that some amount of pain was normal. But this lactation consultant assured me that breast-feeding should not be this hard, that I should not be in pain, and that we needed to troubleshoot the situation.

She diagnosed you with a posterior tongue tie. These are somewhat controversial, as many say that they do not exist or are overdiagnosed. But I was desperate and willing to try anything. So, we had a tongue tie release when you were approximately three weeks old. The very next latch was blissful. No pain, you were no longer frustrated, and my milk began to flow as it always should have: painlessly, easily, and increasingly in terms of supply. Thank goodness we pressed on. You breast-fed, my first girl, until you were four years old. You and your sister tandem fed, because you never wanted to give up that wonderful bond that we ended up forming.

However, I wonder if I had not been so stubborn if I would have been happier. While I loved our breast-feeding relationship and journey, I know that the struggle with breast-feeding contributed to my negative mental state after your birth. I probably had postpartum depression; I cried every day and felt like a complete failure at motherhood because I couldn't feed you. You, my angel of a girl, were underfed and therefore didn't sleep as well and would get more fussy than you would have if fully fed. If we both had slept more and spent less time stressing about something I told myself would be natural, easy, and a source of joy, maybe life would have felt different.

If I had entered into my breastfeeding intention with a knowledge that breastfeeding can be difficult, I might need a lot of help with it, and that success or failure in that arena did not make-or-break my concept of being a good mother, we all would have been better off. Your poor dad would get home from work that first month and I would dissolve into a puddle of tears on the floor, feeling like a terrible mother despite my absolute best efforts. Maybe everything happens for a reason, maybe that was the plan from the universe, but I do question if I had been more willing to try formula if we still could have breast fed, just without all the anguish. My own struggles led me to take a course on lactation and become a certified lactation educator. I turned my struggles into strength and hopefully have since helped many of my patients avoid my fate.

If breastfeeding is difficult, if your birth plan doesn't pan out, or if you feel like you are not yourself after delivery, please always remember that your postpartum body is wondrous. It made a freaking human being! You may not recognize it in the mirror and society may shame you for being bigger or less toned or not snapping back into shape like an elastic rubber band, but recall that every stretch mark and skin fold is physical proof that you are capable of contracting and expanding. You are a marvel, you have done something that not everyone can do (certainly not a man), and your body should be revered.

The most annoying saying that you will be told repeatedly is: "It goes by too fast, treasure every moment". Or alternatively, "the days are long, but the years are short". These are absolutely true, but when you hear them in a moment of struggle, they are not helpful at all. Of course, you will treasure moments when you can but that is not always possible. Sometimes it will feel like you are army-crawling through mud that is on fire and you just want to survive and get out the other side. That's OK. Sometimes you will curse or cry or rage at how hard the day was. Even if every fiber of your being loves being a mom, there ARE moments that will suck. Plain and simple. But know this:

There will come a time when your newborn can support the weight of their own head- it will be liberating, and you will be sad.

There will come a time when you can leave their side without too much fuss- it will be liberating, and you will be sad.

There will come a time when no one needs you in the middle of the night- it will be liberating, and you will be sad.

There will come a time when you will not need car seats and strollers- it will be liberating, and you will be sad.

There will come a time when they don't need or want homework help- it will be liberating, and you will be sad.

There will come a time when they won't ask Santa for toys, preferring gift cards- it will be liberating, and you will be sad.

There will come a time when the highlight of our Thursdays won't be rushing out in our pajamas to see the trash truck drive-by- it will be liberating, and you will be sad.

There will come a time when you won't need rides to activities because you drive yourself- it will be liberating, and I will be terrified.

There will be a point where your dad and I can take an extended vacation away from you- it will be liberating, but I will still worry.

You are currently so young that you still want me very close and I am treasuring that time, or at least trying to.

Some parts will be all liberation:

You won't always trip over the baby gate.

You won't always have to plan your day around nap schedules.

You won't always have to wash bottle parts or pacifiers.

You won't always have to sort and fold teeny tiny baby clothes and socks.

You won't always catch every cold they bring home because you are utterly unable to separate germs.

You won't always have to save big topics for journals like this, because one day they'll be old enough to talk about any subject.

Some parts will be all sadness:

You won't always be wanted for snuggles.

You won't always be the first person they want to tell their stories to.

You won't always say certain words in the most adorable incorrect way like "Golilla" for gorilla, "Nank Noo" for thank you, or "Cheebs" for cheese.

You won't always be willing to hold my hand in public.

You won't always be a three-nager, one day you'll be an actual teenager instead and the adorable three year-old tantrums will be longed for and remembered fondly.

You won't always be able to shield them from the dark parts of the world.

You won't always have endless summers to go to amusement parks and swimming lessons.

You won't always know exactly where they are and who they are with.

You won't always live under the same roof and get to see them every day.

I know there are more milestones coming, and faster it seems.

The one expectation that has held up, at least for your dad and I, is the unconditional and overpowering love that a parent feels for a child. Totally different from romantic love, a mother's love is unending, unwavering, and unrelenting. There is nothing you could ever do that would change my love for you. Not to be dramatic, but feeling this type of love is a gift. Knowing I would sacrifice my own life for yours, without hesitation, is a feeling that I wish upon every person on the planet. It makes me a better human, motivates me, and ultimately has changed me for the better (not my boobs or abs, but my emotional parts).

Often I have to remind myself to mother, not martyr. Of course I expect to sacrifice for you and I'm happy to do so, but I can't sacrifice everything. I was not willing to sacrifice my career and I'm hoping not to sacrifice my marriage. Cutting back my work hours has helped, though I still struggle with believing self care is selfish. Call it mom guilt, call it people pleasing, or call it martyrdom. I'm striving to convince myself that there is value in rest and that if I fill up my own cup a bit, I will be a better mom, wife, and doctor. I know that I can't perpetually pour so much of myself into other people without running dry.

I went into parenting full of thoughtful intentions, a deep desire to have children, and careful planning. I have all of the support and resources one could want: parents who live close enough to help with childcare, an attentive spouse, financial security, a home in a safe neighborhood with good schools, etc. I recognize my privilege, which has become your privilege. I can imagine how much more challenging motherhood would be if the pregnancy was unplanned, there was less home-life stability or support, motherhood happened after many rounds of IVF, or a child comes through adoption or being a step-parent. The mom guilt and expectations might be even more difficult. The mental load could be even more complex and with each added layer of stress, the pressure on moms seems to increase rather than dissipate. I hope if you become moms, the expectations from society and ourselves can reach a more reasonable nadir.

I share these struggles in hopes that they will help you. I want you to see a model who is juggling things imperfectly and feel it's important to illuminate my imperfections. I grew up thinking that my mom could do it all and then felt like a miserable failure when I could not. As long as you are doing your best and making decisions that prioritize what actually matters to you, you will be fine and so will your children. Pick your battles; let them have cereal for dinner once in a while, lower your standards for hygiene, and let the laundry pile up. That's the type-2 fun of parenting: the days of complete mayhem, where you either embrace the chaos or let it devour you. Embrace it, take pictures, and weirdly you will look back fondly on that pandemonium. It's not just a circus sh!tshow, it's *your* circus sh!tshow.

51. Testing Your Sanity And Partnership

Having babies will stretch and pull at your insides in challenging and beautiful ways. Sleep deprivation is no joke. In my experience, mom-brain was incredibly real. I felt scrambled from the inside, my head, my physical body, and my heart. Never underestimate the combination of sleep deprivation with postpartum hormones.

In retrospect, I likely suffered from postpartum depression after my first pregnancy. I was ill prepared for the frustration and difficulty of the learning curve. I had expected all rainbows and butterflies, the joy of breast-feeding, the adorable nature of newborns, and the assumption that it would be easy for me because I was a doctor and had some training. I didn't expect all of the uncertainty, the worry, and the physical pain.

For the first six weeks, I suffered cracked, bleeding nipples, and a festering wound in my sit area due to a birth injury. So breast-feeding and sitting caused severe, stabbing pain. Once we fixed your tongue tie (at 3 weeks) and my open wound from birth trauma was treated with silver nitrate (at 6 weeks), all of that got better. However, those first 6 weeks were a hot mess. As I mentioned, every night when your dad got home and would ask how my day had been, I would burst into tears. Poor guy, he had no idea what to do. He was so loving and supportive during that time, and I now try to recollect those days if he has an off day, remembering that he was there when I needed him most.

I think what I had was stronger than baby blues and crossed the line into postpartum depression, but at the time I was unwilling to believe it. It would have felt like admitting defeat. I was devastated and disappointed that things were not easier for me and I think there was some shame and embarrassment that compounded my feelings. To struggle so much was one thing, but I thought to admit and advertise that I was struggling would have made it even worse. Denial isn't just a river, as they say.

New moms are also inundated with questions about the baby, but few people genuinely check in on them. Instead, people offer what they hope to be helpful advice from their own experience. Take all advice as a new mother with a grain of salt. People are trying to be supportive and helpful, and do not realize that unsolicited advice is the last thing you need. Obviously here I am giving 300 pages of unsolicited advice, but know that it is done with misguided love and a goal to be helpful.

Of course, turn to trusted friends and learn from those who come before you, but typically the questions should be from you and the advice should be given on your terms. Always remember that the most righteous parenting advice comes from people who do not have children. I was the absolute best theoretical parent: no sugar, no screen time, tons of outdoor play. And while I have tried to loosely stick to those goals, reality has also set in and I bribe you with treats to get you to go outside and allow screen time more often than I would like.

Also, beware of older generations who say "I used to do XYZ and you turned out fine". Their metric for parenting success is "turning out fine". I guess I have higher hopes for you to be better than fine. And that phrasing ("I did this, but it didn't ruin you") is very troublesome to me because it casually acknowledges that whatever they did was not ideal, but you survived in spite of it. It would be far wiser to admit your mistakes and shortcomings, take some responsibility for childhood micro-traumas you contributed to, and attempt to see that there is a better way. Set the bar higher, please, boomers!

So, for a bit when you are postpartum, you may need to just embrace the chaos. Go into survival mode, never leave your pajamas, and know that things will get better. Hopefully if you are struggling with postpartum moods, you won't be so proud that you'll be unable to ask for help. Help is there via therapy, medication, or support if you are willing to take it.

When you bring a new baby home, it also changes your romantic partnership forever. Those first six months with a new baby were the most challenging in our relationship, for a variety of reasons. My tearful and disappointed postpartum state, feeling self-conscious about my postpartum body, and being consistently sleep deprived did not make me the most fun partner. I made assumptions that everything would be easier because I was a doctor with extensive experience around newborns. But the physical challenges with breast-feeding and my birth injury, combined with the mental challenges of sleep deprivation and postpartum hormones made everything feel incredibly difficult.

Now, we have systems to ensure we get one on one time to keep our union strong, but we hadn't figured that out yet. It seemed there was not much time for our partnership and, if there was extra time, I felt I should be sleeping. So, any time that I dedicated to your dad came with a small sense of resentment because I knew that I should have been prioritizing sleep for my own physical and mental health.

There are many new tasks to be done when the baby arrives; figuring out who will do what so that everyone feels balanced and satisfied, can be difficult. We actually did OK in that respect because I was exclusively breast-feeding and we knew your dad did not do well with sleep deprivation. Therefore, I took all the night shifts and he did all the cooking (we say I fed the baby and he fed me). I had three months of maternity leave and luckily medical residency had trained me to be sleep deprived while still functional, so I was able to wake up multiple times in the middle of the night and then fall back asleep quickly. If your dad had been woken up, he would not have been able to fall back to sleep and then his moods would have been impacted as well. We discussed it and made a conscious decision to have one person in a weakened state (lucky me!) and another person strong, to support the other. It was a bit unconventional, but worked for us. Every morning, my delirious and downtrodden self would be up at 4:30am with you and then your dad would wake up at 6:00 am to make me a big breakfast and provide some normal adult conversation before he went to work. The healthy food and positive attention are probably what kept me afloat. So figure out a system that works for you, even if the grandmas advise you to do things differently (ours thought we should BOTH stay up all night, but we didn't see any value in making your dad exhausted and cranky along with me; that type of solidarity did not seem useful).

The harsh reality is that you will have less time for your partnership after kids come into the picture. Your partner will have less of your undivided attention, which can be frustrating. I think men can feel a bit neglected by their wives after a baby is born. Women give so much of their mental energy and physical body to their children, and their partner will have less. A strong and confident man, such as your dad, will be able to adjust. They will understand that it is not personal, the baby is not competition, and that the full love is still there, even when the time and physical touch may be diminished.

As a mom, you want to feel competent and confident, so there is a tendency to do everything yourself. While you CAN do it all, protect yourself by allowing and asking for help. Maternal gatekeeping is a concept where moms feel that they do everything best, and therefore do everything themselves. At work, when you want something done right, do it yourself. However, in motherhood, you will be happier and maintain more sanity if you allow others to help and reach out for support. Let someone else change the diaper, even if it leaks later. Let someone else feed the baby, put the dishes away in the wrong spot, and trim the terrifying baby fingernails. The more you relinquish control over your mothering, the less alone and overwhelmed you will feel.

This especially applies to your partner: get them involved, let them do all the baby stuff (the fun/cute and the difficult/gross). If the mom makes all the snacks, gives all the baths, and does all the bedtimes then the partner won't know HOW to do those things. The mom will become the default for everything. Don't create or allow a situation where your partner is helpless and uninvolved. Let them know it's OK to make mistakes and that we all fumble a little bit in the beginning. Encourage them in their learning curve so that you have a true partner in parenting. When they put on the diaper that has a blowout, let them know you've been there and that they should keep trying until they feel more confident. Don't let them default to you when they make mistakes. Help them without enabling them. Oh, and make sure they clean up their blowouts, it helps them learn where the diaper failed so they know where to tighten it next time.

I share all these struggles to help with your expectation management. You may see postpartum pictures where I am smiling or joyful and assume that was all there was. But I did not allow pictures of the tears, of the bleeding and cracked nipples, of the oozing and raw perineum tissue, and there is no way to encapsulate the anxiety and uncertainty of newborn care. Were you getting enough milk? Was the noise you made while breathing normal? Was your belly button stump supposed to smell that bad? Was I losing my mind repeatedly standing over your crib to make sure you were still breathing? If I see postpartum moms in my medical practice, I always tell them that anxiously watching their sleeping newborn, to make sure they are still breathing, is completely normal because no one told me that. I didn't realize it was a universal new mom activity. If I had known, perhaps I would have felt in communion, being initiated to this amazing sisterhood. Perhaps I would have been less depressed, and not questioned my sanity, but rather embraced the new path that I was on.

52. Battling Birth Order Dynamics

I am the baby of the family and I can see how that has served me through my life. Your dad is the oldest and fits that mold. Despite my best efforts, you all display classic birth order dynamic tendencies. The oldest: you tend to want to be in control, to be a natural leader, and to have difficulty when you lack control. Your father is similar: happy making decisions and having people follow him willingly. The middle: you go with the flow and go along to get along. The baby: you try to keep up with the bigger kids, get a lot of attention for being the littlest and cutest, and are good at being a follower. Your dad and I are a great match because he is a natural leader and I am a natural follower.

As the oldest, you once had all of the love and attention, so it is natural to want that as your norm. You also are the leader of your siblings; you know the most and have come the farthest so far in personal growth and development. You can do things that others cannot do, such as fine motor tasks, which puts you in a place of elevated status and as a helper. We have tried so hard to never make you, our oldest, feel like you have caretaking responsibilities for your siblings, but you so love being in charge of them. This is a difficult area to navigate and I don't have an answer yet as you are only eight, six, and three years old while I am journaling this message.

My sweet middle girl, you are so loved and treasured. You have the benefit of being an older sister and a younger sister. You can choose if you want to lead your younger sibling or follow your older sibling. You also have a certain relaxed, go with the flow attitude that I envy. I do worry, though, about how that go-with-the-flow translates into people pleasing tendencies. I see you wanting to make others around you happy and at times compromising your own wants for others in order to keep the peace. I am trying very hard to force you to have a voice and not allow you to fade into the shadows in order to let others shine.

And then there is your baby brother. He is surrounded by women who worship him: his mother and his sisters. He is the classic baby of the family, with things being brought to him on a silver platter and expecting that everyone will think he is adorable. I was a baby of my family and somewhat the golden child. I felt growing up that there was very little that I could do wrong and knew I was adored. This was wonderful and I'm not sure how much of that is due to their parenting in general, or due to the fact that I was the baby. Your baby brother is going to have very high expectations as he ages. Currently, he is three years old and has people eating out of his hand. The baby is not only used to following the leader and having people plan things for them, but also having people help them with things. I definitely have suffered from that, hoping that someone will complete a task on my behalf that I find frustrating, or at least show me the way. I consider my expectation for help and guidance a weakness, perhaps due to being the youngest. You dad, the oldest, instead has an independent I-can-do-this attitude of figuring stuff out on his own. I hope all of you can adopt that attitude instead of my sometimes helpless one.

As I have mentioned with your dad and I, sibling dynamics come into play in romantic relationships. I don't know if another youngest child and myself would survive. I am a leader at work, but prefer not to be a leader in other settings. It is easier and more peaceful for me to follow. For your dad, it is easier and more peaceful for him to be in control and make the hard choices. I hope that birth order dynamics are something that we have not forced onto you and you will break the mold in order to be your most authentic self.

I have been reading about birth order dynamics and implementing ways to avoid them, but you all display the classic signs of your birth order. I wonder if it is worth fighting the birth order dynamics or if they are inevitable due to developmental age differences. As your dad always jokes, at least this will give you something to talk about with your future therapist. I want each of you to be a team player, to be confident enough to express your opinions, and flexible enough to go with the flow when it is best for everyone. You each deserve the adoration of the baby and expectation that those who love and support you will help you when needed. I want you to have the confidence of the oldest child, who is willing to approach tasks and figure them out, because there may not be someone around to help. And lastly, I hope that you each have the wisdom to know when to lead and when to follow, when to struggle on your own and when to ask for help, and when to assert your opinion and when to go with the group.

53. Kids As Catalyst To A Better Self

I can't help but reflect about the time and energy I have spent worrying about my parenting mistakes, despite my best efforts. I can't help but wonder, does everyone worry about this? For those who do not seem to worry about this, have they not started on their journey of self reflection, or are they past the point that I am currently at? Is there a pendulum that swings between total ignorance or irresponsibility for how our actions affect others, and feeling a pervasive responsibility for your children, their experiences, and their future neuroses? I hope a wiser person will one day be able to answer these for me. Perhaps I can graduate through the stage of maternal worrying into one of acceptance and ownership for my words and actions. Perhaps, in writing this all down, it will help to clarify my goals and focus, make me less neurotic, and give you the mom that I hope to be.

Tone and culture are two buzzwords currently associated with toxic workplaces, but the home environment's tone and culture are the most pervasive of all. As the mom, I set that tone and create the culture. It can be one of humor and fun, one of quiet contemplation, one of independence, or one of team effort.

Our home is loud. I wonder if there are actually people with three small children whose homes are not. Non-parents and grandparents feel that our home is excessively loud. Sometimes I hear it when they comment, and other times, I don't. I would like to think that our noise level is a reflection of your enthusiasm and sense of freedom.

I was always told that I was too loud as a child and that I talked too much. I remember having vocal nodules from yelling and screaming, and consistently being encouraged to lower my volume. While it was absolutely true that lowering my volume was needed, being constantly told to quiet down hurt my soul. Being shushed was akin to being told that people did not want to hear what I had to say. So it pains me to ask you to lower your volume; I would rather go deaf than have your words feel unheard or your soul feel shattered.

I recall from a young age feeling that I was 'too much' for people to handle or tolerate, that I was wearing on their nerves, and that I should be quiet, disappear, or make myself small. I never, ever, ever in one hundred million years want you to feel that way. It's hard, because of course you are loud. All three of you. Sometimes, I do have to ask for the noise to be reduced, but I try to do so in a loving way. Literally, sometimes the volume level hurts my ears and I worry about tympanic membrane damage, but I cannot always bring myself to say something because I know how it may be misconstrued and interpreted as a lack of appreciation for who you are and your enthusiasm for life. So, I embrace having a slightly loud and chaotic household. I want you to feel like children, feel accepted in your own home, and feel free to express yourself in a variety of ways. I want our home's tone to be one of acceptance, authenticity, fun, and laughter. Shushing you isn't consistent with that.

Hopefully, despite the chaos and noise, we are also honing in on a culture of gratitude, mutual respect, and kindness. We try to sit down for dinner together every night and share our 'peaks and valleys', the highs and lows of our day. Those shares are a valuable look into your school day, your struggles, your mindset, and your outlook. My generic "how was your day?' is pretty low yield for actual information. There are so many micro traumas that can happen during childhood: a sibling says that they wish you were never born, you have no one to play with at recess, a parent doesn't have time for you at an important moment, or two siblings pair off and reject the third. Trying to micromanage and minimize all of those seemingly small, but potentially devastating, interactions can be exhausting. And, I'm not certain that preventing them is the right course if we are trying to build resilience. Perhaps, rather, let you all figure it out as you go, encourage you not to take things personally, and comfort you when you do feel hurt.

The true gift and simultaneous curse of parenting is seeing yourself reflected back, via an adorable mirror. Somehow, all of my worst traits seem to be the ones most obvious, screaming out at me from your tiny bodies. Either you inherited (nature) or I imprinted on you (nurture) my loud volume, being sensitive to friend rejection, people-pleasing/perfectionism, and my awful sweet tooth. I see these traits and rather than wanting to fix them, I want to tell you that it is OK. Despite being undesirable habits, there is no ill intention behind them. I never want you to feel any part of yourself is bad or unlovable. You are perfectly imperfect, and I love and accept you as you are.

You also inherited some of my goodness: when you repeat loving little phrases to your brother, verbatim of what I say; when you go into fits of deep belly laughs; when you get super excited about nature, science, and animals. But, recognizing my own good is difficult. Seeing the ways in which I have inadvertently passed down my flaws and faults is much more obvious. Perhaps because I am still working to accept those parts of myself, and I am pretty certain you learned them through my modeling.

Regardless, having you as a reflection of things that I am still working through is the absolute best catalyst for change. If there is something I am saying or doing that I am not proud of, and then I see you do it, it motivates me to rapidly work on that behavior. I have always lacked a head-to-mouth filter, but now that my words are repeated back to me, I finally have the willpower to bite my tongue. So, thank you for shutting me up sometimes. Being a mom makes me hyper-aware of my words and actions, because they are emulated. It's a lot of pressure and I plan to rise to the occasion.

Being a mom genuinely helps me to be my best self, because I am determined to stay healthy, to be able to play with you, and be present for your future life events, if I am invited. Having children has brought out my inner child; the silly and playful parts that I don't get to express in everyday life were finally reborn and nurtured through parenting. I love pushing you on the swings at the park, playing soccer, baking cookies, gardening, and seeing the world through your eyes. You are so observant and I admire that. Your dad always notices every little thing, and you have thankfully taken after him in that regard. Sometimes on walks, I will walk right by an interesting animal or plant, but you will stop and pull me back to examine it closely and appreciate its beauty. Thank you for that. Thank you for bringing out my inner child and for emulating and reflecting back all of my good and bad parts, so that I can continue to become a better person day by day and a better mom hour by hour.

54. Where's The Line?!?

It's a legit question and here I am asking, not telling.

Sometimes, I think everything is going OK, you kids are playing and then an argument happens. Before I know it, one sister is telling the other that she wishes she were an only child and that her sister didn't exist. Do I intervene? Is this going to turn into a core childhood wound, to feel unwanted by a sibling? Is it harmless, and every sister says that at one point or another? I definitely know mine said it more than once. If our relationship had "turned out fine" I probably wouldn't overthink this, but we are NOT fine, not even a little bit. So, where's the line?

How much do I let you struggle with something before I help you? I know the value of struggle, but where does it cross the line into micro-trauma and lifelong damage? How long will your frustration and perseverance last before you give up and create an internal dialogue that you are a failure at that activity? I want you to figure things out on your own rather than build mental blocks that you are incapable of doing certain things. One of your friends has already decided that she's "not good at math" and I live in fear that if you struggle too much at a certain task, your confidence will erode away and that task will never be attempted again. But, how much help is too much help? If you want to try something that I don't think you are capable of doing yet, do I let you or encourage you to wait?

When does a sibling battle turn into a war? What sisterly scratches will scar you forever? Words can hurt, certainly, but when do they cross a line from hurt to irreparable verbal abuse? I am trying to let you siblings navigate your own relationships and I know kids can be brutal, but some of the things that you say to each other break my heart and I don't want them to break yours.

Where is the line between encouraging second chances for a friend who had a bad day and failing to recognize a bully? When does something that could be character-building cross a line into a deep emotional wound? Where do I cross the line from being encouraging to being pushy? How can I hold certain things in reverence without taking them "too seriously"? Do you know I'm overthinking things, or do you think I'm "smooth waters"?

How can I find the tipping point between you being a fun-loving rascal, and then being totally dis-regulated and out of control? When can I be confident that you're testing healthy boundaries, versus being utterly disrespectful and not listening? At what point, if any, do I rush in and rescue you while I am watching you flounder or struggle? When there's a slippery slope, where is the black ice and where is the solid footing? At what age, if any, do we switch from the blissfully easy independent Velcro shoes to the time-consuming and frustrating struggle of shoelace sneakers? How can I choose between being easy-going with skipped naps or homework and holding to a routine that encourages your success?

When should I stop chasing and trying, and instead move on or let go? When do I allow you to quarrel and when do I try to keep the peace? What is the difference between trying to meet all of your needs and enabling you? Can someone be spoiled with too much attention? What amount of competition is healthy? Is the competitive spirit you seem to have from nature or nurture?

Do I share that the real world can be a terrible place, or let you discover that yourself? If I share, how much detail should I go into? How do I warn you about bad people without destroying your wonderful child-like worldview? How can I teach you about stranger safety without scaring you? How can I prepare you for the active shooter drills at school?

I ask myself these questions all the time. I wish I had answers. I have a close friend who seems to have such clarity in these moments. When her children are swarming around her and their emotions run high, she seems cool as a cucumber. She says the exact perfect response, straight from the pages of the best parenting books. I've read the same books (she recommended them), but have zero recall when my head is spinning.

I admire that she can process what is happening, in the heat of the moment, and figure out what it all means in the bigger picture. I don't have that ability... yet? I have trouble seeing the forest through the trees and start to feel anxious when you kids inevitably spin out of control. I am never sure when to let you spin yourselves out, gently and calmly slow your velocity, or pull the plug to snap you out of it before you hurt yourself or someone else. I literally DO NOT KNOW. And it haunts me. It's probably the biggest downfall in my parenting. I despise being wishy-washy, but here I am uncertain what to say or do in the most stressful mom moments. I wish I knew exactly what the moment needed and then could execute that flawlessly, but alas I do not.

While I have learned a lot and made great strides, becoming a mother didn't magically turn me into a sage. I still get flustered and am uncertain what to say or do. Even when I have a clear thought in my head, I might stumble over my words and fumble the message. I hope I can eventually find the sweet spot to recognize the difference between lighthearted teasing and disrespectful insults; sibling wrestling and overt violence; tight-knit friend groups and exclusive cliques; healthy disappointment and lasting micro traumas; social struggles and borderline bullying; character building effort and relentless pursuit in vain; humble appreciation and rampant entitlement.

How can I guarantee you will be good people, who contribute to society and always do the right thing? Is that even possible? How can I get comfortable in letting go of those expectations? How can I stop letting my overwhelming love for you cloud my judgment, so that I can see more clearly and be more objective? Please, someone out there or the universe, give me some answers!

Is there a Bluey or Daniel Tiger episode that can teach me this? I don't want to be overbearing, micromanaging, or stifling. I will try to hold back those tendencies in favor of trusting that you are perfect little beings on the right path, which is peppered with learning opportunities unless I rob you of the chances for growth and enlightenment.

Get excited! I have another analogy for you! Swimming lessons! Yes, I said swimming lessons. Water safety is important, because I have heard too many cautionary drowning stories. Even from physicians, whose children died in the bathtub. So, obviously we enrolled you each in swim lessons.

There are different approaches: "survival swimming" or regular lessons. Survival swimming involves throwing a young child in the water every day for 10 minutes, and letting them figure it out with the help of an instructor. Talking with other moms who tried this, the kids were screaming and terrified initially but ended up confident after the crash course. It seemed extreme to me and, as a working mom, attending daily lessons during daylight hours was not feasible. So, we went the traditional route of weekly 30 minute lessons and started you young.

At 6 months, we embarked on our journey for water safety. Spoiler alert: I was teaching you too soon. After 2 years of lessons, you, my oldest angel, could back float but not much else. You were still two years old, after all. Then there was the year long pandemic-pause on all life outside the four walls of our home. When we restarted your swimming lessons at the ripe age of 5, we went to a new swim school and you picked it up quickly. You had the patience and mental capacity to listen, learn, and recall what you had done the week before. Furthermore, the more experienced teachers had a step-by-step approach to teach you. It all just clicked.

So, when are you ready to learn "swimming"? At what age is your brain developed enough to learn certain skills and concepts? Do we let you figure it out on your own, terrified "survival swimming" style, or do we enable learning by hiring the best teachers? How many of my parenting choices are intentional choices, and how many are haphazard results of being a busy working mom? At what point are you, truly, water safe?

We refuse to use arm floaties in pools, because the experts say it creates a false sense of confidence and increases drowning risk. However, when kayaking or swimming near an ocean, we use a life vest. We taught you to swim in warm, calm waters but want you to be able to survive in frigid waves. When do we start to decrease the temperature and increase the tide, to help prepare you for what's ahead? These are the questions I ask myself about most of my parenting choices. I am hoping you will have the skill, will, and endurance to keep swimming in all waters of life. And here's hoping that we gave you enough practice to prevent drowning.

Maybe there is no getting it exactly right. Maybe I will always be between not quite enough and too much; between lazy and trying too hard; between depriving you and spoiling you. Maybe I will just relish in the fact that I am parenting in an age when all of this self reflection is encouraged. That at least I am evolved enough to allow vulnerability and willingness to admit faults. So hooray for questioning, progress, mistakes, learning, and hopefully getting enough of it right that you aren't irrevocably damaged. Universe, if you've got answers to any of these questions, please help them to find me.

55. If You Choose Not To Have Kids

Not everyone desires or is destined for parenthood. It is a monumental undertaking that changes the very fiber of your being, on a cellular level. You will never be the same and some may choose not to make the leap. I fully respect that. Do what you feel in your deepest soul is meant for you and your life.

I was raised with the expectation that as a woman, if I were successful, I would be a mother. Part of that may have been in my head, but I do recall believing that my own mom was a great woman partly because she had propagated and created children. I'm not sure if that assumption was taught to me outright or generated by what I was seeing. Nevertheless, I never doubted my own desire for children. They were a given, something I knew that I wanted in my core from an early age. With that said, I do hope that it is a decision you consciously make and not a predetermined destiny by society or anyone but yourself.

I have spoken above about all of the struggles of parenthood, but also some of the benefits. Not having children will avoid the struggles, but please don't avoid the growth that comes from being a parent. I want you to question your upbringing, question me, and rage against the machine, so to speak. Re-parenting is a process that I believe is beneficial to everyone, even those who are not mothers. Hold a microscope up to your childhood: the language that we used, the tone and culture of our home, the activities that were praised or punished. To fully understand and know yourself is a beautiful thing and close introspection about how you came to be may lead to wonderful discoveries. Knock me off my presumed pedestal eventually, question how you were raised, and hopefully we will move on from our youthful parent-child dynamic into a new era.

Children also force us to be the best version of ourselves, because they are emulating our every move and learning from us as they grow. If left to your own devices, still hold yourself to high standards. There will be no Santa Claus nor elf on the shelf monitoring your behavior, but still do your best. If you don't have a mini me to demonstrate your faults, you have to go looking for them on your own or surround yourself with people who are honest with you. As I have said, holding up the mirror is a slippery slope for friends. It is more easily held up by partners, and effortlessly and mercilessly by your children. So, make sure to fill your life with people who will hold you accountable, help you to become the best version of yourself, and not be afraid to call you out on your bullsh$t.

Children give us a greater purpose by remembering us long after we are gone. They provide a posterity and sense that you have left your mark on the universe. Of course, marks can be left in many ways, so make sure to leave yours. You can leave that mark on other humans, on your community, on the environment, etc. Being a doctor, I hope to do this on a daily basis through interacting with my patients. It can also be done by volunteering with children, for the elderly, with the homeless, with animals, or to save mother earth. Whatever you choose to do, and however you decide to make your mark, do so joyfully and knowing that you will not be forgotten.

I want you to know profound love, full of sacrifice while expecting nothing in return. This could come from children, pets, volunteer work, or mentoring. To experience selfless giving without any intention of receiving gives you a sense of agency. It shows you how you are a cog in the wheel of the universe and lets you see that your spirit can live on, even after your body is gone.

Wellbeing: Health and Respect

56. Age Gracefully

I'm barely forty, but I can already tell that getting old is going to be rough. I remember when my mom turned forty and had to start doing daily piriformis stretches; I thought it was so lame and now I have the exact same problem. When we bought our house with the tile floors, she said it was too hard on her knees and had to wear house shoes to cushion her feet; I rolled my eyes thinking she was being dramatic. Now both your dad and I wear house shoes, too. Karma is truly a b$tch.

Aging is something that should not be feared, but should be planned for. When I run I can feel little twinges in my knees and when I reach back just a little too far I feel a tweak in my shoulder. I know these little hiccups will get more pronounced as I age, if I am lucky. My work reminds me that to age is a privilege since no one is guaranteed another day; everyday I get to spend with you is a gift to me.

Part of aging gracefully is accepting your changing body. I like to think of it as exchanging immense emotional and spiritual growth for physically withering away into a raisin. My patients have taught me not to wait to live my life. I have had more than one patient be diagnosed with cancer the year that they retire. I have had others start travel adventures upon retiring, only to realize that their knees cannot handle walking on cobblestone in the small towns of Europe that they dreamt of exploring. Or worse yet, someone who dies before they ever get to retire and leaves all their plans and dreams on the table. So, I am trying not to wait too long to do the things that I dream of doing outside of mothering and my career. Right now is not the season in my life for big trips or adventures, but I plan to knock some stuff off my bucket list with you three children in tow, eventually.

I am also lucky to be inspired by some truly bada$$ older female patients. I always ask for their secrets. Typically, they eat a lot of fruits and vegetables and have stayed very physically active since their middle age. They speak of yoga and pilates, walking and hiking, and helping care for their grandchildren. The beauty of multi generational families is that it provides mutual benefit for the kids and the older adults. The kids have an additional network of support and the grandparents stay active, both physically and mentally when they are caring for others. Part of me wishes we lived closer to our parents so that we could see them more often. But your dad and I both like to have our own space, so cohabitation with our moms has never been on the table.

I want to stay mentally sharp and I believe the key to that is always learning and growing. Learning new things and maintaining social relationships are important as we age. I have always dreamt of learning to play an instrument or work with wood. Creating something with my hands from scratch seems elusive but appealing. I'm hoping to learn those things after I retire. I'm also hoping to travel and explore little corners of the world to experience the people, music, art, and food. Lastly, I dream of returning to my roots in underserved medicine, hopefully volunteering with the homeless.

With age comes wisdom, they say. I don't want to harp on the drawbacks of growing older, because there is beauty in aging, as well. We get more time to learn from our mistakes, to zoom out and gain perspective on our lives, and to deepen our connections with others and our planet. Seeing how the world is changing, even since I was a kid, is astounding. In my lifetime, we have started to use computers, cell phones were invented, the 'me too' movement happened, we had the first black president, and the concepts of gentle parenting and healing from generational trauma have been given rightful attention. I am eager to see how the world continues to evolve and hopefully become a better place for our children.

REPARENTING MYSELF

With age will come heartache, loss and grief. We will lose those who are close to us, inevitably. The only guarantee in life is death. While that is a somber fact, it is one that I witness firsthand at work and makes me more grateful for each day remaining. I express my gratitude to the universe by attempting to be present, live fully, and prioritize how I spend my time. Time is the most precious commodity in life so spend it wisely by surrounding yourself with people you love, doing work that makes the world a better place, and choosing actions that bring yourself and others joy.

57. People Pleasing And Patriarchy

I've talked quite a bit about my people pleasing, but I already see some of those tendencies in you girls and I am hoping to stamp them out, STAT! This is easier said than done, because sometimes the person you are trying to please is me.

Sometimes you are cleaning up your mess, because you know that I like a tidy house. So far I am failing to have clean ups be internally motivated, but I continue my attempts at convincing you that you like it tidy, you feel good about your ability to tidy, and our minds are more at peace when we can all see the floor. Sometimes you are doing what I ask, even when it is not what you want to do, like putting your shoes on for school. So, it's tricky. I want to encourage you to be your own person, have strong opinions, and state your needs, but also be able to work as a team and go with the flow. Hopefully you will know that your needs are important and valid so that you find a balance between pleasing others and pleasing yourself.

The fact that people pleasing is more common in women is very frustrating. When my mom was growing up, the message to young women was to be a 'nice girl', to be seen not heard, to take a backseat to men, and to make everything pretty and easy for others. That time is coming to an end thankfully. I was raised during the in between.

When you assert your needs or choose yourself, the patriarchy will have you believing that you're the bad guy. Women are finally claiming what has always been theirs: education, power, jobs, credit, money. There's currently a lot of discussion about the mental load in motherhood, which is completely valid and simultaneously intimidating for me. Sometimes, everything feels unfair. Other times, I realize that we have a lovely and sustainable balance within our family.

When I find myself regressing back to a people-pleaser state, I remind myself that the origin of people pleasing is manipulating others into liking you. It's about controlling others perception and being unable to deal internally with hard feelings, such as being unliked. When I consider this view, it helps convince me not to people please and to look within for approval rather than to others. When you adjust yourself in order to be liked, people don't like the real you; instead they like the version that you are pretending to be. It's like Julia Roberts' character in "The Runaway Bride", who bends and twists who she is for each fiance, until she finally figures out who she is. Once she knows herself better and stops contorting herself for others, her life finally takes flight.

I would be remiss in discussing "good girl" conditioning without addressing the Patriarchy. Ah, the patriarchy. What to say that isn't all curse words? Women are still paid less than men. Let's take my career in medicine as an example: women are paid $0.80 to the dollar for their male colleagues. Women in medicine have better outcomes, spend more time with their patients, and get higher visit satisfaction scores. Women in primary care have lower MORTALITY RATES than male doctors. That means less of my patients die compared to male colleagues and is pretty much the best possible outcome a doctor can have. Lady doctors are published and promoted less than male counterparts. Women surgeons have lower post-op complications. Finally, and not so funny if you're me, women in primary care get consistently more inbox messages from their patients. They receive longer messages asking for more things to be done outside of a formal office visit, for free. Their time is not valued.

We do more and do better but get paid less. It is frustrating, but as a woman, I catch myself bending over backwards to please my patients and it's a tough cycle to break. The list goes on. I believe we HAVE to be better than our male colleagues in order to get an ounce of respect. I can't count the times I have been called nurse, while wearing my white coat with large, clear MD initials. Fun totally related side note, women in medicine suffer exponentially more from burnout than male counterparts. Go figure. Despite being years after feminism, we are still working overtime to prove our worth. When will it stop?!

My career is just one example of patriarchal culture and how it affects women. I hope your experience will be different. To start, everyone needs to acknowledge that the system is broken and was created by white men to be unequal for women and persons of color. If we deny that, there is no moving forward for progress. So, I hope that the world you inherit has come a long way from the world that I grew up in. Take your seat at the table, make no apologies, and know that you are worthy. Your wants and needs are valid. You deserve the best and you have a right to speak up to get it. The patriarchy needs to be dismantled, and unfortunately there are large, powerful forces working to prevent that. Unite with other women, use your power for good, and notice the pendulum slowly swinging toward justice.

58. Respect Nouns!

RESPECT, a good song and an important concept. Somehow, I have failed to talk enough about respect so far. I have emphasized authenticity, kindness, friendship, self improvement, and work ethic. How the heck did I miss respect? Respect is the core of kindness, in my opinion. Respect is what makes friendship and marriages work, and I hope that I am demonstrating respect towards you as children and reinforcing respect toward others.

It may seem like a paradox to love yourself while respecting others, but the two are not mutually exclusive. Sometimes I meet someone who is striving so hard to meet their own needs that they become blind to the needs of others. And while this is easy to do, I urge you to be conscientious of what is going on around you, without getting too in your head about it. Again, easier said than done. The sweet spot is honoring your needs while seeing how you are an integral piece in the jigsaw puzzle of the world. Strike a balance between boundaries in the name of self-love, and reaching beyond yourself to help others. By respecting people outside yourself, you begin to see the interconnectedness of humanity.

Don't let respect stop at humanity, extend it to animals, the planet, and the universe. Respect for the earth is at the center of environmentalism and a tenant that can be learned from native populations. If you eat meat, try not to take too much. If you are contributing to processes that take water from land, suck oil from the earth, and kill plants or animals, please do so with hesitance and reverence for the things that you destroy. As humans, we are typically not productive members of our ecosystem. We take more than we give, but I am trying to be better about that. After paused my environmentalist efforts for motherhood, I desperately yearn to return to being a better human.

I try to demonstrate things like minimalism, recycling, avoiding fast fashion, and decreasing single use plastics, but I am not perfect. I do not expect perfection from you, but being aware of our surroundings and appreciative of them goes a long way to decreasing our carbon footprint and environmental impact. If we respect mother earth, we are less likely to burn her to the ground. Hopefully, we can contribute a little to putting out the fire and tilling the soil for the next generation.

Having respect for other cultures also makes us better humans. There is currently a lot of hatred and racism in the world. I don't think any human is born with hatred in their heart, but it can be planted there by their family or culture. If we seek to understand other cultures without judgment and get curious about their traditions and beliefs, perhaps we can appreciate them and approach differences from a loving place. It all begins with respect.

With respect, we are more likely to gain knowledge and understanding, and less likely to develop resentment or bitterness. Just because we don't understand or agree with something does not make that thing wrong or bad. Many "American" habits are viewed as wrong in other cultures: our consumerism, our separatist nature, our nuclear families (rather than multigenerational households), our processed carcinogenic foods, our lack of rest/siesta time, our excessive work hours, our dismal maternity leave, and our lack of early childcare support. All of these are absolutely bonkers to other cultures, but accepted by us as the norm. Perhaps we should begin to question our own habits and look to other cultures for better ways of living, while keeping some of the good concepts that America has adopted (freedom, democracy, welcoming immigrants, opportunity, etc).

Recognizing that everyone has their own sh$t they are dealing with can help cultivate compassion and maybe help you cut them some slack. We never know what is going on inside of someone else, even if they are close with us. We can't possibly increase our understanding through judgment. We can only do so through putting our love and acceptance out into the universe and hope it comes back through karma. All good things will come from a baseline level of respect towards everyone and everything, including yourself. Treat your body as a temple, speak to yourself lovingly, and choose your company wisely. Let respect guide your choices and thoughts. Lead with respect when you embark into the world and it will steer you in the direction of righteousness.

59. Know Your Addictions

Everyone's got something, right? There are obvious addictions that have rehab available and less obvious ones that may be more difficult to recognize. Lots of things could be a "drug of choice": love, sugar, food, actual drugs, alcohol, adrenaline, social media, video games, shopping, gambling, drama, approval from parents or the opposite sex, etc. Be wary of what you are drawn to do when times are tough, stay vigilant as to how that temptation may negatively affect you, and ask for help if you need it.

My addiction is sugar, absolutely. I have a sweet tooth and when I am stressed I will buy myself a treat, sneak a candy, or somehow binge. I was raised with food as a form of therapy and an emotional band aid. When someone was sad, we would eat ice cream; when we wanted to celebrate, we would eat ice cream; when it was hot or we were bored or groups would gather, we would eat ice cream. See the trend? And ice cream could be other forms of sugar ingestion: cookies, candies, baked goods. It didn't matter as long as it spiked my insulin, which developed a direct gut to brain feedback loop that haunts me to this day.

Despite my best efforts, I have made many of the same mistakes with you: using treats to make you happy or augment your feelings. I have used food as a reward and I am not proud of that. When you scored your first goal in soccer, we went out for ice cream to celebrate. When you have not eaten your dinner, we say that you cannot have dessert. When it is a holiday or grandma is visiting, we punctuate the event with a sugar rush. I know how messed up this is, and I am trying so hard to reverse it. Food is a big motivator and a seemingly convenient bribe. I wish that I were above bribing you at all in my parenting, but so far, I have not succeeded in that. I continue trying to phase out sweets and reward-systems in general, in favor of words of affirmation, but then I neurotically worry about people-pleasing so the cycle continues.

Where's the parenting book that will help me get you to do your homework, eat your dinner, and hustle to be on time for school, but does not involve bribes, people-pleasing, or disrespecting your autonomy and strong will? I've looked for it but can't find one yet. Gentle parenting is great, but sometimes life has to go on and endless patience is not possible. I can only be late for work so many times, eventually you just NEED to put your shoes on. So, I apologize if I pass down my sugar addiction to you and I vow to do better as you age without giving you any diet culture messages or body image issues in the process. Lord help me!

The obvious addictions of alcohol, drugs, gambling, or sex are easy to recognize. Consider what you are drawn to when you are in despair and what you feel you have earned or deserve when you are seeking a reward. That's your Achilles' heel. For drugs and alcohol, there are support groups or rehabs, but for other addictions there is often not much recognition and not much help.

My mom likely has a shopping addiction. Even when she is short on money, she will buy things on layaway programs. Even when she does not need something, she will buy it. Even when I have told her I do not want something or explicitly say "don't buy that", she does anyway. I like to dig deeper into the why behind things, and I can't quite figure hers out. She grew up in a middle class family, but I assume must not have felt she had the things she wanted, because as soon as she was making her own money, she was buying them come hell or highwater. I imagine that buying what she desires makes her feel accomplished or powerful or fulfilled. Sometimes, she is chasing a fantasy, such as "I will cook more if I have XYZ kitchen gadget", but then it doesn't pan out. Is she trying to improve herself through shopping? What emotional void does it fill? I may never understand it and it's not something we can discuss openly, as she becomes defensive. The result of her consumerism has led to my minimalism goals, so I suppose I turned her negative into my positive and learned from her mistakes, which I sincerely hope you will do from me. So, fingers crossed my sugar habits will lead you to clean eating?

My dad's addiction is approval. It has led him to be a people pleaser and seek validation from external sources. He needs to be liked and to hear that you think he is doing the right thing. I guess when it comes to addictions, this may be of the lesser variety, but it has the ability to make someone absolutely miserable. My deepest wish for my dad is that he could feel good enough on his own, because he is pretty great. I wish he had more self-love and more confidence in his niceness and achievements. Sometimes people take advantage of him because they know him well. He grew up in the Midwest, where I am told the words of affirmation were few and far between. His whole life, he has offered constant loving words and enthusiastic approval to me. I believe that's what his inner child is still screaming out to receive. In his 7th decade, he is finally starting to see that people pleasing is harmful to him and gently putting his foot down once in a while. Even the lesser addictions, such as his, will cause suffering and taking power over them will enrich your life.

If one day I get diabetes or am unhealthy because of my sugar intake, I know that I will need to stop. I have tried cutting back here and there, which seems to work for a minute and then regress. For even stronger addictions like drugs or alcohol, I can only imagine how difficult moderating or quitting those would be. I don't have answers, but I do have endless support. If ever you're in a situation where my support is required in that way, I hope that I can enable you to get help without enabling you to continue toward rock bottom. Above all, know that I love you no matter what. We are all flawed humans and addictions afflict every single one of us, whether it is recognized or not. You will be stronger if you come to know your addictions and muster the courage to manage them. I will be cheering you on every step of the way and be there to celebrate your baby steps and big triumphs, with ice cream.

60. Find Your Purpose

As you grow and learn who you are, hopefully you will increasingly know and honor your priorities. If you are married, you prioritize that relationship over others. If you have children, you prioritize family over friends and work. Often before you meet your spouse or have your children, you might focus on your career.

Your dad and I both chose our careers and interests while we were in college. That was the pressure placed on our generation: to figure it all out when we were not fully cognitively developed. I definitely didn't know exactly who I was yet, but "higher education" forced me to pick a major and then expected to spit me out of the college machine with a solid career plan. I'm not sure that that is the way the world was meant to work. In medical school, there were some nontraditional students who had one or even two careers before deciding on medicine. They tended to be the most motivated, the most organized, and the most passionate for what they were doing. I think having more deeply considered their career path and lived in the 'real world' for a minute before dedicating their life to a specific field emboldened their choice. They had a calm confidence about them and hopefully are still happy and thriving in their medical practices.

As you age and life brings more responsibilities, you will realize how valuable time is. There are twenty-four hours in a day; hopefully you will sleep for eight of those, more or less. That leaves 16 hours to squeeze in all of the things that are necessary to survive and thrive: cooking, exercise, hygiene, parenting, flossing your teeth, maintaining friendships and partnerships, and parenting.

The largest taker of your time will likely be your job; perhaps of the sixteen hours, eight hours might be spent at your workplace and some additional time for the commute. That's half of your waking weekday life, if you work a traditional 9-to-5. I personally couldn't do it and had to cut back to part time, but for many careers that might not be an option or the hours are more sporadic. I tried working four longer days per week, five days per week from 8-to-3, and hybrid office and work-from-home models. I couldn't sustain the full time hours. But I love my job and luckily the universe lined me up with the part-time schedule of my dreams.

Because we spend such a large portion of our waking hours working, it would be lovely and convenient if your job is something that fills your proverbial cup. Your dad and I are both lucky enough to have careers that we enjoy, that pay well, and that speak to our calling. And while I hope that you will find a career that pays well and fulfills your passions, I also live in reality.

You might have a passion that does not pay the rent, such as art or music or something else. Hopefully, you can parlay your passions into a related career. If you love children, perhaps become a teacher. If you love art, perhaps work in a museum or as an art teacher. You, my oldest girl, currently love party planning, perhaps you can be an event planner or wedding consultant.

It is also worth considering that doing what you love every day, but with added pressures and deadlines, might suck the joy out of it. I never want your dreams to be crushed by the realities of work, so carefully consider if your enthusiasm would be at risk by turning a hobby into a career. Even if it's your dream job, it's still a job. The job you love will sometimes be the job you can't wait to clock out from, the job you complain about to your partner, and the job that feels laborious, even when you enjoy the work.

In medicine, this is often true. I went into it wanting to hear people's stories, help them, and use science as a tool to better their lives. I am fortunate that I am able to do those things, but it involves so much giving that I see burnout in colleagues all around me. The medical visits are too short, the paperwork sucks, and the back-and-forth with pharmacies and insurance companies is soul-sucking, at best, and deadly, at worst. I feel surrounded by threats to suck the joy out of my patient interactions. This was one of many reasons I decided to cut back my hours.

I didn't want to suffer compassion fatigue, as I saw happening in colleagues around me. I didn't want to miss the moments of awe in medicine because I was rushed or burned out. And I didn't want to miss the school plays, sick days, field trips, and summer fun because I was always at work. I didn't want to look back in fifteen years and see that I was toiling away at work and missing your childhood. Now that I cut back my hours, I can see the forest through the trees again. I have more to give both to you kids and my patients, which both finally feel sustainable, plus a bit left in the tank for myself. I was either drowning or treading water when working full time with three little kids, but going part time has allowed me to swim confidently and even float once in a while.

So carefully consider how you want to spend your work life. If you work forty hours per week, you may spend more time with your coworkers than you do with some of your family members. You will certainly spend more time at work than you do with your friends, so hopefully your colleagues are people that you enjoy. If you are working for a nonprofit in a subject that you are passionate about, you might actually find your tribe at work. How cool would that be?

Let me set aside my immense privilege for a minute to recognize the sole purpose of a "job": to fund your life. Work is work and having a job with a greater sense of purpose or with your tribe is a privilege. You might be better off to protect your passion projects and find reasonable work that pays the bills. Hopefully it is not something that you despise, but if you are able to get a union job as a janitor for a university, and it allows you to pay the rent and the freedom to pursue your passions outside of work, that might be a good call. There are so many jobs that I never considered that have awesome benefits or pensions: mail carrier, trash collector for the city, other city or university employees, teachers, nurses, really any union job. I hope that in choosing your career you can think outside the box, and if it is not working out, be brave enough to change course and try something else. And pay attention to the benefits: 401k matching, vacation days, and maternity leave policies all speak to the general attitude toward employees; listen closely to those messages, as they can make or break a job.

The culture of a workplace will influence your day-to-day life. Even if it is a wonderful organization, doing amazing work, and you love your colleagues, as I did at my last job, an off workplace culture can ruin all of that. I still believe strongly in the work that my former employer is doing, but because they are trying to save the world and fix all of the problems in healthcare, employee satisfaction is not on their radar. I felt unappreciated and at times disrespected when working for that organization. As those feelings grew, I could not continue to work for them and it was part of what led me to seek out my part-time work. I couldn't reconcile giving my time to a place that didn't appreciate me, when I knew I was needed and wanted at home by you kids.

At that job, I felt my hard work went unnoticed. Striving to do the right thing was overlooked and working overtime was paid the same as those who left early. Handing in my resignation felt like standing up for myself. I felt proud and hopeful for my future and I genuinely believe the universe charted me on that course to get me where I am today. So, if workplace politics or organizational shenanigans are making you cringe, listen to that inner voice saying maybe it's not the right place for you. Aim for job security, but don't be afraid to cut your losses if things are not working out. Have faith in yourself and your ability to bounce back; know your worth and that you deserve to be treated with respect.

Picking and choosing your career and how to support yourself and your family is an extreme privilege. Not everyone is so lucky to be able to change careers, go to college, and pursue their passions. Sometimes, people struggle to get by and put food on the table. There is no room for organizational ethics, giving the finger to a toxic workplace, or speaking up when people are being taken advantage of. Those are all privileges, and if you are ever in any place of power (either the power to leave or the power to speak up), please do so knowing that others may not have that luxury.

I hope you find your own unique way to make the world a better place, whether that be: more joyful, more beautiful, more organized, advancing science, teaching kids, aiding animals, helping humans, or something else. I hope you can maintain your passions, whether inside or outside of work. I hope you don't take sh$t from anyone, at least not for too long, and not without standing up for yourself or others. I hope you explore your gifts and use them as a force for good. I hope your job provides stability, a reasonable income, and good benefits. I hope you look forward to going to work some days and other days you can't wait to get home to whatever life you have built there. Each of us have unique gifts and sharing those with humanity is our greater calling. If done right, it will put you in communion with the universe and help you feel connected to others in the best ways possible. I can't wait to see the awesome ways that you will make your mark on this world.

61. Recognize Your Privilege

Let's take a minute to formally acknowledge privilege. I hope it is a continuous source of reflection for you; it is a current source of guilt for me. Growing up, my mom instilled a passion to help others, specifically those who needed help most. She was not just a teacher, but a special education teacher for children with "severe disabilities" (that's what it was called then, but I realize the terminology is likely out of date and no longer inclusive).

So, when I decided to become a doctor, I didn't want to be just any doctor, I wanted to serve the poor. When I switched jobs from full-time underserved medicine to part-time for-profit medicine, I lost a small part of myself. As a working mom, I don't spend as much time toward social justice efforts as I would like. Previously, my work was my greater contribution to the world. Now, while I am helping individuals on a daily basis and take pride in that, I don't feel that I am using my privilege to help those less fortunate. I feel a growing need to focus additional efforts to help those without privilege, to satisfy my soul. I am still figuring out how to reconcile this. I try to put my money where my mouth is by donating to organizations that are doing good work. Furthermore, you girls need to see social justice passion in action, in order to spark your own flame.

So, the first step is to recognize your privilege and how it works in your life and the greater world in general. Your socioeconomic privilege is obvious. You have a house, food, clothing, and access to all the things a child could need and want. You also have advantages when it comes to education. We bought a house in an amazing school district and you will receive a wonderful education. It is unlikely that you will slip through school not knowing how to read, not having preparation for college entrance exams, or not being able to write a grammatically correct and coherent job application. These are all benefits that you have, that others do not.

You are American citizens and with that comes many benefits. You were privileged both by the family that you were born into and the country. Family wise, I won't say you were privileged by a lack of generational trauma, because you are still so young, but genetically there are no big red flags. Some people are born with a strong predisposition to cardiovascular disease, cancer, or addiction. These are beyond their control but can alter the course of their life.

Of course, we cannot discuss privilege without discussing race. I hope that you will understand systemic racism and injustice. Slavery ended, then segregation purportedly ended, but there are still many laws that disadvantage people of color. Furthermore, there are loud and large groups in America right now who are outright racist. In order to be anti-racist, we have to deeply examine our own assumptions and thoughts, to recognize where there may be unconscious biases. I'm not an expert on this topic, but I am trying to learn more. I am trying to educate you. We should all, at all times, aim to do our best. We have chosen to raise you in a diverse and multicultural community and school, and hopefully that will help. Having friends and neighbors of different racial and ethnic backgrounds, who speak different languages at home, bring different foods for school lunch, and celebrate different holidays, hopefully will help you to see a broader picture of the world and appreciate other cultures.

If you need proof as to how privilege impacts you and benefits you, here are a few examples: living in a neighborhood where you can safely walk at night for exercise; living where there are trees to clean our air; not living directly near powerlines or polluted water; having the means to buy organic food, which may have health benefits; having parents whose work schedule accommodates an appropriate bedtime for children; feeling secure, which allows for a lower lifetime cortisol level; having safe play spaces readily available outdoors; having space at home to run and play; having a car to transport to activities, visit relatives, and attend birthday parties; getting good rest (which increases academic performance) because you have a bed to sleep on, rather than a floor; not suffering from a food scarcity mindset, which is known to contribute to obesity; growing up with two loving parents and nearby extended family; taking vacations and seeing the ocean, which some will never do; having the means to join a soccer team, where you can learn about sportsmanship and teamwork; the list goes on and on.

I do not share this list with you to make you feel guilty, but rather to help you to see how others are not so lucky. When I hear someone deny that systemic injustice exists or that those in lower socioeconomic brackets should just "work harder to pull themselves up", I think they are missing many points. The inequality in our capitalistic society is widening and it permeates every aspect of life: healthcare, food, education, and the possibilities for the future.

So, recognize where injustice exists and do everything in your means to help remedy that. Small things like tipping well, giving land acknowledgments, or giving a wave and smile to someone who may not feel safe walking down your street, can all go a long way. Because of your privilege, you should be the one extending an olive branch, always being a loud and outspoken ally while never talking over those who are oppressed.

My love for you is endless, so please hear these next words with a loving intention: you are not more deserving of the benefits that you have received from conscious and unconscious biases than others. The odds are ever in your favor, due strictly to luck. My hope is that you use that luck to lift others up and champion their causes. I have a degree of guilt about my own privilege, but if you can use it as a force for good, then you are doing right by the universe.

62. Spirit, Worship, And Communion

I used to go to church twice a week. You wouldn't know it now, though. As a child, I was taken to church on Sundays but did not experience much community there. I did enjoy the music and the after church donuts, if I'm being honest. In college, I found the most amazing church. There, I found spirit, worship, and communion all rolled into one. I've never been able to find one like it since. You can find these three separately, but it is a rare and wonderful gift to find them all together.

I'm not sure what to tell you about believing in God. I do believe in a higher power. Sometimes I call it the universe, sometimes I call it God, and sometimes I attribute it to mother nature. I have always had a deep interest in religion and spirituality, because I believe they can hold great value in times of need. I've known people who were deeply religious and seem to derive a great sense of self-worth and honor from that. I am not inclined to believe that the name one gives their God is important. Rather, I believe that having a relationship with something bigger and something outside yourself is an important construct.

There are many types of communities, such as teams, schools, and neighborhoods, but a spiritual community feels different to me. Everyone is united in hope and positivity; there is an ingrained expectation of support and understanding. In society, people can be frankly rude. In church or other spiritual gatherings, kindness prevails.

Awe is an experience that I hope you have on a consistent basis. It's hard to describe, but I will try. Awe is being overcome with emotion, reverence, and wonder. I have experienced awe at the sight of beauty in nature, in hearing elders share their stories, while listening to live music, and from a church pew. Wherever you can find it, hold onto those moments of awe, savor them, seek them out, and be present enough to fully immerse yourself in the moment. They are rare, but I believe them to be a moment of vibrating at the same frequency as those around you. They are a fleeting moment where you feel connected to humanity as a whole and can sense that the separateness we discern is a mirage or optical illusion.

I like the ideas of Zen Buddhism, though I have not studied them enough to practice. I like the Lutheran Church, its beautiful songs and rebellious history. I also appreciate various religious texts (the Bhagavad Gita, Tibetan Book of the Dead, Gnostic Gospels, Tao Te Ching, and stories from the Bible). I would like to read all of those texts in full, and more, as time permits. I started reading many in college, all for different classes in nonviolence and religious studies. Reading those texts as fictional stories with moral values can be helpful. Seek out the poetry and useful lessons, and feel free to leave the parts that don't vibe with you.

Belief is a choice. One chooses to believe in their religion. Those who try to scientifically prove their theology are missing the point. The choice that you make to answer to a higher power or believe in its existence is an act of faith. There are few things more beautiful than an act of faith. Marriage is an act of faith. Moving away from home is an act of faith. Becoming a parent and being responsible for another life is an act of faith. They are all small miracles in everyday life that should not be taken for granted.

So, believing in a God is an act of faith. Acceptance occurs when something is proven by science: it is black and white, there is a singular correct answer, and it is indisputable. Acceptance of religion is something that children have, when it is forced upon them by their parents: children accept what they are told by the people that they trust. For this reason, I have not been taking you to church regularly. I want religion and spirituality to be something that you discover and foster on your own. I never want to tell you what you should believe. I hope that you'll be interested in these subjects, because they are something that I am interested in and would love to discuss with you when you are older. If you request to go to church, surely I will take you. If you would like to visit a Buddhist temple, surely I will accompany you. If you would like to passionately discuss the premises of atheism, surely I will discuss with you. Belief is a choice you make when there is no proof.

Explore your spiritual side to your heart's desire. You get to pick and choose what has deeper meaning for you. In my own religious upbringing, the things that resonated with me and increased my vibrational frequency were the following:

1. Singing Holden Village Evening Prayer with my college church group, by candlelight during lent. We sang "Let My Prayers Rise Up Like Incense" in a round and I highly recommend it, both for its beauty and the message that the song presents.

2. Also during lent, there was congregational Taizé chanting, also sung in a round by candlelight. I remember many of the songs, but the one that has always stuck out is called "Da Pacem Domine". It is the most beautiful song I have ever heard and brings me to tears when I sing it. I have shared it with friends, sometimes awkwardly, but in the right group it can be magical.

3. Walking a labyrinth. Labyrinths seem to find me, or the universe puts them in my path. Does everyone come across labyrinth walks on a regular basis, or is it the crowd I hang with? I have stumbled upon labyrinths since my teens: visiting a cathedral in college, at an interfaith retreat, on a hospice elective, at a conference, in a hotel courtyard, and of course there was one at my redwoods retreat. The most amazing labyrinth walk occurred when I was revisiting the redwoods, years after my month-long retreat. I was walking the labyrinth with two close friends and a third woman with fantastic energy that we had all just met. When we reached the middle of the labyrinth, without speaking, my two friends and I sat down and began crying our eyes out. The three of us held hands, but there was an open space. The fourth woman had already departed the center and was walking outward, but when she saw us she turned to head inward again. She sat down and completed the circle, all four of us linking hands and crying together. We did not speak. We must've cried for about ten minutes before we were ready to walk out, cleansed of the burdens that we had carried in. It's hard to describe those silent moments that scream so loudly. I felt both homecoming and longing, vulnerability and safety, and grief and joy all at the same time. It was a beautiful moment and I hope you have similar spiritually enlightening experiences in your lifetime.

My wish for you is that you appreciate a deeper connection to the universe and others, that you are unafraid to go deep, that you have a healthy amount of reverence, and obviously that you avoid cults. There can be power in having a 'higher power'. Some people need an elf-on-the-shelf/big-brother-is-watching mentality in order to make good choices. I believe that may be because they were raised believing that external validation was important. However, there are many other benefits to believing in a higher power: moments of awe and connection during worship, a sense of support and community, and feeling an unconditional love that one otherwise may not experience.

I applaud the version of God that is accepting, compassionate, and merciful, but I do not vibe with a vindictive or vengeful God. I think the concept of forgiveness is a beautiful one, but the concept of a final judgment is flawed. The takeaways from my time in church that I try to hold dear are: forgiveness is for you and not them, judgment is not your place, love is unconditional, do the right thing even when noone is watching, and at times it can be valuable to relinquish control to a higher power. Maybe you will find some peace in church, maybe in the mountains, maybe in music, or elsewhere but I hope that you continually seek it out and explore the complex and beautiful spiritual parts of yourself.

63. Role Models And Mentors

There are so many awesome women in this world, yourselves included, and some appear as shining lights guiding you like a beacon. When you encounter them, don't be blinded by the light but rather follow it and let it illuminate your world.

Drew Barrymore is the poster child for resilience. I'm so glad that she has her own TV show right now, because I didn't know how ridiculously awesome she was until I watched her be so unapologetically herself. Her openness and vulnerability are inspiring. Hopefully her story is well known to you, but she was a childhood actor, was drinking and taking drugs at a very young age, and went to rehab. Her mother was more of a friend than a parent/protector. She now has two little girls, is divorced and sober. She does not see her past in a negative light at all; in fact, she sees it as a road that got her to the person she is today. She can laugh at her wild times, like when she flashed David Letterman on television. I think there is a particular beauty in being able to reminisce fondly about our former selves, even if we have grown immensely from that person. She is a living example of the beauty of being authentic.

Drew also brings a magnificent energy to her discussions of childhood, growth and mistakes. She seems to be perpetually in a state of awe and exuberance. I just love her vibe so much. She has been open about her struggles during motherhood, her struggles with alcohol, and the importance of finding oneself. If you don't feel like reading this book, watch some of her segments on YouTube, if that still exists. Notice how she admits mistakes without being mad at herself, embraces former parts of herself that she has outgrown, and remains open minded about the future. She is a wonderful active listener to her guests, displays consistent compassion and thoughtfulness, and is a master at holding space for others. She is truly a marvel.

Note something important that Miss Drew can illustrate: Resilience is NOT perfection. Resilience is falling down and getting back up. It's perseverance in the face of failure; hope in the face of disappointment; and adaptation in the face of change. You must move with the tides to avoid being pulled in by the rip current. It is getting back on the proverbial horse. Trying again, and again, and again NOT until you get it right, but until you are satisfied with your efforts. It may include accepting defeat, but doing so gracefully. It may include confidently moving on if your efforts are in vain.

Another person who I think is a model for authenticity and empowerment is Taylor Swift. I know, I know, another millennial obsessed with Taylor Swift. I didn't become interested in her until recently, because the more I see her interviews the more I am impressed. She celebrates other women and prioritizes her friendships. She is giving a finger to the patriarchy and creating her own economy in any country she visits. When her artistic work was bought out from under her, she re-recorded her earlier albums to regain control over her own art. She has been incredibly generous, donating to food kitchens and giving huge bonuses to her tour workers, which hopefully will set a precedent for other artists. She has spoken about the criticism she has faced and her resulting attempt at perfection, her heartbreaks and shortcomings, and is utterly genuine and goofy. Oh, and her music rocks. I love the vulnerability that she allows in her songs, the humor, the hope, and the heartbreak. I eagerly anticipate watching her grow, hearing her new music, and observing the grace with which she handles it all. She is a shining example of rooting for your fellow females, being unapologetically yourself, and not being afraid to break the mold.

There's so many other women to look up to: the energy and novelty of Oprah, the intelligence and perseverance of Hillary Clinton, the work ethic and honesty of Serena Williams. There are men who can be role models too, but I think as a girl it is more important to have females to look up to. Challenges for women are unique and until the patriarchy is burned all the way to the ground, we ladies need to have each other's backs.

Aside from celebrities, there are real people who have strongly influenced my life. I have had mentors at work, who I would like to emulate or who have inspired me to be better. Some have been incredibly giving and kind, others have told hard truths. I have also encountered anti-mentors, the kind of doctors I want to avoid becoming, which may be equally important. They may have had what I consider terrible bedside manner, they may have fumbled a difficult patient conversation, or they may have treated support staff with something less than respect. I like to remember those instances and write them down, so that I can be sure I do things differently.

If having an example for the path you would like to take is important, having a counterexample for the path to avoid is helpful, too. In short, there is something to learn from every single person that you interact with. You may emulate the way someone dresses, a figure of speech, or an act of kindness that you can pay forward. Mentors can help propel your personal growth, highlighting characteristics that you value and those you'd like to avoid.

When I was considering changing jobs from full-time to part-time, in order to be with you kids more, I called one of my mentors and asked her opinion. I was, quite inappropriately, also asking her for a letter of recommendation while bawling my eyes out at the thought of leaving my underserved patients. I discussed my crisis of consciousness, knowing that the reason I entered medicine was to help the poor and that the thought of leaving them felt like a betrayal. However, at the same time, I knew that I needed a change and wanted more time with you kids. I had imagined that she would discourage me from leaving underserved medicine, as she had dedicated her life to the same thing and was nearing retirement. I thought she might talk me out of it. But what she said was exactly what I needed to hear: that if I left my job, there would be another young, passionate, smart doctor to take my place and give my patients all of the things I was giving them, but that there was no one else who could be the mother to my children. She offered understanding in a moment when I feared judgment, and I am eternally grateful to her for that.

I am lucky to have had many awesome women doctors as mentors: some who continue to inspire, some who have reached a well-deserved retirement, some who have disappointed me, and some who have left medicine all together. I have collected little bits of each outstanding woman and try to honor them by doing my best and emulating their ways. None of them were perfect, but each has many pieces that I want to carry forward and integrate into the fibers of my own being.

It is OK to be disappointed by parts of a role model or mentor. No one is perfect, everyone has different motivations for their choices, and just because we do not understand someone's actions does not mean they are not justified. When someone who you look up to offers to take you under their wing, gladly accept and glean whatever wisdom they have to offer.

Having people apart from your family who support and inspire you is imperative. Seeing people do things outside your comfort out zone can be the spark that lights you up and sends you rocketing into orbit. You need people who you place on a pedestal and watch from a distance, but do not know personally. They are aspirational. I have talked about social media being a highlight reel and the pitfalls of that. But, seeing another's highlight reel can also serve as inspiration and you can learn how others are doing things.

You also need actual human beings that you can know up close, where you see their little imperfections but can learn something anyway. There are opportunities for learning and growth all around us, if we are humble enough to look and patient enough to listen. So, keep your eyes open and your antenna up, pay attention to how people make you feel, and observe the energy that they are putting out into the world, some of which can be absorbed by you.

I believe that the closer you are to someone and the more you know them, the farther they drop down off of their initial pedestal. In reality, being on a pedestal isn't even a metaphor (you're welcome!). Literally, for someone to be on a pedestal, they are far away and you do not see them well. To see them more clearly, they need to come down off of the pedestal in order to be examined up close. You never quite know all the details about someone who is on a pedestal. So, when you see someone up close and notice their inevitable flaws, realize that seeing someone's shadow parts is actually a gift. It is viewing Michelangelo from inches away, without the red velvet rope keeping you back. Go forth with a snapshot of all the people who inspire you; who you would like to emulate and who you prefer to disregard. Feel free to adapt their characteristics to your own needs and don't be afraid to be completely different and unlike anyone you have ever met before.

Grief: Sickness & Death

64. The Ocean Of Grief

Enough already with the metaphors? Well, not yet. Grief is a multi-headed monster that will creep up at various points of your life. Many people assume that grief only relates to death, but grief applies in many situations. You will feel grief at the loss of friends and partners, at unexpected disappointments, and at things you have done that you wish you could take back. It comes in many forms and for many reasons. One helpful construct for processing grief is as a metaphoric ocean.

Grief is like the ocean because it comes in waves. At first, you will know to watch out for the waves, because you will be freshly exposed to the trauma. You will watch your back, knowing that you may be pummeled at any moment. Then, as time passes, the waves may calm and you will gain a sense of security and relax. But beware, you are still in the ocean and turbulence will find you once again. I say this not to frighten you, but to set up realistic expectations. Especially when it comes to death, after losing someone you never quite get over it. It stays with you, both memories of the person and the hurt at losing them. Remembrances may come when you can anticipate the swell of emotion, such as during anniversaries or birthdays, in small unexpected waves when you are triggered by a memory buried deep in your body, or when you enter calm, still waters and are abruptly pulled under by a rip current. Knowing that these are possibilities can help you to ride them out.

One beautiful aspect of surfing, in my mind, is that the human is distinctly aware that the ocean is a greater force than themselves. There is no pretense that they can control their surroundings. They watch and wait patiently for the right wave to come, knowing that they can't ride and conquer them all. As you proceed forward through your grief, know that there are stages. You can look those up, as a way of anticipating your progress and knowing what to expect. When you are in the ocean, denial is dangerous; so while it is a normal stage of grief, try not to stay in denial for too long.

I hope that this metaphor is helpful, and that if you experience grief, I am there to support you through it. Keep watch for the waves and understand when grief unexpectedly pulls you under. Allow yourself to dissolve into a puddle of tears if that's what you need, and at other times swim strongly. Eventually you will be able to float again in life. The vastness and unimaginable depths of the ocean are hopefully analogous to the love that you feel or felt for the person that you lost. After all, to grieve and feel immense loss means that you once had something great.

65. If I Die, Know This

If I die: know that you were loved, I did my best, I'm sorry, you're allowed to hate me (sometimes, at least), and my spirit and energy will linger around to support you even when my physical body is not present. Hopefully this book is a good start to my apology tour for any generational trauma I have passed down.

In my best moments, I hope that I was loving, supportive, present, and fun. I hope that I instilled in you being inclusive, kind, confident, hard-working and having a strong sense of self. However, in my weaker moments I know that I manipulated with prizes or punishments, tended to be a bit neurotic, over analyzed when I should have let it go, and didn't demonstrate friendship, sisterhood, or emotional maturity as well as I would have liked. I hope that those are not your most lasting memories of me as a parent.

I also know that at times I was staring at my phone too much and I let you have too much screen time. I leaned into my toxic positivity when I should have embraced the tough feelings instead. I sometimes made assumptions about what other people were thinking or feeling that then fueled an imaginary war in my mind; all that time planning my retort to defend myself was wasted because the other person was never a villain and in fact could not have cared less. I wish I could go back and change all that.

I never took you to church and haven't talked to you enough about spirituality. I hope that that is something you will want to explore when you're older, but not having sparked that interest in you, how will you know to do that?

I also have not been as social justice oriented as I would like. I have tried to discuss current events and politics with you, but it always goes horribly wrong. I did take you to the women's march as a baby, and our selfie there is one of my favorite pictures of us. After that, I cheered on the social justice movements from the sidelines but didn't show up to protests because of violence that was happening there. That was a selfish move from a place of privilege. If I want to be an ally, I have to be willing to assume some risk and speak up for what I believe in.

It is still so early in my parenting, that it's hard to see what my biggest mistakes have been. Maybe the things above have been trivial, but I have made some other huge errors. Maybe the way that we approach drugs and alcohol will be devastating to you; maybe the ways that I have approached health or school will be detrimental. It is hard to know at this stage. But please know this, I apologize for whatever mistakes I make moving forward. I hope that when I am older, I will be able to take ownership of them and apologize for any damage that I have caused. I will take responsibility for my words and actions, and try to do right by you in the future..

I like to think of myself as a counter-culture hippie vegetarian, but I have not truly been that person for you. I started eating meat when I was pregnant, and now continue to do so out of convenience for your dad, who does most of the cooking. I have not visited my college town in more than a decade, but long to take you there and show you the vibrant urban culture which is so different from our suburban bubble. While I still think of myself as a hippie, if you looked at me from the outside, you would see a frumpy, boring, vanilla, suburban soccer mom instead. I dream of matching my insides to my outsides more as life moves along, and fully growing into the person I want to be both for myself and for you girls

Unfortunately, I am unable to demonstrate the siblinghood that I so desperately wish for you to have. I pour my energy into fostering your sisterhood with each other. Hopefully this is the only area in which I am semi-pushing my own perceived shortcomings onto you, hoping you will triumph where I have failed. I know that's not fair, but it matters too much to let nature run its course.

I have tried my absolute best to not speak negatively about others in front of you, though I do catch myself at times. My mom bad-mouthed all of the stay-at-home moms in the neighborhood when I was growing up, and it just didn't sit well. I am trying to speak positively about others, demonstrate girl power, and teach you to avoid comparison culture and celebrate others instead. Lift other women up, rather than trying to knock them down a peg; you'll smash through that glass ceiling beside them not on top of them.

I can't think of all my bad moments; I try to block them out honestly. I am doing my best and I hope that you will see that. I always knew my mom was doing her best, even though in my perception she made some mistakes. I still love her and am close with her while trying to reroute the generational path, rather than walking the same road because it is easy and familiar. Your dad and I talk openly about our intentions and curate messages carefully. I hope that the good has outweighed the bad in my parenting, so far. You are still so young that I have lots of years left to make mistakes and amends. When you're a grown adult, I hope that we will still have a great relationship and transition into an adult-parent relationship that is mutually enjoyable.

66. The Body Dies, But The Spirit Lives On

We honor those who have passed by living life fully, with reckless abandon at times and meaningful caution during others. When I pass, I hope that you tell stories about me, both respectful positive ones and troubled cautionary ones. I fully believe that our spirits live on after our physical bodies have decomposed. My paternal grandmother's spirit lives on in making pot roast and holiday cookies. The smell of onions in a slow cooker beckons her presence into our house, even though she has been gone for many years and you will never meet her in the flesh.

Family traditions help us to know that our loved ones stay with us through space and time. We can keep physical mementos, like the little wooden whale that sits on your shelf from my mom's mom (the cool, beachy minimalist with exquisite taste, who was a mid-century modern, recycling, NPR-loving, cool cat before the cool kids were even born). I don't have cool knick-knacks (your dad despises them), but I'll leave behind my wedding band and engagement ring that you can have to remember me.

When my grandmothers both died, I found it more difficult to select keepsakes from my midwest grandma, who had an overwhelming amount of stuff, compared to my hip beachy grandma, who had a minimal amount of carefully curated items. I try to Swedish Death Clean regularly, so no one will suffer from my accumulated junk in the future. The British have a word called gubbins, which is the clutter of life or the stuff that takes up space. It can be defined as bits and pieces, or paraphernalia. But it also means the hidden insides of something, like the inner workings of a clock. It's intriguing to think about all of the knickknacks mixed together with the purposeful pieces. That somehow the junk and the art seamlessly blend together to comprise our surroundings and influence our consciousness. I hope I have curated our home carefully enough that it is a calming place to live. If I strike the right balance, our paraphernalia won't get in the way of what's important, but will provide a little flair and character. Fingers crossed our gubbins are good and you'll feel free to take or trash whatever suits you. The fate of the physical objects left behind won't matter to me, but rather the pervasive energy that greets you when remembering me.

Some believe in heaven, some believe in reincarnation, and others believe in ghosts. No matter what you call that vital energy that is inside all of us and can be exchanged between people, look for it. You can usually find signs of loved ones watching over you, supporting you, and along for the ride. I think heaven is a very useful construct, if it can exist without the threat of hell. Believing that your loved ones are in a sacred place that is free of pain, stress, and the toils of humanity is a beautiful concept. And, just like belief in God, you can choose to believe that your loved ones are in a better place where they are reunited with other lost souls and awaiting reunion with you. If those thoughts help you to sleep at night, then by all means embrace them.

You might also consider the scientific principle of atoms; they comprise our universe and are not as separate as we make them out to be. Our physical atoms can scatter and become other things. When we conceptualize humanity in this way, our interconnectedness can be seen and our separate bodies become illusions of the mind. Atoms are forever and finite, only their structure can be perpetually rearranged. That whole 'you are dust and to dust you shall return' trope is not only a great poem, it is quite literal.

Hopefully, if you desire, my spirit can be remembered through stories, pictures, and in the ways I influenced the people in my life. Retell silly stories when I did something stupid or totally overreacted; when I was a huge dork or a big inspiration; and when I was there when you needed me or totally flubbed a major moment. I believe that remembering someone helps to keep their spirit alive. Speak the name of the ghost and they will appear.

Hopefully I live long enough that my death does not take you by surprise, but accept that eventually it comes for all of us. However long I live, I made the most of it and found a lot of joy on my journey. My greatest joy was with you kids, stumbling through being your mom, striving to be better for you, and watching you develop into who you are meant to be. So, thank you for being my kids and letting me mother you.

67. Honoring The Dead

As the soul that remains living, you may be moved to do nothing in your grief, you may need to laugh, you may want to process things you did or didn't get to say, or you might rejoice the parts that you won't miss (goodbye overbearing, long-winded lectures!). Feel free to remember me with an eye-roll or a smirk.

The best way to honor me, personally, is to seek out joy again. Live life to its fullest, laugh often, and stare up at the sky from the base of a redwood tree to ponder your place in the universe. Listen to my playlists, which were curated with an inordinate amount of love. If you bury me, for some reason, come dance on my grave in the pouring rain, blasting good music, and leaving behind happy tears and cookie crumbs. Of course, humor me by being a tiny bit devastated, but I don't want that feeling to last too long. Go live your life, find your truths, and put out loving energy into the universe. When loving energy or luck comes back to you, I hope you can sense a bit of it is from me.

I tried to create a full family through siblings because we don't have much extended family. Thus, you will need to find a chosen family, since your genetic family is kind of small. Gather friends and tribe-members; share holidays with them, include them in your life, build trust, and go through hardships together to cement your bond. This provides me an opportunity for another metaphor. Ready? Excited? Redwoods!! My favorite tree has some really cool facts that I must share. I will let you read between the lines for the relationship and life lessons they can provide.

1) Despite being 300 feet high, over one million pounds, and living for 2000 years, their roots are wide (50 feet from the base) but NOT deep (only 6 to 12 feet underground).

2) These massive trees have teeny tiny pine cones. New growth is sparked by the smallest seeds planted in fertile soil. They each grow at their own rate.

3) New trees can grow from seeds, branches, roots, or STUMPS. Imagine a million pound towering tree that can originate from a stump, literally a remnant of its former self!

4) Because new trees can sprout from the roots, baby trees grow in a circle around a parent tree. Over time, the parent tree will disintegrate and return back to the soil, thereby nourishing the baby trees. What's left behind is a ring of redwood trees, called a cathedral ring (aka fairy ring or family circle).

In cathedral rings, the young trees know to branch outward from the circle rather than inward toward the center, as doing so would rob itself and its ring-siblings of sunlight.

5) In cathedral rings, the trees are not identical clones of the parent, but have genetic diversity and can actually be separate species of tree. Diversity helps the circle survive and thrive, by making it more resistant to pests, fires, and other stressors.

6) Redwood roots are intertwined with neighboring redwoods. They hold onto nearby roots to increase stability for both trees. This allows them to withstand earthquakes, landslides, floods, strong winds, and other trees falling against them.

7) Giant sequoia redwoods actually NEED fire to reproduce (it releases seeds from cones, fertilizes soil for seedlings to take root, and creates gaps in the forest canopy for sunlight to reach seedlings). So a seemingly destructive fire actually serves a greater purpose long-term.

8) They grow upward from the top, but outward at the bottom (the base/foundation does not move-you can come back to the same knot at eye level years later). They can grow in different directions at the same time, expanding in one area while seemingly staying the same in others.

9) Bark flakes off over time so that scars can heal, holds water inside to feed the tree, and can be up to one foot thick with tannins, helping the tree to withstand fires. Thick skin has many benefits.

10) The up in the air canopy has its own little universe and ecosystem. Some plants and animals spend their whole lives only in the canopy and certain trees can grow ON the redwood branches, reaching up to 40 feet tall. Thus a separate tree can grow solely from the branch of a bigger, older tree. There is an internal life above that we can't really know or appreciate from the base of the tree.

11) They drink fog, which they themselves create via their heavy canopy. The shallow roots also prevent root rot and are able to absorb water from overlying morning dew. If allowed to grow and thrive, they will create a universe where they sustain themselves.

I will not insult your intelligence by extrapolating from the above metaphors. Suffice to say: create a support system and grow like the redwoods. A chosen family is a gift you give yourself. Find a group with which you can rest, travel, revel in nature, experience joy, and celebrate milestones. I hope to be there, too. But just in case the universe takes me away, build out your network so that you have a safety net and bring in others who need a net, too. The best way to honor the dead is to keep on living and keep memories alive by speaking them aloud.

68. Funeral Requests

This is hard to say/write, but I figured I'll put it out there into the universe, hopefully to alleviate your stress in the event that something unexpected happens. I have pretty specific thoughts about death, after doing multiple hospice rotations and seeing my own grandparents and many patients pass away.

If I suffer from dementia and no longer know who you are, and cannot experience any joy or become a consistent drain on my family, please feel free to let me go. I believe in physician assisted death and never want to be a burden to my family, especially if there is no hope for meaningful recovery. Similarly, if I become very ill and something like chemotherapy would not meaningfully extend my life and could diminish the quality of what's remaining, I may choose to forgo and make the most with what's left. Hopefully, that will not be seen as giving up, but rather giving my all to the time that I do have.

Death is the only certainty as humans; I am an eternal optimist guilty of toxic positivity but the buck stops here. Death cannot be taken lightly; as a physician, I've seen too much and witnessed too many families have a negative experience to not have a very strong opinion.

Once I'm gone, don't waste effort, time, or money on planning a big funeral. No open casket for this gal! As much as I revel in the concept of you joyfully dancing on my grave, I would like to be cremated. It's just easier. I would like my ashes divided into four equal parts, one for each child and one for your dad (assuming he still wants anything to do with me by that point). Then, it is up to you what you do with those ashes. If you'd like to plant them under a tree in your yard, keep them on your fireplace mantle for your cat to eat, or spread them in nature, do what you will. Hopefully, someone will sprinkle a little bit of me in the Pacific ocean and in a redwood forest somewhere, as I believe a part of my soul belongs in those two places. But beyond that, I am yours for the taking.

We are in the process of making our will, which has been so difficult. Imagining you children with anyone but us is gut wrenching, heartbreaking, and impossible. With my relationship with my sister being what it is, we have chosen your dad's sister as your potential guardian. She does not have children, but is a good person with similar values, and I believe would carry on our goals for adventure, time in the outdoors, and encourage you to be good people. Hopefully, it doesn't come to that and I die of old age like my grandmother's both did.

As for a funeral, I don't have that many friends to begin with so just have any people who would like to pay final respects gather and listen to the playlist that I created (see music therapy). If they want, they can bring a dessert for a sugar-fueled potluck in honor of my sweet tooth. And, if anyone feels moved, they can share a favorite memory, funny story, or a poem of their choosing. Keep it short but sweet. Try not to be too sentimental or sad. We all live and we all will die. My hope is that writing this book will help keep the peace and be with you always.

Ideally any memorial or funeral type setting will be filled with laughter more than tears, funny stories more than sentimental ones, and good music and food. Like a wedding, but a separation not a union. Interestingly, in my experience, parents are on a pedestal when their children are young, come off the pedestal when their children are teenagers and young adults, and then return to their pedestal once they have died. Feel free to continue acknowledging and reflecting on my mistakes, even after I am gone. I don't expect denial as a form of reverence and don't need a pedestal. Speak freely and honestly about me, acknowledge my imperfections and humanity.

There are no rules, but I encourage you to feel all the feelings and stages of grief: love me, hate me, burn me in the flame, sprinkle me around, and then move forward knowing that my spirit will linger in love. You can always return to the Pacific Ocean or the redwoods to feel the little parts of my soul that are left there. I also have had breastmilk necklaces made for each of you kids, so you can physically wear a part of my body, if you would like. It's meant as a symbol of my intention to nourish you, give of myself, and create beauty for your lives. I figure resin-preserved freeze-dried milk inclusions are better than a lock of hair, a snaggle tooth, or ashes which could spill and make a mess. You're welcome for being such a complete and total weirdo.

Enlightenment: Insights & Intentions

69. Perpetual Growth Goals

In my third decade of life, I finally understood that the process of personal growth could occur without seeking an end goal. My wish for you is to reach that place sooner than I did. Take the pressure off of feeling like you need to get from point A to B (while resenting A and longing for B), and instead recognize you are moving forward and making effort. There is beauty in endeavoring to better yourself, regardless of how slow the progress might be.

As you age your internal world becomes more refined, while your outer body gradually deteriorates. There is a bell curve of living: as a baby and in old age we don't expect as much, while that sweet middle spot is the bulk of our time on earth. From our 20s to our 70s, hopefully we have awareness, strength, flexibility, and momentum. To "live in the present moment" is one of my ultimate goals. To gain control over my thoughts, where they wander, and where they lead me. I want to be more aware of what is happening around me and within my own mind and body. Sometimes I am ignorantly blissful, but I also miss little glimmers of beauty. You girls always notice them. You must be looking around more and I'm laser focused on what's ahead, but I would love to stop and smell those roses with you.

If I can gain more awareness and control over my thoughts, perhaps I will not waste time, my most precious commodity, on worry. Of course it happens, but I try to reflect on any ACTION I can take to change a situation, and then take those actions and release the worry. Worry is NOT living in the present, action is. When it comes to thoughts, past thoughts are either regret or nostalgia and future thoughts are either worry or hope. Of those four, worry is the most pointless. Regret can help you learn from mistakes and make better choices in the future. Nostalgia can bring you back to a place of comfort or joy. Hope can propel you forward and help you sleep at night. Worry will ruin your sleep and I can't find a positive purpose that it serves. I aim to plan ahead, take the actions that you can to ensure success, and then release the worry; of course like all mental gymnastics this is easier said than done.

Living in the present can be tough. Currently, the world is pretty dark and scary. It is easy to fall into a spiral of despair and hopelessness. I worry about the environment, the hatred that is becoming more outright in people's actions, and the disappearing sense of community and kinship among humans. But there are always little rays of light, if you seek them out. There are people in the world who are working to make it a better place, in direct opposition to those trying to destroy it. Hopefully you will be one of the forces for good.

Look to people like Bill and Melinda Gates, who are donating their riches to charitable causes; to Oprah, who is educating young girls in Africa; to Reese Witherspoon, who is championing stories by and for women; and nameless people who are protesting water resources on native reservations, doing land acknowledgments, promoting persons of color on social media, and supporting small businesses. There are a million small acts that can contribute to the greater good, as well as larger visible efforts. Both should be applauded.

Always act in good conscience, making ethical choices for yourself and others. The right thing to do is almost never the easy thing to do, but do it anyway. There is no silver lining with the current wars and people dying in the world, but I remain hopeful that there are good people working on this from many sides, the violence and hatred will diminish, and recognizing each other's humanity will prevail in the end. I do not say this naively, but rather desperately. I feel powerless and all I can cling to is hope. MLK says "the arc of the moral universe is long, but it bends toward justice", and I choose to believe that is true.

My personal growth has led to oscillations in my level of civic engagement. At one time, I attended the rallies and protests, volunteered at the refugee clinic, and engaged passionately in discussions; at other times I have turned off the news and buried my head in the sand. I would like to regress back to the most engaged version of myself, but that currently exceeds my bandwidth. I am learning to be OK with that, temporarily. I plan to re-activate in the future.

In the meantime, I help with my dollars by donating to conservation efforts, political groups that I believe in, and giving the likes and follows to people doing good work in the world. It's not as much as I would like, but there are seasons in life and I am trying to accept that the current season is less politically active or social justice oriented. My inner hippie activist is not dead, she's just resting. I'm expecting that once you're old enough, having girl kids will help to reignite my passion and advocacy efforts. I want to pass down activism and engagement to you, since it is vitally important that you feel power and agency in this changing world. I envision passionate future discourse with you about these topics. Yay for things to look forward to, little sparks to light our fires!

70. Karma

Not just a kick-butt song by Taylor Swift. It is also a very useful philosophy and concept. In Christianity, I was taught to "do unto others" as I would want done to me; but in Buddhism and Hinduism, the philosophy of karma is that your past and present actions will determine your future fate.

If you put out positive energy, kindness, and generosity those things will find their way back to you; and if you perpetuate negativity, hate, or injustice then those will later knock on your door. It both gives us internal motivation to do good and helps us relinquish control or concern for others' negative actions toward us. In short, it is finding peace in the belief that justice will prevail and that the arch of the universe is toward fairness.

When you genuinely accept that construct, you will sleep better at night. Karma relieves any burden of trying to make others take responsibility for their actions. In reality, we only control our own actions and despite our most insightful and persuasive words, we can't control others. When you choose to believe in Karma, you let Miss-Big-Bad-Universe even all the scores, so that you don't have to worry your pretty little head about it.

When someone else seemingly does something negative to you, in actuality they are often doing it to themselves. That's not to say that others should not take responsibility for how their actions affect you, but they have to own their actions and you do not play any role in that. They should apologize if they've done you wrong or attempt to make it right, but some people will never do that and that is on them. They are the ones who have to live and sleep with their poor choices; don't waste your energy on convincing others to do the right thing. Just lead by example by doing the right thing yourself, and hope that they follow or learn. This does not apply to crimes, which should be prosecuted to the full extent of the law.

When I was a teenager and I felt the world revolved around me, I would become irate when someone had done me wrong. As I have grown up, I realize that many of those situations had nothing to do with me. I was an innocent bystander in the other person's drama. The sad or relieving fact, depending how you look at it, is that most people are not thinking about you nearly as much as you believe that they are. Most people are caught up thinking about themselves and it is rare that someone has genuine ill will and purposeful wrongdoing. The person may accidentally do you wrong and when we see it that way, it might take away the sting just a little bit. Karma helps with that; you'll get yours and they'll get theirs. It keeps you from sinking to someone else's level and from screaming down criticisms from your high horse.

When I have had interpersonal conflict in the past, part of that was due to my assumptions about the other person's intent. I assumed they were consciously trying to insult or hurt me. I thought that the only way forward was to over-explain my point of view until I could convince the other person that I was right and they were wrong. While I still do this all the time, because I am human and also sort of an idiot, I know that it serves no purpose. While it feels good to justify my thoughts and feelings, most people do not need those illuminated for them. Your dad is the exception; I think it is helpful for him to see where I'm coming from at times. That poor guy will never hear the end of it, ha ha ha. However, the somewhat random friend, classmate, or coworker from my past did not need me to justify or over-explain myself to them. Most of the time, whatever has happened is already in the past and no one is thinking about it except for me.

The concept of karma helps me to move on. When someone adds stress to my life or showers me with their toxic energy, I try to let it go and know that that person's negative energy is inside of them, eating away at their soul and does not need to eat away at mine. The negativity is not inside of me, unless I allow it in. That is where our control lies, in what we allow into our hearts and minds. I believe that karma is a form of energy transfer. When there are good vibes flowing, everyone can share them. However, when there are bad vibes around you do not have to partake in them. I hope you embrace the concept of karma, as it can save you many hours of spiraling in your own thoughts and trying to control the uncontrollable, others thoughts or actions. Karma is a way to relinquish a sense of power that we never had and never will; it is a form of self acceptance and self-love. Learn it, use it, sing the Swift song!

71. What Money CAN Buy

Before I get into my boring advice on finances, I want to be very clear on the things that money can and cannot do for you. MONEY does not make you happy! There are actually many studies on this. It is a bell curve, where the happiest are those in the middle class or upper middle class. There is a point at which increasing your wealth actually decreases your happiness.

We try to teach you to be smart with money. Being financially secure gives freedom and that is the true blessing of working hard and making a living wage. I am not a big lover of fancy things: purses, shoes, clothing, cars. They have never appealed to me nor your dad. We do enjoy travel, which of course comes at an expense. I believe the most worthwhile things to buy are experiences: performing arts, zoo memberships, soccer team fees. Money can buy you opportunities for life experience.

Money also enables you to take risks. If you are earning enough to live and eat, there is a certain amount of ease or calm that can wash over someone. In that state, one may realize their passions and take risks to do what they love. I am very fortunate that my job, which I love, also pays extremely well.

As I have mentioned, you may find out that your passion is not well paid and have to supplement with a 9 to 5. Hard work that is rewarded should be appreciated, but working should never come at the expense of living well. Also, never compromise your morals for money. Lying, cheating, and stealing may be the easier route, but of course they are not just ones. You'll make a lot more money chopping down the forest, then fighting to save the trees. Save them anyways.

With wealth comes some responsibility, in my mind. If you are comfortable financially, use any extra to vote with your dollar. Support slow fashion, organic produce, companies that pay a living wage, fair trade organizations, and companies who uphold ethical practices. Some people do not have the luxury of doing these things, but if you have the luxury then it is a moral imperative that you take that responsibility seriously. Donate to organizations doing good work. Pay it forward by being a good tipper and lifting others up.

While money can never buy you happiness, it can buy a sense of security, a level of confidence to take risks or go after what you want, an ability to have adventure, and the privilege of safety. These are the things that you can buy and that I would recommend you invest in, because they will add immeasurably to your well-being. Don't get it twisted, being rich does not guarantee joy, it does not automatically eliminate struggle, nor can it magically illuminate your purpose or passions in life. Those are all inside jobs that have to be done for free, with time and personal growth. Sometimes, money can buy time, as I did when I exchanged a bigger salary for part-time work. I literally bought back time with my young kids: best purchase EVER! I see clearly that I am far better off with less in my pocket. Hopefully, you can find a balance between internal riches and a stable bank account.

72. Financial Advice

Money, money, money, money, money..... MonAyyy! I'm no expert but your dad and I share some common saving and spending values that we hope you inherit. They're pretty simple: live as cheaply as possible, spend on experiences and not physical items, be a saver not a spender, and start investing as early as possible to take advantage of compounding interest.

Currently, many people are unable to buy houses because of inflation, high interest rates, and not enough inventory. We opted to buy a smaller house (half the budget of what we were approved for) and do a shorter term loan (15 years), in order to free ourselves of having to work for 30 years in order to pay off the house. Your biggest expense will likely be rent or mortgage, so make your housing decision after deliberate consideration and number-crunching. We decided we would rather have a smaller house, but ensured a family friendly neighborhood with good public schools. Once you're a parent, good public schools are a major savings. A house only needs to be enough. Ours is small, not fancy, and that is fine. It is an extreme privilege to have housing stability and live in a safe place, so that's really all we sought.

Keep costs down, the largest costs are typically housing and perhaps cars. In college, I always shared a room and found relatively cheap apartments. I took over a friend's lease in residency to keep costs down; it was a dumpy apartment but in an awesome neighborhood. I figured I was working 80 hours per week and all I needed was a safe bed. I have always taken the minimum school loans to pay for education. I know people who took extra education loans to live better, buy cars, travel abroad, or fund a lifestyle they otherwise could not sustain. Please avoid that.

Do NOT open credit cards to live beyond your means; it sets you up for failure, as a bad credit score will haunt you into adulthood. Please do not let your incompletely cognitively developed 20-year-old self screw over your future hard-working wants-to-buy-a-house self. In your teens and early 20s, your brain is not programmed to be future-oriented and the worries of tomorrow seem far, far away. I plead with you to protect future-you as an act of self-love, even if it puts restrictions on current-you and feels like a killjoy buzzkill that causes FOMO.

Avoid any debt possible: cheap rent if you can find it, used cars that you drive until the wheels fall off, and care for your possessions so that they last. Once you have some debt, make it a priority to pay it off. I performed public service loan forgiveness to pay off my medical school debts quickly after graduation. If you get into the mindset of not having fancy things, it enables you to splurge when it really matters. The most important thing is to know how much money you will be making, in order to budget. Even though we now both make good money, we are so accustomed to living cheaply that changing our habits seems silly. We don't eat out much, don't get Starbucks, and don't look or act like people with money. They say true wealth is quiet, not flashy, and in our case that is definitely true.

The other day you came home from school asking why we weren't rich, since I'm a doctor, and I've never been so pleased by a question. We are secretly very financially secure but I don't want that to be obvious to you or anyone else. I hope you're not pissed when you grow up and find out we did have hidden money. Instead of buying lavish cars or clothing, I opt for reasonable and functional. Buy those Costco jeans and pajamas, they are fabulous! Caring about what others think and spending money to influence someone's opinion of you is futile and an unwise use of funds. The only opinions that matter are based on who you are on the inside and how your actions reflect your values. If someone judges you for not having a cool car or designer clothes, let them; they are not worth your time nor energy and you will never have their approval, nor does their approval hold any genuine value.

Your dad's job is more tenuous than mine. It could evaporate overnight, so we have prepared financially for that. You should always, always have a 3-6 month emergency fund saved up. As soon as you start working, build that fund first. Having a financial buffer gives you freedom if the economy goes upside down, opportunity if a job isn't working out, or relief if you need to take leave for sickness or family reasons. Saving, of course, is easier said than done. There's a balance between delaying gratification until you can afford something and living fully in the present moment. We see renters in our neighborhood who want to buy a home, but cannot afford the house they are renting and whose spending habits prevent them from saving for a down payment. It's tricky, so just make sure your spending habits align with your goals, that your long term goals are reasonable, and that you are confident and secure in your financial choices.

Pay off your credit cards in full every month if you can, learn to say no, and analyze your budget until you are living well within your means. Maybe home ownership is a thing of the past and the housing market will be impossible to navigate. Who knows. Maybe I am speaking from an unreasonably privileged place and this advice is unfair. I hope you will witness and learn financial responsibility from me. Of all my more lofty and convoluted life goals for you girls, this one seems straightforward and attainable.

If you do have extra money, start your 401 early. Look up some Internet charts about compounding interest and you will see that the sooner you invest, the more your money will grow. When I worked for ten years at a nonprofit, I was not able to contribute as much and now I am kicking myself for having lost a decade of compounding interest. Start your 401k as soon as you can, max out as much as you are able, and consider it an integral category in your budgeting. You are literally investing in your own future and there is nothing better that you could invest in.

If you do have extra after contributing to your 401, invest in stocks, specifically the S&P 500. Your dad and your grandpa have spent time researching and investing in individual stocks, but even Warren Buffett will say nothing beats S&P so just do that. I've read a few financial books and of those I would recommend: "Rich Dad, Poor Dad" and "The Simple Path to Wealth". They keep it simple and make a dry subject readable.

Generational wealth is tricky. As Warren Buffet says, "give your children enough money to do something but not enough to do nothing." I would hate for any generational wealth to inhibit your drive or create a sense of entitlement. Work ethic is one of the most important things that we can teach you; I want you to correlate hard work with reward. I do not want to pave an easy road for you, because it will not benefit you long-term. Instead, I want you to walk the uneven cobblestone path of your choosing while I attempt to put up helpful little road signs reminding you to stay the course and avoid deadly cliffs. The best that I can hope for you is that you will work hard, find a passion, and that that passion will be able to sustain a reasonable lifestyle.

I'm about to repeat myself, but some things are worth repeating: use any financial wealth you may acquire to vote with your dollar. Be the person to support small businesses, women run businesses, businesses run by persons of color. Buy organic, avoid single-use plastics, reject fast fashion, and shop ethical brands. If you have the means to do so, the responsibility to support good causes lies more heavily on your shoulders. Those who are barely getting by do not have the luxury of picking and choosing the brands that they support.

The most important thing to remember when it comes to finances is to differentiate wants versus needs, and to remember that your self-worth is not reflected in your bank account. Never get fooled into thinking you NEED something shiny and new. Don't be a victim of our consumer culture that would have you living in perpetual debt in order to be viewed as having it all. Don't get sucked into the hamster wheel of momentary pleasure from the dopamine hit that you get when clicking "complete purchase". Buying something can be useful and enjoyable, but that momentary high is far outweighed by the long term decrease in your stress levels that comes from having an emergency fund and knowing that you can pay rent. Having confidence and security is better than any Prada purse or trip to Vegas. You'll sleep better after a free day at the beach than a debt-inducing night at the casino.

So here's where it gets hairy, as all things do. Spend a little bit, don't squirrel away every penny and deny yourself everything. My dad passed down his spending values to me and was/is a major saver. In fact, he's been very generous with his kids and grandkids, but I doubt has spent a dime on himself, ever. I admire how he has saved so much of his money, but now that he's older I wish he would have known when to loosen the purse strings and live a little. I wish he had traveled more before his knees went bad. I wish he had allowed himself to experience some of the finer things in life, which he deserves. I wish he knew that our love for him is because of who he is and not related at all to what he gives. So, treat yourself once in a while because you deserve it, just find a sustainable balance.

Remember that joy is free. Awe is around the corner waiting for you and cannot be bought. It costs nothing to be kind, patient, and helpful. Your best investments will be in the company you keep, the choices you make, and the wholehearted belief in yourself. The people who truly value you will not care what you wear or drive. So, find a balance between investing in your future and making the most of the present. Bet on yourself, every time. Put your heart on the line, exhaust all your efforts, but maybe save a little money just in case it doesn't work out. There's no shame in having a backup plan. You'll figure it out and hopefully these tips will save you some of the mistakes I have made and set you up for success by giving you a road map rather than a trust fund.

73. Regrets

We all have them. I don't have any huge regrets, but have quite a few small ones that I would like to share, as a cautionary tale. While I fully support making mistakes, I hope you won't make these same mistakes.

Firstly, I have taken myself too seriously for far too long. In high school, my perfectionistic approach to sports and academia led me to treat every test like the SATs and every race like the Olympics. And ironically, not one of those tests or races actually mattered at all, ever. I wish I had goofed off more, laughed more, gone to more parties, and in general been more of a rascal. It's too hard to rascal when you're trying to be perfect all the time. There were times when someone would make a joke at my expense and I would become angry because I couldn't laugh at myself. I wish I could have relaxed a little bit and allowed more chaos into my life. It would have better prepared me for motherhood.

There is also a list of silly physical things that I wish I had tried, like dying my hair a neon color or shaving my head. I have had the same hairdo since I was a child. I wish that I had tried bangs, even though I know I would've hated them because I am a low maintenance kind of gal. If I had dyed my hair a neon rainbow when I was young, no one would have cared. I wish I had tried a nose ring or a belly button piercing when my stomach was flat. Now, I am too old for those things. The window has closed on body experimentation, until I retire at least. Fair warning, I plan to be the grandma who shows up with rainbow hair and a clip-on nose ring.

I do not have tattoos, and that is something I'm fine with since I can't think of one singular item that I desire permanently on my body. But, I have friends with tattoos that I really like and I admire. One has a tree on her foot. The tree is a symbol in almost every religion and is a wonderful metaphor for growth: the roots are your birth family and connectivity, the trunk is your strength and individuality, and the branches are your continual growth in various directions. The leaves may fall in the winter and regrow in the spring, they may change color over time, and they may blow in different directions. The leaves can be wiped out by a fire, but if the trunk is resilient, it will regrow or bend with the wind. I love the metaphor of the tree and therefore the tree tattoo that my friend has. I have other friends with matching sibling tattoos to eternally symbolize their bond. If you feel moved to do so, feel free to mark your body forever, just maybe avoid your beautiful faces.

Another big regret that I have is not studying abroad during college. I was in such a rush to finish in four years, because that is what everyone said I should do, that I didn't stop to consider any alternative options. In retrospect, college was the absolute best time of my life and I had the gift of knowing that fact as I was living it. Studying abroad would have extended it to last another semester. Once college is over, that stage is gone forever and you cannot get it back. I nearly had a double major, in a non-science subject that I was very passionate about and would have completed it had I studied abroad. Instead, I graduated on time with a minor in that subject. If I had sat down to think about the big picture, I could've graduated "late", taken that extra semester abroad, had a double major, and added what I assume would have been a transformative, life-changing experience to my life. If you ever have the chance, study abroad or join the Peace Corps or go to a foreign country for an extended period of time, I can only imagine it would be sublime.

Drugs, man. I am probably one of the only people I know who has never tried drugs. Your dad has tried marijuana, but it made him anxious. All of my friends in college and med school smoked marijuana, but it never appealed to me. I was raised to be very worried about addiction and believed that drugs were scary. I never touched one and now that I'm older, there's deadly Fentanyl in everything so the window has closed. Marijuana is now legal, so maybe I'll try that when I retire. I have high hopes that mushrooms will be legal at some point in the future, as well, and think those would be safe to try. Of course, please avoid what I consider the big 3 dangerous drugs: cocaine, methamphetamine, and heroin. Also, the jury is out (medically) on ecstasy and LSD; there may be some longer-term cognitive issues with those, so please avoid until further notice.

I said to avoid the big three because the amount of dopamine released when you do those drugs will be the largest dopamine release that you ever feel. Those drugs, as well as nicotine, totally flood your reward system receptors in a way that will never be replicated. I do not say that to make those drugs appealing!!! Keep reading!! If you try those, you will end up in one of two positions: 1) you may be chasing that high for the rest of your life and become addicted to the drugs, in a downward spiral that will lead to ruin. Each drug use will disappoint you, because it will never replicate the first high and eventually you will get high just to return to your prior neutral pre-drug dopamine levels. 2) you may not chase that high and never use the drug again, but your body will never experience another dopamine hit like it. It will rob you of future joy.

Because I have never done drugs, my largest surge of dopamine and oxytocin was giving birth to each of you children. That's actually pretty awesome, when you think about it. My highest high was seeing your newborn faces for the first time. You will rob yourself of all the future dopamine hits if you try one of those big three drugs. Climbing to the top of Everest will not be as exhilarating, having your baby latch to breast-feed will not be as elating, and crossing the finish line of a marathon will not give you the runner's high that you rightfully deserve. So, avoid those three drugs and find other natural highs; they are more sustainable in the long run.

Of course, I have already discussed my regrets when it comes to friendship and siblinghood. I'll spare you the replay. As I mentioned, I do regret the multiple missed opportunities for leaning in to a kiss or an arm. So, heed my tales: if you have an opportunity to kiss someone that you would like to kiss, do it! Kiss all the frogs; it might be fun and you will likely only regret the shots you don't take. I wish for you a life of only small regrets and no big ones.

74. Parting Wisdom, Words, and Wishes

Before this was a book, it was a series of journals and lists. I wanted to create a "family mantra" to put on our entry wall that we would see every day. But, of course, I had too many ideas and couldn't narrow it down so it became too long to read. Then I started wanting to elaborate on each idea, which led to the journal entries. I took that idea and ran with it, I suppose. Here we are. Below is a little summary of what I hope you have taken away from this book.

First, the family mantra/wall art, which I still have not finished because I want to make it pretty and can't quite commit to the wording.

Be Kind
respect all people & things; be a friend; never speak negatively of others; believe in karma
Be a Team Player
support each other; celebrate victories & comfort defeats; give more than you take; remain humble
Be Joyful
revel in nature, music, & friendship; enjoy the journey not the destination; laugh at yourself
Be Responsible
take pride in your words & actions; own your mistakes & feelings; be honest & sincere
Be a Hard Worker
always do your best; strive for progress over perfection; never stop learning & growing
Be Thankful

be present & patient; avoid comparison & judgment; find the good in
others
Be Ethical
stand up for what is right; use privilege to fight for justice; reject
consumerism
Be Resilient
handle challenges with grace & grit; learn from adversity; don't take things
personally
Be Yourself
know who you are; believe in yourself; love yourself and other
unconditionally

<u>**Traits I hope you have:**</u>
   Gratitude
   Authenticity
   Confidence
   Kindness
   Respect
   Hard-work

<u>**Concepts I hope you'll remember:**</u>
   Happiness is the journey not the destination
   Type 2 fun
   Admit and learn from your mistakes
   Practice gratitude
   Seek out fellow weirdos, they are the best
   Embrace the mess, find peace amidst chaos
   Some people's bridesmaids will sleep with their fiancé
   Wants versus needs

REPARENTING MYSELF

<u>Mantras:</u>
Their Negativity Isn't Mine
Don't Take It Personally
All Humans Are Beautifully Flawed
There are no mistakes in art, just opportunities for creativity
Perfection doesn't exist

<u>Metaphors, oh the metaphors!:</u>
Dandelions (for perception)
Losing Your Teeth (for rates of personal growth)
Baking (for how little ingredients can make-or-break a recipe)
Musical harmony as demonstrated by Gospel Choirs (for teamwork and collaboration)
Swimming Lessons (for parenting)
Being on a Pedestal (for only being able to see flaws when up close)
Ocean (for grief)
Redwoods (for support networks and communing with your environment)

<u>Recommended Poems:</u>
"Dust If You Must", by Rose MIlligan
"For a New Beginning", by John O'Donohue (a poem I have read at every transition point in my life)
"When the Pawn", by Fiona Apple
"Breathe" by Becky Hemsley
"The Quality of Mercy", (The Merchant of Venice, Act IV, Scene 1) by William Shakespeare
"Do Not Go Gentle Into That Good Night", by Dylan Thomas
"The Road Not Taken", by Robert Frost (So cliche, I know!)
"Like A River Finds the Sea", by Whitney Hanson

<u>Fun Quotes:</u>

"To talk without thinking is to shoot without aiming", by Greg Clarke

"Every dead body on Mount Everest was once a highly motivated person, so maybe calm down" - unknown

"You gotta be tough, If yer gonna be stupid", by John Grisham

<u>Items to consider purchasing:</u>

Feelings Wheel

Values Card Deck

When times are hard, I want you to feel surrounded by support. Even if I am not with you, whether in this world or at that time, I want you to feel enveloped in maternal loving energy. Even if you are sitting alone in a dark corner, I am always rooting for you no matter what. I will haunt you like a friendly ghost, to make sure that you know I am always there for you. If you cannot talk to me directly, look up at the sky and find me in a fluffy cloud. Close your eyes and picture the ocean, the calming waves washing over you. If you cannot picture the ocean, look at a dog or cat to see the kindness in their eyes and know that my eyes see you with that same energy.

One generational trauma that I hope to break is people pleasing and only being encouraged to express positive emotions. As your parent and captain of the proverbial ship, I feel a responsibility to encourage you to accept and embrace the good and the bad. Hopefully I can set a tone where feelings are respected and processed in a healthy way. Be just as in touch with your inner state, as you are with the outside world. Never make yourself or your needs smaller to help someone else feel big. Understand that family and relationships require a beautifully complex exchange, where equality and fairness are not synonymous. If someone is unkind or not their best self, I hope you can still find good in them. I hope you can forgive them, knowing that everyone has off days and hopefully those days don't define them. However, if a person is repeatedly unkind, know that you deserve better.

REPARENTING MYSELF

I hope that I raise you with resources of gratitude, resiliency, ability to handle disappointment with grace, and perhaps most importantly the ability to reach out and ask for help. The darkest times are the times when we learn the most about ourselves and the people around us. You may have friends who you think will support you, but they don't. You may have strangers step up in those moments and become your chosen family. It is not the moments that we conquer and win that define us, it is the moments of loss that will show us who we are and who is important in our life.

In so many ways, the pendulum is always swinging: parenting strategies, health and fitness trends, fashion styles. In my lifetime, I've lived through the low-fat diet craze, but now there is science to support whole fat dairy. In my youth we laid in tanning beds trying to achieve a sunkissed glow, but now I never let my skin see the light of day. In parenting, right now gentle parenting is highly revered. I'm not sure if my parents, or anyone in the 80s and 90s for that matter, followed a "parenting strategy". Looking back, it feels like parents were more intuitive, less worried, less contemplative, and seemingly more happy. It was a simpler time, but in retrospect NOT better.

As time passes, the world collectively grows more aware and our past failures become crystal clear. So, I know that my own parenthood will be viewed with the clarity of hindsight. I accept it, I respect your critiques, and I will do my best not to carry forward my parenting habits into my potential grand-parenting habits. I promise to stay open to new ideas and not cling to my past parenting as if it was the best or only way to do things. I will try not to be so fragile that I am unable to reflect on my best efforts as having had shortcomings and being imperfect. I solemnly swear that I will continue to grow, and once you are an adult, I will be willing to hear your feedback and take it into consideration.

I anticipate and eagerly await your generation's critique of gentle parenting, which we are all so convinced of at this time. It feels like the right thing to do, but I am certain past generations believed wholeheartedly in their parenting methods, as well. After all, spanking was once the norm and now we call it child abuse. So, it will be interesting when we learn all the glaringly obvious pitfalls of this approach, which I cannot fathom at this time. Sorry, in advance.

Thank you for being my child. You owe me nothing moving forward. Being your mother was the highlight of my life and watching you grow is the absolute greatest gift I could have. In my job there are no guarantees or promises. I cannot guarantee we all get to live another day together, but I can promise that my love will always be there for you. It exists outside of space and time, it extends beyond our physical bodies, it is more infinite than our concept of the universe, and it is yours to have, forever and always.

Love, Mom

Afterword

If you read this far and were not birthed from my hoo-ha, thank you! I hope that you can take something away from reading this: a belly laugh, a good ugly cry, a solid eye-roll, kindling for your next bonfire, or perhaps feeling enveloped in loving maternal energy. If reading this was entertaining or thought provoking, I hope you will pass it along to other moms and daughters.

If you enjoyed reading this book, as a brand new and self published author, I would be eternally grateful for you posting any reviews on Amazon (https://www.amazon.com/dp/B0CY5Y29C9) I promise to read every review and appreciate the time and energy that it takes to write them.

Lastly, if you would like to connect with me, provide feedback about the book, or join in discussions with fellow readers, my book group can be found on Instagram (@ReparentingMyselfBook) or I can be reached by email (MotherLodeJournals@gmail.com).

Sending well wishes and positive energy for you out into the universe!

My sincere thanks,

-Anony Mom, MD

Acknowledgements

Thank you to my parents for being incredibly giving, loving, and always doing your best. Thank you for believing in me, encouraging me, and liking me so that I could like myself. If you ever read this, I hope that you can sense all of my love and respect despite any critiques. I appreciate that, like me, you are each a product of your upbringing and perfectly imperfect humans.

Thank you to my husband for putting up with me. Thank you for making me laugh, being a sounding board, and parenting alongside me. If you ever read this, I will finally admit it was more than a "little side project" (insert wink). I love you so much and you are a great dad to our kids. Thank you for keeping me sane with your admirable middle finger to people-pleasing, amazing humor at the best times, and supporting words when I need them. I'm sorry that my personal growth is not always in your best interest, but I hope eventually that I find a happy medium that is less of a P.I.T.A. for you.

To the universe, thank you for all the little signposts along my way. Thank you for extending outside the bounds of my comprehension, occasionally turning me upside down, and somehow keeping me in orbit. Your frequent absurdity and hilarity have made my life better.

To all the YouTube self-published authors who have posted videos on how to format books and figure out self publishing, thank you! This book would look like total crap without your very helpful tutorials.

Lastly to my kids, I'm pretty sure I've already said it all. I love you to infinity.
-Mom

About the Author

Ugh, writing this in third person is going to be supes awks! Obviously I'm self published so I'll be writing this part, but third person is the convention and I'm a rule-follower, so here it goes:

Anony Mom is a married 40-something mother of three and primary care doctor. She stumbles often in her parenting but is enthusiastically figuring it out as she goes.

Growing up in a middle-class suburb and a product of divorce, her childhood was filled with tree climbing, soccer games, pink sprinkle donuts, repressing her feelings, and obsessive people-pleasing.

She "found herself" in college and has prided herself on being a work in progress ever since. She journeyed miles of baby steps through medical school, residency, meeting her life partner, and starting her post-graduate career in medicine.

Despite that great deal of personal growth during her twenties, becoming a mother hit her like a ton of bricks as she was inundated with evidence of inner work that still needed to be done. All of her faults were reflected back to her by the adorable little humans she had birthed.

"The Mother Lode Journals" series dissects her thoughts about those faults, via letters to her daughters. It is her attempt at building a bridge from where she is now to where she would like to be, and reconciling her efforts in excruciating detail.

Anony Mom has used journaling to express herself since her late teens and started journaling to her daughters when they were born. She decided to share them with the world in hopes that she might find other moms on a similar journey.

She has chosen to publish anonymously to ensure online privacy for her kids and to avoid patients googling her name for reviews and stumbling upon these incredibly vulnerable stories.

She currently identifies with being a recovering people pleaser, embracing imperfections, attempting gentle parenting, and wishing everything came more naturally and the world in general was a better place. She believes in strong female friendships, trying your best, humor as therapy, and that nature is sometimes the best medicine.

She would love to engage with any readers book-club-style on Instagram (ReparentingMyselfBook).

Don't miss out!

Visit the website below and you can sign up to receive emails whenever Anony Mom MD publishes a new book. There's no charge and no obligation.

https://books2read.com/r/B-A-QEOEB-EOVYC

BOOKS 2 READ

Connecting independent readers to independent writers.